The Physical Environment at Work

WILEY SERIES IN
PSYCHOLOGY AND PRODUCTIVITY AT WORK

Series Editors
D. J. Oborne and M. M. Gruneberg

The Physical Environment at Work
Editors — D. J. Oborne and M. M. Gruneberg

Further titles in preparation

Occupational Fatigue
by *I. Brown*

Occupational Safety and Accidents
by *T. Cox and C. Mackay*

Hours of Work
edited by *S. Folkard and T. Monk*

Computers at Work
by *D. J. Oborne*

Psychology of Employment, Underemployment and Unemployment
by *G. E. O'Brien*

The Physical Environment at Work

Edited by

D. J. Oborne and M. M. Gruneberg
Department of Psychology,
University College of Swansea

JOHN WILEY & SONS
Chichester · New York · Brisbane · Toronto · Singapore

Copyright © 1983 by John Wiley & Sons Ltd.

Library of Congress Cataloging in Publication Data

Main entry under title:
The Physical environment at work.
   (Wiley series in psychology and productivity at work)
   Includes index.
   1. Work environment. 2. Human engineering.
I. Oborne, D. J. II. Gruneberg, Michael M.
III. Series.
T59.77.P78 1983   620.8'2   82-23743

ISBN 0 471 90123 7

British Library Cataloguing in Publication Data:

The Physical environment at work. — (Wiley series
   in productivity at work).
   1. Psychology, Industrial.   2. Industrial
   productivity.
I. Oborne, D. J.   II. Gruneberg, M. M.
658.3'14   HF5548.8

ISBN 0 471 90123 7

Phototypeset by Dobbie Typesetting Service, Plymouth, Devon
Printed by The Pitman Press, Bath, Avon

Contributors

L. J. BELLAMY   *Department of Applied Psychology, University of Aston, Birmingham*

GORDON R. BIENVENUE   *Environmental Acoustics Laboratory, Pennsylvania State University, USA*

DAVID CANTER   *Department of Psychology, University of Surrey*

BERNARD J. FINE   *U.S. Army Research Institute of Environmental Medicine, Natick, Massachusetts, USA*

JOHN G. FOX   *Department of Employment, Social Affairs and Education, EEC, L-2920, Luxembourg*

M. M. GRUNEBERG   *Department of Psychology, University College of Swansea*

JOHN L. KOBRICK   *U.S. Army Research Institute of Environmental Medicine, Natick, Massachusetts, USA*

K. H. E. KROEMER   *Ergonomics Laboratory, Virginia Polytechnic Institute, and State University, Virginia, USA*

E. D. MEGAW   *Department of Engineering Production, University of Birmingham*

PAUL L. MICHAEL   *Environmental Acoustics Laboratory, Pennsylvania State University, USA*

D. J. OBORNE   *Department of Psychology, University College of Swansea*

Acknowledgement

We would like to acknowledge the considerable help provided to us while preparing this manuscript by Mrs Jackie Davies, who completely re-typed the manuscripts submitted by individual authors, and by Mr Paul Wood, who prepared all of the diagrams in this book.

D.J.O.
M.M.G.

Contents

Editorial Foreword to the Series

This is the first book in the series 'Psychology and Productivity at Work'. The aim of the series is to illustrate to managers, students, and others who are interested, the contribution of psychologists to an understanding of human behaviour in the workplace. It is probably fair to say that psychology and psychologists have not earned themselves an enviable reputation as major contributors to the well-being of organizations. The reasons for this are many. It may be due to a feeling that psychologists are concerned only with the welfare of employees even at the expense of organizational efficiency; it may be due to the premature application of underdeveloped and impractical theories of human behaviour in organizations; and it may be due to a failure of psychologists to communicate adequately to a relevant audience what is known of behaviour and what can be done effectively in organizational settings to improve not only human welfare but also organizational efficiency.

This series, therefore, is concerned not only with looking at the quality of working life, important as this is, but at how psychological research and principles can help to improve organizational efficiency and productivity. As has become abundantly clear over the last few years, these two aspects are not independent. The individual who works for an inefficient organization runs the risk of losing the quality of working life because there is no working life! The series will aim, therefore, not only to look at questions such as satisfaction and employee welfare, but to consider organizational efficiency and productivity.

This first book in the series does just this. It shows in a number of ways how the physical context of work, from the built environment to environmental qualities such as temperature, noise, etc., all have effects on both efficiency and satisfaction. Future volumes will look at other aspects of working life with the aim of helping the manager and the student to understand better what psychology can and cannot do to help him or her.

The Physical Environment at Work
Edited by D. J. Oborne and M. M. Gruneberg
©1983 John Wiley & Sons Ltd.

The Environment and Productivity: An Introduction

D. J. OBORNE AND M. M. GRUNEBERG
Department of Psychology,
University College of Swansea,
Singleton Park, Swansea, UK

The physical environment is all around us; it constantly affects our behaviour. If it is cold outside, we put on extra clothes; if it rains we carry an umbrella; in strong sunlight we wear sunglasses; and if we get too close to a road drill we cover our ears. Just as it affects our daily living, aspects of the environment at work are also able to influence our working behaviour and efficiency to a greater or lesser extent. As the chapters in this book will illustrate, excessive environmental noise can interfere with an operator's ability to hear important messages; too much light (or light in the wrong place) can obstruct the perception of fine detail; the thermal conditions which prevail can impede cognitive and manual functioning; and levels of vibration arising from the mechanical environment can hinder adequate manual and visual dexterity. In addition we should not forget the physical constraints of the actual working place; the ability to reach controls, to pass through doors or to find the easiest way through a factory complex. Any of these environmental factors can interfere with the normal flow of work output and can thus obstruct work productivity.

THE CONCEPT OF PRODUCTIVITY

Although defining what is meant by 'productivity' may, at first, appear to be a simple task, on closer examination it becomes clear that an adequate definition and explanation of the nature of productivity at work is not easy at all. Increasing productivity is not simply a case of increasing the amount of material produced by any particular operator, unit or process; definitions of productivity which are couched in such terms as 'output per unit time' must

1

beg the question of how much has had to be put into the system to produce the output (Ruch and Hershauer, 1974). A number of factors such as new machinery, investment in manpower, or even investment in worker comfort may have to be included in the simple productivity equation. For example, for a firm to invest £10 million in a new plant to produce an increase in production of one unit per month would not necessarily be considered to be either desirable or a productive change. In addition to the input–output relationships, therefore, a sensible concept of productivity must also consider the *efficiency* of the production—the utilization of the resources available. As such it needs to be couched more in terms of the economic, physical, and manpower resources to hand.

In its most basic form a simple model of a work process would involve three main stages: materials being put into the process, operations being carried out on the materials, and the completed product being available for outside consumption. The first two of these operations (the material and the process itself) could be considered as being the input phase of the productivity equation; it is these which cost money and energy. The rewards gained from the acceptance of the product by a consumer could then be conceived as the output phase. It is only at this point that the organization is able to determine the value of the finished product, which can then be offset against the cost of producing it.

It must be accepted from the start, however, that such a model is extremely simplistic; it glosses over the multitude of factors which go to make up each of the above three processes. In addition each has important sub-factors, and the cost or the benefit of each of these must be assessed before the equation can be completed.

The costs involved in any process are more than simply those of the raw materials used to produce and to sell the product; the steel, the bolts, the paper, the machines, etc. They also include the manpower needed to operate the machinery and to control the process. It is at this point that the debit side of the equation becomes complex, since manpower costs do not stop simply at wages. They include training costs and those involved in ensuring that the workforce are motivated to perform at their peak and to remain at their jobs. In this latter respect, of course, sickness and accidents may diminish the workforce. Even if a worker is only temporarily hurt by an accident and takes perhaps only an hour off work to visit the sick bay or a doctor, wages are still being paid and the productive time is reduced by at least that hour and possibly more.

The problem of safety provides an excellent example of the multitude of sub-factors which need to be taken into account for just one aspect of the cost side of the productivity equation. Bearham (1976) suggests that the costs of any accident can be divided into direct and indirect costs. Direct costs are those incurred through such aspects as the settlement of claims for damage to equipment; compensation for loss of earnings, pain and suffering as a result of injury; legal liability under health and safety acts; and insurance premiums.

Whereas these costs are readily understandable and accountable, indirect costs are more difficult to evaluate since they tend to be hidden. Bearham's list includes costs for safety administration, medical centres, welfare payments, ambulance services, other employees whilst helping the injured person and giving evidence, replacement labour, loss of production, damage to machines, and accident investigation. In addition, unsafe environments can lead to members of the workforce leaving — so increasing turnover.

If an adequate list of the total costs involved in a productive process is difficult to obtain, it is often the case that definitions of the benefit side are equally difficult to produce. This is particularly so when the output is difficult to quantify; rather than being couched in concrete terms such as particular produce units, for example nuts or cars, the output is more of a qualitative nature. Examples of such occasions occur in teaching or research where quality is more important than quantity, or in situations where the critical product cannot easily be attributed to any individual in the organization but rather to the result of a group process.

Problems also exist when attempting to define the time scale over which any performance measures are to be taken. 'Short-term' measures of output may often be misleading. For example if high output in the short term is 'bought' at the expense of worker 'well-being' or safety, then the short-term gains may be more than outweighed by long-term losses in the form of accidents or industrial unrest.

From the above it is clear that the concept of productivity is by no means simple. The appropriate definition depends largely on the context in which it is used. Since this book focuses on the relationship between human behaviour and the environment in which work is carried out, however, the term will generally be used to consider the more *efficient* use of human resources.

THE ENVIRONMENT AND EFFICIENCY

In essence the environment can affect behaviour in one or more of three ways. First, under extreme conditions it can degrade health. Noise can cause deafness, too much or too little temperature can cause hyper- or hypothermia, intense light can blind, etc. Even at less extreme levels, however, the environment can reduce safety by its effect on performance. The chapters in this book will each discuss how this can occur and how reduced performance can lead to reduced output. Thirdly, less than optimum environments can interfere with comfort which, in turn, can lead to reduced efficiency and safety. As will soon become apparent, however, each of these three effects can be highly interrelated.

The environment and safety

In many countries the need to ensure that a workplace is safe is a requirement embodied in law. The legislative aspects apart, however, the value of ensuring that all of the workforce remain at their workplace and do not have to take time off due to sickness or injury should be readily apparent. It must be the case that overall productivity will decrease with a reduced workforce, all of whom still need to be paid.

Many aspects involved in ensuring a safe workplace lie outside of the range of influence of psychology and more in the sphere of occupational medicine; for example, making the environment free of carcinogenic gases, or reducing noise to levels which will not cause permanent deafness. These are interactions with the environment which are at a physiological level and involve no, or very little, behavioural inputs from the operator. From an occupational viewpoint, the input of psychology occurs at the point at which the operator is required to perform tasks in the environment. An accident occurs when the environmental conditions demand more of the operator than is able to be given.

A simple behavioural model of how an accident can be caused is shown in Figure 1. The lower trace illustrates the total, fluctuating demands which are made by the environment. For example when driving a truck, the environment is likely to demand a high level of controlling skill to make the truck actually move, a high degree of visual ability to enable the operator to perceive obstacles, etc. The upper trace indicates the operator's ability to perform these combined tasks: momentary levels of vigilance, of hand–eye coordination, of cognitive capacity, etc. For most of the time that the task is being performed, the operator's ability will exceed the environmental demands; the obstacles will be seen, the vehicle is controllable. As long as this state of affairs remains

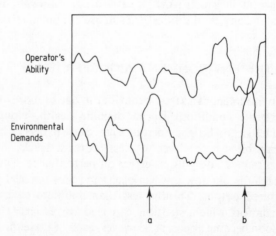

Figure 1. A simple model of accident causation

there will be no accident. Even at point a on the figure, when the environmental demands increase—perhaps the driver is suddenly blinded by the glare of oncoming headlights—no accident occurs since the operator still has the capacity required to respond to the situation. At point b, however, the total man-environment situation is different. Perhaps the same environmental conditions prevail—oncoming vehicles—but, in this case, the abilities required to react successfully to this situation are momentarily lacking (perhaps the driver is fatigued) and are not sufficient to meet the sudden demands of the environment. When this happens an accident occurs—the environment has demanded more than the operator can give.

Although this model is clearly simplistic in its approach, it does emphasize the complex interaction between the operator and the environment, and the role that both play in producing a safe, and therefore efficient, environment. The model suggests that safety is not simply created by considering the environment alone; by reducing the noise level, or increasing illumination. Safety is created by the operator's behaviour being able to match and exceed the environment's demands. Furthermore, the model argues that neither of these components are static in their level. The environmental demands are task specific: the demands made by driving in heavy, built-up environments are different from those made whilst driving along the motorway. In the same vein, the operator's abilities vary both with individuals and, more importantly, within an individual over time. Fatigue, for example, is an obvious factor which could detrimentally affect an operator's ability.

The environment and performance

The effects of the environment on operator performance are clearly less dramatic than they are on safety. They are clearly no less important, however, to work productivity.

The relationship between task and environmental demands and the resultant operator performance can be fairly simply described by an inverted-U function as shown in Figure 2. Thus when the demands of the environment are particularly low—perhaps the job is boring—or when they are exceptionally high—under conditions of stress, then performance is reduced. Only when the environmental demands are within a narrow, middle range will performance be optimum.

Although the inverted-U relationship has been explained so far in terms of the task and environmental demands, the actual continuum which underlies the function is that of operator arousal. This concept of arousal refers to the amount of brain activity in the operator and, indeed, is often measured using electroencephalography (EEG). Thus when a person is asleep or drowsy then brain activity or arousal are low; when under stress the arousal is high (this is often accompanied by such physiological reactions as sweating).

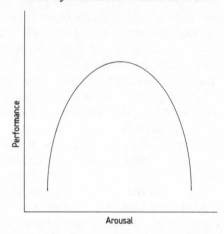

Figure 2. The performance/arousal continuum

The importance of this relationship to considering the effects of the environment lies in the fact that the level of individual arousal is related to the amount of external (and internal) stimulation which a person receives. The environment at work is clearly a source of stimulation. Thus with low stimulation, perhaps from a boring job, from environments with little noise or illumination, in situations which are 'ideal' so that heat and cold receptors are not being stimulated, or when signals from the task are few and far between (such as inspecting objects on an assembly line), performance will be low. Similarly cases in which the stimulation is too high can cause reduced performance. Too much noise, in environments which are too hot or too cold, with extreme glare levels, can all act to increase the operator's arousal levels to produce less than optimum performance. Only when the situation is 'ideal' will performance be at a maximum.

Unfortunately the inverted-U arousal/performance curve is only a general relationship. Both the shape of the curve and the level of arousal at which performance is optimum are dependent on the characteristics of the operator and of the type of stimulation. Personality and intelligence are just two individual characteristics which can alter the relationship. For this reason it is not possible to provide 'tables' of optimum arousal/stimulation levels. All that can be done is to recognize the existence of the relationship and to ensure that the levels of stimulation in the environment are neither too high nor too low for the individuals concerned. If the environment is found to be less than optimum, then steps can be taken either to increase or to reduce the stimulation. For example in a later chapter Fox discusses the value of industrial music as a means of increasing arousal for boring, repetitive tasks.

Before leaving the discussion of the arousal/performance relationship, it should be emphasized that the level of stimulation which an operator obtains from the work arises from a number of factors: physical, physiological, social, personal, etc. Each can operate to raise or to lower the overall arousal level. The implication of this is that the value of an otherwise 'ideal' physical environment may be reduced if the operator's arousal is increased or lowered by, say, bad social relationships with colleagues or by worries at home. Since it is the *total* arousal level which is related to performance, any one factor which makes up this total may affect the final arousal level on one occasion but not on another.

In addition to describing this relationship between environment and performance in terms of an arousal model, attempts have also been made to model the effects in terms of 'mental capacity'. In essence this model suggests that an operator brings to a task a limited capacity to perform that task. Provided that the capacity is not exceeded, the task will be executed efficiently. Performance is reduced, however, if the task demands more than the operator is able to give. This model, therefore, is similar in concept to the accident causation model described earlier.

The essential value of this model, however, lies in the fact that it suggests that when performing a task some sort of trade-off often takes place between the demands of the task and of the environment, and the capacity of the operator. The spare mental capacity model, therefore, suggests that requirements made by less than optimum environments can be compensated with more operator effort. Thus when operating a lathe, for example, adverse conditions may well be able to be accommodated by the operator without any performance loss simply because more of the limited capacity store is used up — the operator 'works' harder or 'concentrates' more. If the task and environment demand too much, however, the spare mental capacity which was otherwise used by the task will be exhausted and so performance will be reduced. The model predicts, therefore, that a difficult task, which leaves less spare mental capacity, will be affected quicker and to a greater extent by adverse conditions than would an easier task.

The implications of this model, therefore, are clear. Operators are able to adapt and account for less than optimum environments but only at a cost. Provided the environment does not demand more spare mental capacity than the operator is able to give, performance will be maintained. Too much of a demand, however, will reduce efficiency.

The environment and comfort

Comfort is the most subjective, least easily definable, aspect of the environment to consider. Unlike safety and performance its units of measurement are not easily observable. Thus the effects of the environment on safety, for example, can be measured fairly simply in terms of the number of injuries caused or accidents that occurred. Although more difficult, the effects on performance can be defined in terms of some type of output, according to some measure of speed, accuracy, quality, etc.

With comfort, however, the position is different. Indeed it may well be that comfort cannot even be defined, and without adequate definition there cannot be adequate measurement. Branton (1972), for example, suggests that the problems with the concept of comfort are very similar to those when defining health: it is only possible to declare that a person is healthy when he/she does not have any illnesses. Thus comfort and health can only be defined in terms of their negative qualities—discomfort and ill-health.

The importance of maintaining comfort, or a lack of discomfort, when dealing with working efficiency is apparent when one considers that 'man' is a 'comfort-seeking'/'discomfort-reducing' animal. For example, discussing the concept of sitting behaviour, Branton (1966) formulated a theory of postural homeostasis. Homeostasis is a concept which is widely understood by physiologists and concerns the self-regulation of body functions. A common example is body temperature regulation: if the body temperature rises sweat is produced which, when it evaporates, has a cooling effect. When the body becomes cold, however, the blood is routed away from the skin to the warmer, central, parts of the body. As far as sitting posture is concerned, therefore, Branton suggests that to maintain comfort a person will seek stability from the seat. By doing so, however, over a period the very stabilizing aspects of the seat (the arm rests, back rest, crossed legs, etc.) will tend to compress the fleshy parts of the body (for example, the buttocks and thighs) so reducing blood circulation through the capillaries and possible numbness. This causes the impetus for a posture change, so reducing stability, and the circle continues. The homeostatic behaviour of the sitter, therefore, is constantly to alter posture to maintain comfort (or reduce discomfort). In this way, Branton argues, fidgeting can be used as an index of sitting comfort/discomfort.

Although postural homeostasis was advanced to explain sitting behaviour, its concept can be extended in a similar vein to describe comfort-seeking behaviour when interacting with any aspect of the environment. It can also be used to illustrate how 'uncomfortable' environments can affect performance and safety. Thus, by actively taking steps to seek comfort (or reduce discomfort) the operator is likely to be presenting reduced attention to the task. The more 'uncomfortable' the environment, the more homeostatic behaviour patterns are likely to be exhibited. The need to seek comfort, then, is likely to affect task performance in some cases by using more of the store of spare mental capacity, by interfering with the efficient performance of some tasks (for example typing is difficult if the typist is also fidgeting), or by increasing arousal to levels above the optimum.

SUMMARY

The purpose of this introduction has been to set into context the following chapters of this book. As will be seen, each of the authors considers in detail how different aspects of the environment can affect operator performance. As this introduction has illustrated, however, translating the performance effects which are described into productivity terms must be both difficult and, at the same time, applied carefully to specific situations. Thus the very nature of productivity is that it is an extremely individualistic concept. It must be defined by the situation in hand. This being said, however, this introduction has also described the three ways in which aspects of the environment might affect overall efficiency — by affecting safety, performance, and comfort.

REFERENCES

Bearham, J. (1976). *The Cost of Accidents Within the Port Industry* (London: Manpower Development Div., National Ports Council).

Branton, P. (1966). *The Comfort of Easy Chairs.* Furniture Industry Research Association Report No. 22.

Branton, P. (1972). *Ergonomic Research Contributions to the Design of the Passenger Environment.* Paper presented to Institute of Mechanical Engineers Symposium on Passenger Comfort, London.

Ruch, W. A., and Hershauer, J. C. (1974). *Factors Affecting Productivity.* Occasional Papers No. 10 (Tempe, Arizona: College of Business Administration, Arizona State University).

The Physical Environment at Work
Edited by D. J. Oborne and M. M. Gruneberg
©1983 John Wiley & Sons Ltd.

The Physical Context of Work

DAVID CANTER
Department of Psychology,
University of Surrey,
Guildford, Surrey, UK

Consider a not uncommon situation. The productivity of the workforce has been at a steady level for years but, for economic reasons, profit margins are falling. Any additional urging by management is fraught with difficulties, not least due to the ever-watchful unions who are keen to ensure that no-one is seen to be exploited. In a search for a way out of this impasse a member of the board comes across an article in a management magazine on the power of colour in the environment in influencing worker productivity and motivation. This is welcomed as a cost-effective way forward at last. For little more than the price of a few cans of paint, it is believed, the factory can be transformed. Furthermore, the director who puts forward the proposal can show that it is based on 'scientific' principles. After all it is probably graced with a label like 'Milieu Motivation' or 'Colour Psychology'.

The lot of the manager, and possibly the workforce as well, would be so much easier if the scenario above was likely to have a positive outcome. If we could shape people and their behaviour by the simple expedient of painting their rooms, or by giving them more space, then management could be reduced to a simple check list and skills and sensitivities could be kept for the golf course. If the physical environment had a direct and simple effect on worker productivity then people and automata could be easily interchanged and the complexities of decision making and people management would be a thing of the past.

It is possibly because of this vision of a manager's utopia, in which people do not need to be understood but just manipulated, that there is such a constant quest for the formulae which will show the physical influences on behaviour and why some of the less scrupulous consultants can make a good living out of the sale of such unsubstantiated cures and potions. Myths, such

11

as those dealing with the effects of colour on performance, feed on ignorance and confusion. It is with the intention of clearing away this source of mystery that the present chapter is written.

In the opening scenario the likely outcome of redecoration, far from being a happier and more productive workforce, could possibly be a less satisfied and more disruptive one. It is quite possible that the workforce share some of the mistaken views about the effects of colour and believe that they are being manipulated against their will. Or it may be that they think the redecoration is a sop in lieu of more urgently needed, but more expensive, modifications in working conditions. The workforce may well have different tastes in colour and design than the management, as well as different requirements, which will also add to their dislike of what has been done for them. In other words, the dominant influence of the physical surroundings, in this case, is via its significance. It is what the existing surroundings and proposed modifications mean to the people involved which carry their influence, much more than any direct effects on behaviour.

What is true of colour is true of space and layout, light and sound. Within the levels of normal experience, the consequences of the physical conditions of work are subtle and complex. Yet although this was first demonstrated over half a century ago with the widely known Hawthorne investigations (Roethlisberger and Dickson, 1939), the old myths still surface again from time to time. They take many forms, such as beliefs in animal-like 'territoriality' or 'defensible' space, the need for contact with nature or faith in the profound significance of daylight. As with all myths they contain a grain of truth but to find that truth we must first clear away the confusions and secondly not expect it to take the form of any simple, magical formula.

CONSIDERING THE PHYSICAL CONTEXT

The first step in considering the role of the physical surroundings in an organization is to move beyond over-simple ideas about productivity, its nature and consequences. The legacy of Taylor's 'scientific management' approach (discussed very clearly by Schein, 1965) dies hard, especially when it offers hope of rules of thumb and direct courses of action which can be applied to any situation without too much effort. The view that people can be treated as machines which will produce more if they are kept in good condition, stoked up with the appropriate fuel, and allowed to run only within their optimum working strains, is a view which although not often explicit is frequently behind discussions of working conditions and considerations of pay. Yet if there is one clear message which has come out of a century of psychological research in organizations it is that there is no simple relationship between the conditions of work and productivity. We must, as a consequence, turn away from looking at how much is produced for how much effort,

Very important could be used for Vivian's paper.

i.e. how 'productive' the workforce is, and look at other aspects of organizational effectiveness if we are to understand the role of the physical environment in the organizational process.

Of course, it can be argued, and often is, that because the conditions of work have so little direct bearing on worker performance these conditions can be ignored. If jobs are scarce then people will take work where they can. If people enjoy their job because of the personal challenge it offers or because of the social framework it provides then they will put up with abysmal working conditions. The challenge to the logic of this argument comes from two directions. The first is that the physical context of work is frequently one of the major capital outlays an organization must make although it contributes a relatively small amount to regular recurrent costs — salaries and wages usually being by far the largest component of recurrent costs. Thus any contribution that the physical environment can make to increased effectiveness is remarkably good value for money. Its benefits accumulate over the lifetime of the capital expenditure and modify the consequences of the much larger sums of money spent on keeping the organization going.

The second argument in favour of taking the physical environment seriously is that although the direct consequences may not be so obvious the indirect ones may be very important indeed. Thus although, for example, the official channels of communication through a factory, office, hospital or school may consist of memoranda and meetings, job sheets and telephone calls, none of which are usually dramatically influenced by the design or layout of the workplace, the informal contacts which enable an organization to adapt to changing circumstances, or which are an essential ingredient of organizational morale, are very likely to be a function of how spaces are connected with one another and what their ambience is. Furthermore the interrelationships between aspects of the surroundings and their consequent cumulative effect on the work situation should not be underestimated. For example, how easy it is to have a conversation in an office may be directly related to whether it is a warm day or not. On warm days people in the office may feel the need to open the windows to let fresh air through, but this may also admit a lot of local traffic noise thus making it difficult to converse easily.

The simple example of the relationship between thermal comfort and ambient noise level illustrates the much more profound phenomenon that an organization, as manifested by both its physical and social existence, is a closely related set of component parts. Modification of any one aspect is likely to have ramifications throughout many other aspects. Another graphic example of these processes at work can be drawn from the study in a psychiatric hospital of the furnishing of a special space for patients to meet and socialize (Ittelson, Proshansky, and Rivlin, 1970). Note was made of the pattern of activities throughout the psychiatric unit before the room was furnished and after. What was found was that although the absolute amount of, say, solitary activity in the corridor had changed, the overall amount of such activity throughout the unit had stayed fairly constant. Becker (1981) also gives many examples of how technological innovations have frequently not been as effective as had been hoped because of indirect, unanticipated consequences.

APPROACHING ENVIRONMENTAL DESIGN

The opening discussion about the role of the physical environment in the working context has one very important implication. The ways in which decisions about the physical surroundings are made are frequently inappropriate. In effect, what is being advocated here is a change in the planning of and approach to the design of places of work. What follows in this chapter are some of the issues which need to be considered in this process, but experience shows that there are many pressures against taking these points seriously.

Heimsath (1977), a practising architect himself, suggests that one of the reasons for this reaction against what amounts to a psychological involvement in design is a set of related fallacies which are commonly held about the design process. He specifies six of these and they are well worth summarizing:

(1) *The design structures behaviour in a simple, direct and easily predictable way.* As a consequence the designer believes that if he or she can imagine what might happen in a place then that is what will happen.
(2) *The physical design is irrelevant, therefore the designer can really do what he wants and the administration of the building when it is complete is a quite separate issue.* (Fallacies 1 and 2 can comfortably co-exist in the same organization.)
(3) Growing out of the first two fallacies is the third. *Once a genius is recognized in architecture all that is necessary is to follow his lead without examination of the context or purposes he had for his creations.*
(4) *In so far as design is at all relevant to behaviour it can be coped with through flexibility and choice.* The fallacy in this idea is in its implementation rather than its concept. Who is in a position to choose? Are there any mechanisms available to make use of the flexibility?
(5) *If a response is made to human requirements and psychological processes all that emerges is boring 'totalitarian' architecture.* The confusion here is in thinking that a designer who does not consider these issues is 'free'. As can be seen from the other fallacies designers are frequently constrained by much more limiting assumptions.
(6) *It is all too complicated, it is best to just get on with the job!* This is clearly no basis for any professional activity.

These six fallacies, then, give an indication of some of the arguments a manager may have to face when he or she tries to implement the ideas in this chapter and the rest of this book. At least the reader has been warned! Let us now return to less pragmatic considerations of the physical context of work.

METAPHORS FOR COMPLEXITY

Two related metaphors are frequently used to help describe and capture the complex relationships which relate people to their physical surroundings. One is the metaphor, drawn from biology, of the ecology of place use (Barker, 1968). For just as chains of influence can be traced between plants and animals in any given habitat so that, for example, a change in the shrubs available can lead to reduction in mammal populations because of the reduction of animals who feed on animals who live in the shrubs, so the introduction of a new canteen can slow down production because there is less warning of likely stoppages in supplies because people no longer pass each other on the way to the tea room at the back of the stores. The other metaphor which is gaining wide acceptability is that drawn from the development of microcomputers and electronic processors. This is the metaphor of 'systems' and 'information processing'. I call this a metaphor because terms such as 'information', 'feedback loop', 'channel capacity', 'control mechanisms' and so on can be given a very precise meaning in computing and engineering but when they are used about people in organizations they are treated more loosely as analogues or metaphors. This does not weaken their value but it does lead to the warning that the emphasis on the need for a systems approach to organizations should not be taken as a slightly up-market approach to the scientific management of earlier years. Instead it should be seen as a powerful way of emphasizing the importance of thinking about the consequences for the whole of an organization when considering any modification to its component parts.

The major implications, then, of this acceptance of the richness and complexity of organizations, especially when considering the role of their physical surroundings, is the need to move beyond a direct focus on productivity in simple cost–benefit terms. This is *not* to say that organizations should be unproductive, but rather it is to point to the pitfalls of only considering productivity in terms of easy-to-measure, readily apparent components of the total system. The indirect costs of any action should be examined and the consequences for a range of aspects of experience and behaviour always need to be taken into account. This approach has the further advantage of showing the similarities between organizations in industry which have clear products and the many others which do not, such as, for instance, schools, hospitals, and prisons. Their effectiveness can still be facilitated by the appropriate surroundings. There are, as well, all those organizations in which conventional 'work flow' productivity is not easy to measure, such as many service industries and offices. A broader definition of productivity is also essential to include them in our considerations.

BEYOND PRODUCTIVITY

In order to give more detail to the other components of productivity let us consider those aspects of organizational life which are typically related to, but not necessarily directly influenced by, the physical surroundings.

Satisfaction

One of the easiest things for management to forget is that the attractions of working for any given organization must outweigh any competing attractions of not working for it. Further, it has been established in very many studies (see Schein, 1965, for an old but succinct review) that the amount a person gets paid is only one amongst many factors which go to make up the attractiveness of any given job. Relationships with co-workers, supervisors, and management; the intrinsic interest of the job itself, and the individuals' feelings about the extent to which their worth is recognized, all contribute to the overall satisfaction with the job.

Many of these aspects of satisfaction have links with the physical setting. If it is physically easy to see and make contact with others then friendship patterns are likely to be that much easier to establish. Having a room of one's own may be a way of having 'worth recognized'. It is also clear from these two examples that all the different components of satisfaction do not inevitably have similar implications for the physical surroundings. They pull in opposite directions.

Another important point for management to remember is that increased satisfaction does not always mean increased productivity. In a now classic study March and Simon (1958) showed both the logic and the evidence for this. However, they also argued that a dissatisfied workforce is hardly the basis for an effective organization. Their point is the central one of this chapter: that management should not look to productivity as the reason for achieving many additional valuable objectives.

Turnover

Where worker satisfaction does have a direct influence on organizational costs it is in relation to worker turnover. Dissatisfied workers may perform at the same level as satisfied ones when they get to work, but whether they turn up or not will be a direct reflection of how happy they are in the working situation. The costs to organizations of absenteeism and of training people is very considerable, so that turnover is a significant economic factor. Attracting the appropriate people in the first place is also important. Here again the physical setting can contribute to first impressions in important ways.

Communication

Organizations exist on communications. Any text on organizations emphasizes the significance of effective communication systems. This includes both the less structured communications between individuals and the more formal communications between, say, departments. It is this infrastructure which makes the working of an organization possible at all and as communication is, in effect, the transmission of information over a large or small distance, it is directly related to the spatial and physical properties of the building(s) in which work is carried out. This not only includes the distances over which the communications must take place but also what types of communication are possible in various contexts. Polite, subtle guidance as to how a job might be carried out more effectively cannot be given, for example, in a workshop which is so noisy that all instructions must be shouted loudly.

Symbolic identification

The extent to which a setting provides information about the people who are connected with it is identified by Steele (1973) as one of the major functions of the physical surroundings. This emphasis can be seen to have validity when it is realized that both satisfaction and communication can be greatly facilitated if the environment is seen by all who use it as appropriate to its users. It inevitably acts as a label for its users. The consequence of this labelling therefore needs to be considered.

Adaptability and growth

All organizations change over time or stagnate. This may be internal adaptation which adds little new to the organization or it may be actual growth and development. Whichever it is, the physical setting always plays a crucial role. Yet unfortunately, because of the fallacies discussed earlier, designers frequently do not consider this possibility in any but the most general sense. 'Flexible' buildings usually allow for all modifications in general but no modifications which are specifically attuned to particular organizational requirements. Designs which looked more closely at what might change and allowed for flexibility in relation to that, shaping the remainder of the building as appropriately as possible for the present uses, would probably be much more effective.

Competence and safety

There is one further aspect of activity and experience at work to which the physical environment contributes. This might best be called worker competence. It is fruitful to consider this as having at one extreme the provisions for safe working and at the other the limitations the workplace might impose on the handicapped. Bednar (1977) has written at length on what he calls 'Barrier-Free' environments, for the disabled. But it is misleading to think either that these considerations are relevant only for a very small special group in the community or that the benefits of designing with them in mind accrue only to special groups. To put this argument as succinctly as possible: if a child is safe in a factory then it is likely that a worker with a hang-over who is not concentrating as much as usual will also be safe there and that the time lost through minor accidents will also be minimized. The opportunity for employing possibly very highly motivated, disabled workers will also be increased.

What all of these aspects of organizational life have in common is a view of people as striving to achieve something. The individuals at their desks or machines make some sense of the world and attempt to make use of the situation in which they find themselves in order to do what they believe to be appropriate. They thus interpret and assess their situation and form evaluations of it. This leads to feelings of satisfaction and comprehension, views about where it is good to be and where it is best not to be. These reactions also influence whether a person can and will respond positively to changing circumstances and in the end whether the effectiveness of the organization, overall, is high or low.

EXPERIENCING PLACES

Having broadened the framework of 'productivity' to cover salient aspects of many actions and experiences at work we are now in a position to consider the ways in which the physical surroundings play their role. This involves two steps being taken beyond the consideration of the physical fabric of the buildings in which people work. The first step is to realize that the physical fabric of a workplace combines together with the activities which go on there to create an *environment*. It is indeed curious that prior to about 1960 you will find little reference to the environment in discussions of the working situation. The idea that another entity existed, which was an aspect of the working situation, yet was more than just the temperature and noise levels and what the buildings looked like, each considered in isolation, actually took some selling (Manning, 1965).

For the second step it is necessary to recognize that the environment created by the combination of physical fabric and activities in any location is itself harnessed to particular goals, individual and organizational. This relationship was first outlined by the Building Performance Research Unit (1972) using the model shown in Figure 1. This model shows directly that the objectives of the organization must be considered when examining the bricks and mortar, or stone and concrete, which house it.

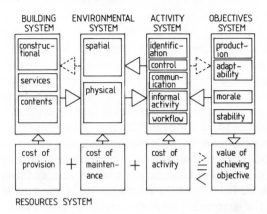

Figure 1. Conceptual model of the system of building and people.
(Building Performance Research Unit, 1972)

Any particular environment, then, takes on a special quality which is a product of its users and *what* it is that they are using and *why* they are using it. In order to capture this more complex phenomenon in one technical term a number of authors have started to use the word 'place' (Canter, 1977; Farbstein and Kantrowitz, 1978). Our original question about the role of the physical surroundings therefore becomes a question of the contributions which places and their experience make to the working situation.

To answer this revised question we need to take account of three different elements of the use of places: *spatial*, *social*, and *service*.

The spatial aspects of interactions in places cover all those concerns with the quantity of space needed for human activities. It is one of the inescapable facts of life that our bodies require a certain amount of space in which to operate. But the minimum amount of space necessary for human activity in a strictly mechanical, or engineering sense is rarely sufficient or appropriate. Thus the ergonomic recommendations discussed in the next chapter provide only the starting point for considering the space needed in any particular context. If all six aspects of organization life discussed above are to be considered, then the consequences of spatial provisions can be seen to go far beyond having enough space in which to 'do the job'. Furthermore, in keeping with the integrated, systems approach being advocated here, spatial provisions should not be considered in isolation from the other elements of places. For example, the consequences for worker satisfaction of the space available will relate to who (and where) else he/she has access to, as well as the general qualities of, the space.

The second element of place experience is the social one. Our use of places always has a social component, even if it is the negative one of the desire to be alone. Thus, as social beings an important aspect of any place is the way in which it and its attendant rules of use help or hinder us in our desires, or requirements for contact with others. This is sometimes forgotten when a technical, manufacturing process is seen to have its own requirements for organization and thus its layout inadvertently imposes a social pattern on those who must work with it. A further consequence here is that the social implications of any place are carried, or reflected, in its physical arrangement and therefore make possible the 'reading' of that arrangement. Hence the symbolic properties which can be so significant in place experience.

In order for a place to be viable for the activities desired in it, it not only needs the appropriate amount of space but also that space must be appropriately serviced. These services are the thermal, luminous, acoustic, etc., aspects of the environment discussed in more detail in subsequent chapters of this book and, for example, in Bell, Fisher and Loomis (1978) or Canter and Stringer (1975). But from the integrated perspective of the present chapter, the way the services contribute to the effective utilization of space and the social implications of those spaces is a necessary consideration.

Before turning to consider each of these elements of place experience more specifically in the context of work, one further aspect of places needs to be clarified. This is the aspect referred to by researchers as the 'hierarchy of place' (Canter, 1977; Russell and Ward, 1982). What this means is that every place gets its qualities both from the places of which it is a part and from the places which compose it. Thus there are always immediate implications to take into account when thinking of places, as well as more distant ones. The private office can be thought of on its own but many of its qualities will derive from where it is in the building. These different 'levels' of place experience, for simplicity taken here as the two *immediate* and *distant*, combine with each of the three elements above to give six distinct aspects of the physical context of work. We shall now turn to consider the consequences of each of these aspects, but it should be borne in mind that each of these aspects has consequences for the six areas of organizational life discussed above.

IMMEDIATE CONSEQUENCES

1. Spatial

Beyond ergonomics

If the worker is considered at all at his or her workplace, getting on with the job, without any immediate need for contact with others, the human components of the design of that workplace may often be thought of solely in engineering terms. The worker is thought of simply as a mechanism with certain proportions and overt physical requirements. So questions are asked such as: 'How far must the person reach?', 'What is the best height to sit at?',

'How bright a light do they need to see the task they are doing?' and so on; ergonomic questions.

Of course, these are important questions even though many organizations still do not think to ask them. Many thousands of pounds, for example, may be spent on new office equipment such as word processors without any thought of the physical design necessary to accommodate this equipment so that its users will be able to utilize it effectively. Cakir, Hart and Stewart (1981) have shown the elementary mistakes which are frequently made with visual display terminals. Indeed, looking at word processors specifically, Canter and Davies (1982) showed that the spatial provisions for this equipment were frequently underestimated in much the same way that a previous generation of management had underestimated the spatial requirements of key-punch operators (Langdon, 1963). It is almost as if many office managers have a built-in misunderstanding of how space is used and that this fundamental misunderstanding has not changed with changing working practices. It is tempting to speculate that in those very early cities, thousands of years ago, the scribes incising clay tablets probably also complained that they had nowhere to keep their chisels or their unused slabs of clay! They possibly also complained to their spouses, when they got home, of a stiff neck from sitting in such an awkward position all day.

Taking productivity in relation to return on capital expenditure, it is clear that ergonomic considerations can have a direct bearing on the effectiveness of equipment, whether that equipment is a new lathe, a new microprocessor, or a new office building. If the acceptability of the equipment to the workforce and their satisfaction with it is also taken into the equation, which in many cases may make the crucial difference in the use of the equipment profitably, then the role of ergonomics becomes even more significant. If people complain about the installation of a new visual display controlled factory process, because of such intangibles as 'eye strain' or 'fatigue', to the extent that it is found necessary to replace parts of the control system, then considerable investment may be lost as well as the cost of the further disruption while the changes are carried out. Yet such problems can often be avoided by careful attention to the principles of ergonomics (cf. Oborne, 1982).

Emergency situations also reveal occasions when ergonomic factors may mean the difference between success and disaster. The most famous example of this is the Three-mile Island nuclear reactor failure (President's Commission, 1978; Malone *et al.*, 1980). According to the official report into this event a major contributory cause was the extent to which the control room design ignored established ergonomic practices. For example it was found that the information required by the operator was often non-existent, poorly located, ambiguous, or difficult to read. Indeed in one control room it was concluded, after the event, that a total of 91 per cent of applicable human engineering criteria for displays were not met. What this all added up to was that when something went badly wrong, the design of the controls did not lead operators to take the most effective action.

This example also serves to illustrate that even when considering workplace design from the stance of human engineering it is not enough to deal with the workforce as passive receptors. Their ability to make sense of their work situation is crucial. They need to understand what is happening and why. The physical context, its design and layout, frequently provides the main cues to aid this understanding. When the task at hand clearly goes beyond physical manipulation, involving problem solving, judgement or decision making, then this more subtle role for the surroundings comes to the fore. It is here that the consequences for satisfaction and turnover and the other aspects of productivity become paramount.

Further, the mundane tasks of assembly and physical manipulation are becoming the province of computer-controlled machines, and as a consequence the distinction between the 'factory' and the 'office' is fading fast. The idea of the office housing 'clean', 'white-collar' jobs as opposed to the overalls of the factory is no longer valid. Factory processes are becoming ever more office-like as factories become automated. Offices are filled with ever more complex and sophisticated machinery. One of the implications of this coming together of forms of workplace is that the research carried out into office design is gaining relevance for other work settings and vice versa. The special human skills of judgement and assessment are becoming more dominant in the workplace and those aspects of the surroundings which contribute most directly to the effective performance of these will become even more important. Having the appropriate conditions for the manager to interview staff, for a designer to consider closely a difficult problem, for maintenance staff to gain access without disruption, or for rare, but rapid decisions in an emergency, all are becoming more significant than, say, setting the appropriate light levels for a task demanding high visual acuity.

Of course any, even casual, examination of existing workspaces reveals that they are only very rarely small, astronaut-like cubicles engineered solely to the mechanical requirements of the human frame. It is rare for the size of space in which a person works to relate simply and directly to the physical requirements of his activities. The vast desk of the chief executive, typically bare, has only to be contrasted with the overflowing little desk of the lowly clerk. It is apparent that forces other than mere 'functional requirements' in any narrow sense are often allowed to play their part in spatial organization. A key point here is that in presenting this example of desk sizes no criticism is necessarily intended. There *are* important spatial issues beyond the 'merely' functional.

In order to clarify these personal uses of spaces, labels such as 'personalization' and 'place-identity' have emerged. These rather jargon-rich terms point to the role which a space has in telling us something about the person who inhabits it. This was shown very graphically a number of years ago by Canter, West and

Wools (1974). They showed people pictures of private offices and asked them to describe and evaluate those offices. They then showed the same pictures to another group of people and asked them to describe and evaluate the people who might work in those rooms. A very consistent relationship was found between the descriptions of the rooms and the descriptions of the people who it was thought would work in them; for example pleasant people were expected to be found in rooms thought of as friendly. Joiner (1976) took this approach a step further by showing that there were distinct differences between people in the way they arranged their own offices and that this difference was a function of the type of organization for which they worked. Academics tended to have easy access from the door to the space behind their desk whereas civil servants were more likely to place the desk as a type of barrier between them and the door. Joiner argued that these differences were a function of different patterns of 'defence of territory' but unfortunately he does not provide any evidence that the actual jobs carried out in these different offices were similar. Nonetheless he does show that simple observation reveals consistent differences between people in the way they arrange their rooms and what they have in them. These differences are then available for others to see and interpret.

It is not surprising, therefore, to find that people are aware of these processes, sometimes labelled as 'impression management' and, implicitly or explicitly, strive to harness them to their own ends. It is also apparent that such processes are not limited to offices. Farbstein and Kantrowitz (1978) cite many examples in and out of work situations. They argue that one of the general skills which people should learn is how to use and interpret these messages more effectively.

Again a warning must be sounded. These mechanisms of personalization should not be dismissed as frivolities. Communication between people depends upon each party to the communication understanding the role of the other in the issues involved. This includes each individual feeling that his role is adequately reflected in the interaction. The shop steward having his or her own room or the manager believing his desk is in the right part of the open-plan office both contribute to the effective performance of their roles. So personal influence on the look or layout of a place can have direct effects on activities, but only if they do indeed relate to the roles and the activities of the individuals who use that space.

Some interesting light is thrown on the effects of context on individual judgement from studies of psychological experiments (first summarized by Rosenthal, 1966). This is a remarkably inbred activity but one of relevance here when it is realized that in many ways a psychological laboratory looks like and is used like a mechanized office. The 'subject' comes in and sits at a desk and is asked to perform some tasks, frequently of a paper-and-pencil type not too far removed from clerical work. For example, in Rosenthal's experiments people were typically asked to rate photographs of other people. As is the way of psychological research this has now become a field of research activity in its own right, the study of 'the human subject' (Adair, 1973). But for our purposes here it is worth pointing out that not only have significant differences in the judgement made been found for the same task in different rooms, but the amount of time the investigators voluntarily spent in the different rooms also varied and thus the type of interactions they had with their 'subjects'.

2. Social

The ultimate 'personalized' space, established for the total benefit of its user, is possibly the private office of a senior executive, especially if he is in a new building for which he was responsible. However, the isolated air-conditioned box has many disadvantages when the social context of work is considered. Contact and easy communication with others, as well as the flexibility to change the spatial relationships between individuals and groups, is a central requirement to many organizations. Hence the reason for most factories and many offices to be designed in an essentially open framework.

But once the individual's membership of a group is recognized, and her or his requirements of meeting and working with others, then there is the need to balance social requirements with individual ones. This is shown by the fact that the whole debate about the value of the open office really revolves around discussions of whether privacy should give way to flexibility of space use, or ease of contact should give way to local control over space (Canter, 1972; Hedge, 1980; Wineman, 1982). This was put in a more dramatic way by clerical workers when they contrasted being treated like battery hens, each in its own cage, in a cellular office block, with being treated as a mere cog locked into a vast machine in an open-plan office (Manning, 1965). Wells, working with Manning, was also able to show that the social networks in large open-plan offices were much looser but fewer people were outside them completely, whereas in the smaller offices stronger but more exclusive networks were found. Out of this potential conflict, management consultants and interior designers saw the value for a creative compromise and the notion of 'office landscaping' or 'panoramic office planning' emerged (Duffy, Cave and Worthington, 1976). Surprisingly these ideas do not seem to have percolated very far into the design of workplaces other than offices although on the face of it there are many important similarities.

What is being recognized, then, in discussions of open plan and the immediate consequences for the worker of his or her social role in the organization, is that there is always a need for some balance between individual privacy and social contact. This, of course, is not unique to the work situation and it is therefore not surprising that some general models have been developed to show the relationship between the mechanisms by which people maintain a balance between the pressures of being together with the others (frequently discussed under the generic term of 'crowding') and the desire to get on with one's own activities alone (usually explored as an aspect of 'privacy').

The most all-embracing and frequently quoted model is that of Altman (1975) who brings together discussions of 'personal space', 'crowding', 'territoriality' and 'privacy', as shown in Figure 2. Altman's model emphasizes that there is a variety of ways in which the social pressures of relating to others can be modified or harnessed, not all of them directly relying on physical, design possibilities but all of them of relevance to the physical context of work. He emphasizes that people strive for a balance in the relationship between the privacy they have and what they want, and that they do this by using a range of mechanisms. These mechanisms open them up or reduce their contact with others. Eyes are averted, doors are left open, signs are put up, and so on. All this is in the interest of achieving the optimum privacy for the context.

The general implications of these processes for productivity have been touched on, but when it is considered that the major reasons for which organizations exist is the benefits which accrue from people working together, then the many ramifications of these social processes become apparent. Being able to gain easy, informal access to senior management may have crucial implications for the adaptability of the organization to changing circumstances as well as the possibility which contact throughout the organization provides for increased satisfaction and understanding by

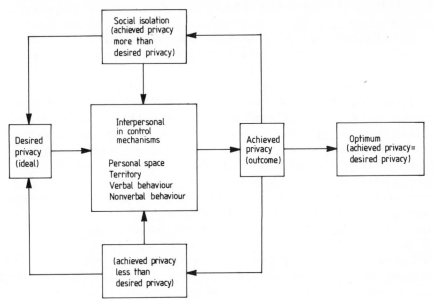

Figure 2. Overview of relationships among privacy, personal space, territory, and crowding. (Altman, 1975)

individuals of their roles. On the other hand, if this easy contact interrupts the work process itself or is quite independent of the decision structure in the organization then it can be counter-productive. Each individual and group within an organization has to strike its own balance, using the variety of subtle mechanisms open to them.

3. Services

Having established a place for individuals which has the appropriate personal and social qualities there is the further concern that the place will be effectively serviced. Other chapters of this book discuss in detail the effects of various aspects of the environment on performance. For the present it is essential to emphasize the integrated role these aspects play in any work setting. This integration comes not only from the way in which, say, heating systems and noise levels in a workplace may interact but also from the way their consequences may interact.

Consider the indirect impact of even moderately high noise levels. Jones, Chapman and Auburn (1981) have produced an extensive review to show the social consequences of noise. For example, the inability to carry out informal conversation in noisy settings can often lead to a feeling of social isolation among employees. The stress produced by noise can also lead to less effective coping with other people, sometimes even after the noise has stopped.

A further important point about the impact of noise levels is the way the size and nature of the space in which the noise occurs can influence the consequences of the noise by influencing the adaptation level. Two processes are involved here. One is the process whereby a general level of noise will act as a mask to hide particular noises and thus make, for example, private conversation possible in a way that would not be the case in a quiet room. This might be thought of as the 'restaurant phenomenon' in which people can have private conversations close to each other without any risk of overhearing because of the high level of background noise. The other is the expectations generated by given noise levels. This could be called the 'spectator phenomenon'. People seem to expect to have to shout to be heard at a football match, for instance, because they associate particular noise levels with that event. People do not complain that the match was too noisy or that they got hoarse from trying to discuss the game with their friends. These expectations about what is possible in a given setting thus influence what people try to do in those settings. It is changes from the expected which produce problems. Notice the way conversation ceases on a noisy train when it comes to a halt and is quiet. People do not immediately lower their voices. They expect the train noise to mask their conversation.

DISTANT CONSEQUENCES

1. Layout

In discussing the consequences of the immediate surroundings it was never completely possible to avoid concern for the larger framework of the organization. In a similar way it will be apparent that when focusing on the larger-scale surroundings the local conditions of which they are composed cannot be ignored. Although space itself can be considered as a resource and so the total amount needed by an organization can be calculated in some general terms, it is more fruitful to consider the range of places which are necessary for an organization to function effectively.

The implications of such considerations can most effectively be seen during the stages of planning a new building, or the modification of an old one. Canter (1982a) illustrates this with the planning of an engineering design centre. Instead of a more conventional approach of establishing the number of people to be housed in the new building and multiplying this by some '*x* square feet per person' factor, Canter and his colleagues carried out exercises with the workforce to establish the major constituents of the organization to be housed. They then carried out further work to establish the size and services necessary for each of these constituents and the relationships they bore to each other.

This approach kills off one of the sacred cows of much workplace design; the idea of total flexibility. All too often such flexibility either means that the physical setting is never appropriate for anything in particular or that resources are wasted on providing for potentials which are never actualized.

The alternative strategy is actually to provide for a specified range of possibilities. This approach produces a range of different types of place rather than some monolithic uniform space. The direct practical advantages of this were shown some years ago by the Building Performance Research Unit (1972). They were studying schools but their findings are relevant to many other workplaces. By simple record-keeping they were able to show that many of the desks available in a school at any point in time were not being used, although teachers complained of overcrowding. Overall, taking the space available during a teaching week, as much as 40 per cent of it was not being used. Yet this space had to be heated and cleaned while the building users complained of being crowded into small classrooms.

The central reason for this 'overprovision' was that the schools were designed with all the classrooms being the same size, thus smaller classes inevitably occupy bigger rooms. Schools built subsequent to this study were designed with a much greater variety of room sizes. But variety of room size only goes part of the way towards solving this problem. The issues of demarcation and personalization also play their part. Once a space has been labelled for a particular use there are strong pressures against changing that use, whether it is teachers wishing to use a laboratory for 'ordinary' lessons, or a manager wishing to store equipment in an 'office'. Putting labels on rooms is one aspect of privacy and control, having implications for communication and satisfaction. Thus any change of the designation of room use must incorporate a consideration of the processes associated with the labelling to ensure that the designations can be effectively changed in parallel.

The constituents of an organization, the places which go to make it up, do function in different degrees of relationship to each other. Some may function with little autonomy, others in relative isolation. The issue of intercommunication will be turned to in the next section, but whilst still focusing on the spatial aspects of the organization at the large scale it is important to distinguish between the size of an organization and its spatial extent. There is now a healthy literature (reviewed some time ago by Barker and Gump, 1964) to show that as the size of an organization increases so various indices of its effectiveness in human terms decrease. For example larger units typically have higher turnover and absenteeism rates and lower indices of efficiency than do their smaller counterparts. There is no full understanding of this consistent finding although some very valuable attempts at explanation have been put forward (e.g. Wicker, 1979). It is clear, nonetheless, that the effects of organizational size are not a direct product of the physical extent of an organization or of the physical isolation of its component parts.

Simply putting parts of a factory in different buildings as a way of reducing their organizational size, whilst maintaining the overall organizational structure of actions and decisions, will not reap the desired benefits of the small scale. Neither will putting many units together in one building necessarily forge them into one organizational unit.

This was shown quite clearly by Mazis and Canter (1979) in their study of children's homes. As might be expected, in general, the larger homes were less 'child-centred' than were the smaller ones, but the number of children in a home itself was not the best predictor of this relationship. The size of the total institution of which it was a part was a more effective predictor; so that a group of half a dozen children in a wing of a hospital were likely to be treated in much the same way as everyone else in that hospital. By contrast 30 or 40 children in a private, independent home would have much more freedom and autonomy. Even the smallest health service based homes were less child-centred than the largest private homes.

2. Interaction

Having accepted that an organization is an agglomeration of component parts which act together to varying degrees, the important question arises of how those parts relate to each other and the consequences of those relationships for organizational performance. A start can be made in answering this question by recognizing that just as the use of space by a few individuals has a pattern and structure to it and is anything but random, so also does the distribution of groups around the space occupied by an organization inevitably have a structure and pattern to it. In other words, the individual civil servant who puts his desk between himself and the door has direct parallels to the administration putting 10 storeys and a lift between itself and the workforce. It is no accident, for example, that top management are usually housed on the top floors of office buildings. The fact that this impairs access and reduces many aspects of communication is thought by those managements to be less important than the status possibilities provided by being literally on top of things.

A number of examples of the representation of status differences by the locations assigned to members of an organization are discussed by Steele (1973). He highlights a building produced for a West German insurance firm in which the organizational hierarchy is rigidly reflected in its stepped building form. The ground floor is large and houses 360 clerical workers and the top floor is much smaller with room only for the president, with ten grades in between. The president is quoted as saying that the design was intended to 'encourage ambition and provide a visual image of our organization structure'.

Perhaps the most interesting point about this West German building is the frankness with which its purposes are discussed. Similar building forms, essentially pyramid, can be found in many other settings such as Japanese mass housing or British town halls, but the symbolic qualities of these buildings and the messages they carry about the relationships between the people within them, are usually hidden behind discussions of daylight regulations and the properties of abstract geometrical forms. But, as Steele goes to some length to illustrate with personal anecdotes, the rhetoric of planners and designers, no matter how earnestly it is expressed, does not blind people to the messages which the building layout carries about the relationships between people within an organization. Steele also rightly emphasizes that the smaller the amount of information (or feedback as he calls it) which people obtain about their roles in an organization from other sources the more reliance they place on the cues given by physical design and location and any changes in it. This latter point accords rather well with the argument made by Hediger (1962), one of the pioneers of research into animal territoriality. He argued very strongly that the maintenance and defence of territories in animals was necessary because they could not talk to each other. He called territoriality a 'speech saving device'. Thus the preponderance of physical cues to position could well be taken as an indication of *weaknesses* in the communication systems within an organization. Management and the workforce could well ask each other why such symbols exist and what purpose they actually serve.

But again it must be emphasized that there may be good reasons for the conscious representation of relationships between people in organizations. One such set of reasons may be that the type of activity in which a group is involved, and the physical location demanded of that activity, inevitably carries its own significance. For example, a research department involved in commercially sensitive development work may inevitably be rather isolated and have more ample space, say, than other departments. However, management have to be vigilant to ensure that people do not read the wrong messages into these environmental cues.

Another set of reasons for the physical representation of social relationships may relate to the possibility that it is actually cheaper, in the long term, to represent status and other aspects of role differences by physical means rather than, say, by salary increases. Indeed given the importance of a person's view of himself in contributing to job satisfaction, it may well be the case in certain circumstances that physical representations of position may be more effective than other means.

One point is worth emphasizing here. In the above discussion the physical representation of *status* alone has not been emphasized. Instead the emphasis has been on the patterns of interactions between people in an organization. The reason for this is that the location and layout of groups within an organization reflects more than just the hierarchical structure of the organization. Consider, for example, a study of a school carried out by the Building Performance Research Unit (1972). In order to understand the relationship of the communication structure in a school to its physical layout and the way different social groups made use of the space, a rather novel survey was carried out. Note was made of which teachers had coffee and where. It was found that, although there were less than 40 teachers in the school, there were six distinct locations to which teachers went during their breaks. This division of the school into small groupings was so institutionalized that the assistant headmaster could provide a complete list from memory of who could be found where during the breaks. There were a number of reasons for this fragmentation of the teaching staff, not all to do with the layout of the building. Some of the most obvious reasons, however, were due to the fact that the courtyard structure of the building made the creation of many little enclaves quite feasible and that the stream of pupils out to the school yard during break times cut across the route which led to the central staff room.

This school example illustrates an active aspect of the 'ecological' processes mentioned earlier. An organization adapts to the consequences of its physical layout. This adaptation may, in its turn, lead to modifications of the pattern of informal social contact within an organization, which can play a significant role in its adaptation and development. But just as an individual has many ways of achieving a balance between individual and group demands so there are various ways of dealing with the consequences of the physical design for interaction within an organization. Increasingly, for example, the mode of communication between individuals is a consequence of the building layout.

Two examples illustrate the way in which mode of communication may also be related to the physical layout. In one prison studied by Canter and Ambrose (1981) the rather dispersed layout and lengthy corridors combined, with the desire to give prisoners freedom of movement within the prison, to make the prison officers rely very heavily on walkie-talkie communications. Thus, although the prisoners had freedom of movement, the prison staff dealt with each other in a much more formal way, as necessitated by passing information on the movement of prisoners over a radio link. Another example comes from the maintenance of modern complex factories, which are controlled from central operating panels. Here again radio links are essential to check with the control room when carrying out operations within the plant.

An important point in both these examples is that different types of information can be carried more readily by different modes of communication. As anyone who has tried the party game of describing a corkscrew without using their hands will know, much essentially visual information is difficult to convey in words. But there are also socially relevant aspects of the communication mode. For example many of the nuances of mood and attitude are carried by how we move, the gestures we make, and our facial expressions. As a consequence procedures may often be noticeably slower and misunderstandings may occur more readily when channels of communication are limited.

The indirect consequences of the mode of communication may help to explain the common finding that when organizations move into a new building there are complaints about how formal things have become and how difficult communicating has become. The informal patterns of communication well established in the old building are sometimes destroyed when moving to a new building and replaced by telephone calls and a proliferation of memoranda. As a consequence the subtleties of interactions between individuals and departments may be lost and the ability of the organization to adapt to changing circumstances may also be weakened.

3. Facilities

In considering the physical provisions local to the workplace, reference was made to the role of the services — especially heating, lighting, and the acoustic provisions. These are not utilized directly for the job at hand but provide a context within which the work can be carried out effectively. In a similar way, taking an organization as a whole, there are a number of such facilities which must be drawn on, but are not productive in their own right. It may be photocopying facilities or storage, central records, toilet provisions, or the works canteen.

Because these are not directly productive components of an organization and cannot typically be 'charged' exclusively to one sub-unit, there is frequently a difficulty in deciding on exactly what to provide and where to put it. Yet there has been remarkably little exploration of the role these additional facilities play or of how to identify what might be needed where. The information technology explosion has certainly not helped matters. It has made intercommunication between people more feasible, at least electronically, but it has made the location and definition of the resources needed much more complex.

Against this background of such a dearth of information one main point may be made. Any centralized resource has the potential for helping communication throughout an organization. If secretaries can meet at the photocopying machine or all management use the same dining room then the potential is there, at least, for an increased flow of information in relation to organizational (and other) activities. Indeed one way of adapting to a building which disperses people is consciously to create centralized facilities. Some organizations moving into new but potentially more formal buildings may decide, for example, that they will have a central management coffee room so that informal contact may be maintained. However, here as always caveats are in order. The use of central facilities cannot be imposed on an unwilling group. If their use goes against other strong pressures in an organization then they may only emphasize inherent conflicts. In the earlier school coffee room example, for instance, one of the pressures acting against the general use of the central staff room was that one group of teachers shared a religious commitment with the head of the school and it was this group which dominated the staff room.

DIFFERING PERSPECTIVES

In much of the discussion so far the interpretation by the individual of the significance of his or her surroundings has been emphasized. The issue of the differences between people in their interpretations and the consequences of those differences has not been explored. The view that there is one best physical layout for any given organization has, as a consequence, been implicit in much of the discussion of this chapter. Indeed this monolithic perspective is almost inevitable when the notion of an *organization's* productivity is the starting point. The idea of tailoring a physical system to optimize the overall productivity of an organization is an inviting one but it has two related flaws. One is that there are always many approaches to the optimization of a complex system. Putting it simply, for example, sales may be improved by better marketing or by a better product. So sales may benefit from redesigning the show room or the factory. The second flaw in the idea is that there will exist within an organization many different views of how that organization is operating and of what is possible for it to do. These differing perspectives will also be reflected in different views of the most appropriate form of the physical surroundings.

The existence of such differences in organizations, with reference to offices, was studied some time ago by Wells (see Manning, 1965). Wells solicited attitudes towards office size from people at different levels of the organization. He found that whereas junior staff liked the idea of small offices, supervisors much preferred large open offices, with management views being between these two. Thus the role of the individual related closely to their view of the building and how it should be used. Other studies have shown that this is a generalizable and repeatable finding. Gerngross-Haas (1981), for example, has shown that the evaluation of a school building varied from headmaster to staff to pupils. Canter and Walker (1980) demonstrated in the case of mass housing that the different individuals involved, such as the architects, the planners, the counsellors, and those who assigned houses to tenants, all had very different views on what key issues were to be considered in relation to the design of houses. Many other examples of these 'differing perspectives' (reviewed by Canter, 1977) can be found in the research literature so that they form a framework with considerable predictive validity.

A number of important points emerge from this consistent finding but they are all based on the premise that no one viewpoint is the correct one. This is perhaps the most difficult premise for any individual to accept. He will be aware of his own viewpoint and have some idea of the reasons for it. These reasons will relate to the nature of the job he has to do and so will have the appearance of 'objective' logic to them. It is only when it is appreciated that each job or role within an organization may make quite different demands on the physical context that the egocentric nature of an individual's view becomes apparent.

Once it is understood that different viewpoints on the physical surroundings are likely to be a product of a person's role within the organization, then the value of harnessing all those different viewpoints becomes clear. Labels such as 'consultation', 'participation' and 'industrial democracy' are now common place. They all derive from arguments about the value of involving the workforce in decisions. In relation to the physical context, it is being suggested here, there is a direct value in involving a wide range of people, if for no other reason than that they actually have a valid, yet distinct, way of thinking about their physical surroundings deriving from their use of it.

One further implication of this argument is that one group of people in particular can be expected to have a perspective on the physical surroundings which is distinct from that of many users, namely the architects and designers. Their dealings with the physical context are so distinct from the building users' that they will often think of it in very different ways. The consequence of this is that an inadequate brief, or programme, which an architect is given for a new building or a modification will lead to a building which is less appropriate than it could be. One of the frequent ways in which such briefs are inadequate is in not utilizing the variety of perspectives available in an organization.

DESIGNING FOR PLACE USE

Throughout the discussions of the present chapter it has been implied that the physical surroundings can be shaped to facilitate productivity in the broad way it has been defined. Clearly work flow, supervision, and other aspects of the working situation which are related to the physical layout can be shaped by appropriate design and planning. One powerful example of this is the introduction of 'office landscaping', described above, which explicitly attempts to reflect patterns of supervision and work flow in the layout of desks. But it is also possible to respond to the other more subtle and complex implications of the physical surroundings by design and layout. However, to do this the planning and design process needs to be informed by more than the fads and fashions of architecture or the narrow focus of O & M.

In the opening section of this chapter Heimsath's views on the needs for a new approach to design were summarized. But even when these views are accepted there are still many myths and fallacies about the psychological contribution to design which get in the way of the effective utilization of psychological ideas. Bechtel (1977) summarized six such obstacles in the form of client and designer attitudes. They are certainly worth summarizing here.

The first set of attitudes Bechtel calls *The Monument Syndrome*. This is the attitude on the part of senior management that the building should really reflect management's own accomplishments, being a monument to their own glory. A good designer will try to utilize this desire for an appropriate image to the building without sacrificing all the other requirements to be made of a design. Closely paralleling the first syndrome and often intertwined with it is *The Control Syndrome*. This is the idea that the building can be used to shape people's behaviour and control what they do. In the present chapter I have gone to some length to show the weakness of this as a starting point for design.

A further set of unproductive attitudes Bechtel calls the *'Bricks-and-Mortar'*, the *'We already know'*, and the *'Here Comes that Jargon'* syndromes. These all point to a dismissal of the contribution of social science on the basis that it is irrelevant or common sense. Indeed frequently the same person will insist that buildings have no relevance to behaviour, then when challenged on particular examples insist that they are obvious and thus are to be dismissed. Yet what is clear, from the many examples throughout this book and in the further reading listed at the end of this chapter, is that if the ideas derived from a psychological involvement in design are already known they are very often ignored. Furthermore, in many cases where they are ignored it is because they are only imprecisely understood. It is by utilizing the more precise language of psychology and its associated measuring devices that these 'well-known' facts can be acted on. This is especially true where resources are scarce, because it is then that a clear statement of what is required will allow choices to be made.

Once these attitudinal obstacles have been overcome, which is no easy matter, there is still the question of what can actually be done to improve the design process. Here the assumption is that knowledge of the issues discussed in this chapter and the rest of this book is not enough. Ways of drawing on this knowledge need to be implemented as well, in other words different forms of design process.

Zeisel (1981) has provided many details of how the design process can be modified to incorporate issues such as those discussed in this chapter. Detailed examples are also given in Rubin and Elder (1980) and in Canter (1982b). Perhaps the one common theme through all these examples is the view, based on experience, that building users and potential building users can make a valuable contribution to design without having any specialist training. One of the stumbling blocks here is that people often erroneously believe that there are very special skills involved in reading plans and understanding what a building will be like before it is built. However, it is clear from a number of studies (reviewed by Appleyard, 1977) that buildings can be simulated in a rich range of ways very successfully as a basis for the involvement of non-architects in design. Plan and perspective drawings, models, and various enhancements of these using television and computers have been used by many people. Nor should the value of a careful examination of who does what where be minimized. Even the simple device of cutting out shapes to represent pieces of equipment and moving them around a sketch plan can open up issues which might not have emerged until after the building was completed.

CONCLUSIONS

In this chapter I have avoided giving any suggestion that if specific design policies are followed then specific changes in productivity can be anticipated. Instead I have attempted to broaden the notion of productivity to include all those aspects of the working situation which contribute to organizational effectiveness in the short and the long term. In utilizing such a broad notion of productivity I have tried to demonstrate that the consequences of the physical context, although many and varied, are nonetheless typically subtle and indirect. I have also sought to demonstrate the interconnectedness of the different components of the physical surroundings and the consequent need for managements to be on their guard for the consequences of changing what might be called the 'ecology' of the work situation.

However, against this admittedly complex and somewhat indefinite set of issues a number of themes have emerged to show the role which the physical environment can make to productivity. These may be summarized as its contribution to:

(1) providing appropriate conditions for the work tasks themselves,
(2) facilitating communications between individuals within an organization,
(3) giving symbolic identification to individuals and groups within an organization as well as for the organization itself,
(4) enabling growth, development, and change to be carried out within the organization.

Finally, it has been argued that, because of the mixture of perspectives on the nature of the workplace within any work setting, one of the major sources of understanding of the contribution of the physical context to productivity lies with the workforce itself.

FURTHER READING

Taken together the following publications give an excellent account of the relationships between the physical environment and behaviour within organizations.

Becker, F. D. (1981). *Workspace: Creating Environments in Organizations* (New York: Praeger). (This book deals directly with how decisions about the physical environment in organizations are made and proposes ways of making them more effective.)

Bennett, C. (1977). *Spaces for People: Human Factors in Design* (London: Prentice-Hall). (Although taking ergonomics as its starting point this elegantly produced little book provides a general framework for thinking about the design of workplaces from the point of view of those who use them.)

Canter, D. (1982). *Psychology for Architects* (London: Applied Science). (An elementary introduction to fundamental ideas in psychology in terms of their relevance to design decision making.)

Canter, D., and Stringer, P. (1975). *Environmental Interaction: Psychological Approaches to our Physical Surroundings* (London: Surrey University Press). (A detailed review of psychological studies of the physical surroundings.)

Farbstein, J., and Kantrowitz, M. (1978). *People in Places: Experiencing, Using and Changing the Built Environment* (London: Prentice-Hall). (A well-illustrated introduction to some of the 'links between our feelings and actions and the settings in which they take place'.)

Parsons, H. McI. (1976). Work Environments. In Altman, I. and Wohlwill, J. F. (eds.) *Human Behaviour and Environment: Advances in Theory and Research*, Vol. 1 (London: Plenum). (A rather dry review of the academic literature dealing with the influence of the environment in the world of work.)

Steele, F. I. (1973). *Physical Settings and Organization Development* (London: Addison-Wesley). (A general overview of the mechanisms by which the physical environment can affect organizational development.)

REFERENCES

Adair, J. (1973). *The Human Subject* (Boston: Little, Brown).

Altman, I. (1975). *The Environment and Social Behavior: Privacy, Personal Space, Territory, Crowding* (Monterey: Brooks/Cole).

Appleyard, D. (1977). Understanding professional media: issues, theory and a research agenda. In Altman, I., and Wohlwill, J. F. (eds.) *Human Behavior and Environment* (New York: Plenum Press).

Barker, R. G. (1968). *Ecological Psychology* (California: Stanford University Press).

Barker, R. G., and Gump, P. (1964). *Big School, Small School* (California: Stanford University Press).

Bechtel, R. B. (1977). *Enclosing Behavior* (Stroudsburg: Dowden, Hurchinson and Ross).

Becker, F. D. (1981). *Workspace: Creating Environments in Organizations* (New York: Praeger).

Bednar, M. J. (ed.) (1977). *Barrier-Free Environments* (New York: McGraw-Hill).

Bell, P. A., Fisher, J. D., and Loomis, R. J. (1978). *Environmental Psychology* (Philadelphia: W. B. Saunders).

Building Performance Research Unit (1972). *Building Performance* (London: Applied Science).

Cakir, A., Hart, D. J., and Stewart, T. F. M. (1981). *The V.D.T. Manual* (Chichester: John Wiley & Sons).

Canter, D. (1972). Reactions to open plan offices. *Built Environment*, October, 465–467.

Canter, D. (1977). *The Psychology of Place* (London: Architectural Press).

Canter, D. (1982a). *Psychology for Architects* (London: Applied Science).

Canter, D. (1982b). Contributing to environmental design. In Canter, S., and Canter, D. (eds.) *Psychology in Practice* (Chichester: John Wiley & Sons).

Canter, D., and Ambrose, I. (1981). *Prison Design and Use* (Guildford: Department of Psychology, University of Surrey).

Canter, D., and Davies, I. (1982). Ergonomic parameters of word processors in use. *Displays*, April, 81–88.

Canter, D., and Stringer, P. (1975). *Environmental Interaction: Psychological Approaches to our Physical Surroundings* (London: Surrey University Press).

Canter, D., and Walker, E. (1980). Environmental role and conceptualizations of housing. *Journal of Architectural Research*, 7, 30–35.

Canter, D., West, S., and Wools, R. (1974). Judgments of people and their rooms. *British Journal of Social and Clinical Psychology*, 13, 113–118.

Duffy, F., Cave, C., and Worthington, J. (1976). *Planning Office Space* (London: Architectural Press).

Farbstein, J., and Kantrowitz, M. (1978). *People in Places: Experiencing, Using and Changing the Built Environment* (London: Prentice-Hall).

Gerngross-Haas, G. (1981). Organizational role differences in the evaluation of an experimental school. *International Review of Applied Psychology*, 31, 223–236.

Hedge, A. (1980). Office design: people's reaction to open plan. In Thorne, R., and Arden, S. (eds.) *People and the Man-Made Environment* (Sydney: Department of Architecture, University of Sydney).

Hediger, H. (1962). The evolution of social behaviour. In Washburn, T. L. (ed.) *The Social Life of Early Man* (London: Methuen).

Heimsath, C. (1977). *Behavioral Architecture: Towards an Accountable Design Process* (New York: McGraw-Hill).

Ittelson, W. H., Proshansky, H. M., and Rivilin, L. G. (1970). The environmental psychology of the psychiatric ward. In Proshansky, H. *et al.* (eds.) *Environmental Psychology: Man and His Physical Setting* (New York: Holt, Rinehart & Winston).

Joiner, D. (1976). Social ritual and architectural space. In Proshansky, H. M., Ittelson. W. H., and Rivlin, L. G. (eds.) *Environmental Psychology: People and Their Physical Settings* (New York: Holt, Rinehart & Winston).

Jones, D., Chapman, A., and Auburn, T. (1981). Noise in the environment: a social perspective. *Journal of Environmental Psychology*, **1**, 43–60.

Langdon, J. (1963). The design of mechanised offices. *Architect's Journal*, **137**, 1081–1086.

Malone, T. B., Kirkpatrick, M., Mallory, K., Eike, D., Johnson, R. W., and Walker, R. W. (1980). *Human Factors Evaluation of Control Room Design and Operator Performance at Three Mile Island—2*. Report prepared by the Essex Corporation for the Three Mile Island Special Inquiry Group. NUREG/CR-1270; 3 volumes.

Manning, P. (ed.) (1965). *Office Design: A Study of Environment* (Liverpool: Department of Building Science, University of Liverpool).

March, J. G., and Simon, H. A. (1958). *Organization* (New York: John Wiley & Sons).

Mazis, S., and Canter, D. (1979). Physical conditions and management practices for mentally retarded children. In Canter, D., and Canter, S. (eds.) *Designing for Therapeutic Environments* (Chichester: John Wiley & Sons).

Oborne, D. J. (1982). *Ergonomics at Work* (Chichester: John Wiley & Sons).

President's Commission (1978). *The need for change—the legacy of Three Mile Island.* Report of the President's Committee on the accident at Three Mile Island.

Roethlisberger, F. J., and Dickson, W. J. (1939). *Management and the Worker* (Cambridge: Harvard University Press).

Rosenthal, R. (1966). *Experimenter Effects in Behavioral Research* (New York: Appleton-Century-Crofts).

Rubin, I., and Elder, J. (1980). *Building for People: Behavioral Research Approaches and Directions* (Washington: National Bureau of Standards Special Publication 373).

Russell, J. A., and Ward, L. M. (1982). Environmental psychology. *Annual Review of Psychology*, **33**, 651–688.

Schein, E. H. (1965). *Organisational Psychology* (Englewood Cliffs: Prentice-Hall).

Steele, F. I. (1973). *Physical Settings and Organization Development* (London: Addison-Wesley).

Wicker, A. W. (1979). *An Introduction to Ecological Psychology* (Monterey: Brooks/Cole).

Wineman, J. D. (1982). Special issue: office design and evaluation. *Environment and Behaviour*, **14**, Nos 3 and 4.

Zeisel, J. (1981). *Inquiry by Design: Tools for Environment—Behavior Research* (Monterey: Brooks/Cole).

The Physical Environment at Work
Edited by D. J. Oborne and M. M. Gruneberg
©1983 John Wiley & Sons Ltd.

Engineering Anthropometry: Work Space and Equipment to Fit the User

K. H. E. KROEMER
Ergonomics Laboratory,
Virginia Polytechnic Institute and State University,
Blacksburg, Virginia 24061, USA

Fitting work space and work equipment to the operator is clearly one of the basic tasks in ergonomics. For this, one must assess the physical dimensions of the human body and translate this information into design specifications. It would be an easy task if all anthropometric dimensions and proportions, of all people, followed a general rule. Thus, philosophers and artists embedded their ideas about the most aesthetic dimensions into ideal schemes of perfect proportions. 'Golden sections' were developed in ancient India, China, Egypt, and Greece, and more recently by Leonardo da Vinci, and Albrecht Dürer. However, such canons are fictive since actual human dimensions and proportions vary greatly among individuals. Hippocrates (about 460–377 BC) taught that there are four temperaments (actually, body fluids) represented by four body types. The psychiatrist Ernest Kretchmer (1888–1964) proposed that three typical somatotypes (pyknic, athletic, aesthetic) could reflect human character traits. In the 1940s, W. H. Sheldon and his co-workers devised a system of three body physiques (endo-, meso-, ectomorphic). The classification was originally intuitive, and has more recently been developed to include actual measurements.

Physical anthropology as a recording and comparing science may be traced to Marco Polo (1273–1295) who described a great number of human races differing in body size and body build. Linné (1707–1778), Buffon (1707–1788), and White (1728–1813) are usually credited with having started the science of anthropology. Blumenbach (1752–1840) reported the complete anthropometric data available, *On the Natural Differences in Mankind.* The statistician Quetelét (1796–1874) is the 'father of anthropometry'. He conducted the first large-scale somatometric survey. Broca (1824–1880),

Table 1. Sample applications of engineering anthropometry*

General uses and examples	Data required	Purpose
Design criteria development and selection		
Determine general and specific population characteristics of users. Measurement of sample subjects, statistical description of sizes, design population selection.	Major body dimensions (height, weight), age, sex, job, national extraction, geographic areas.	Realistic design and evaluation of dimensional specifications. Customer acceptance, maximize sales, minimize legal liabilities.
Design requirements		
Work space design and development — aircraft cockpits, automobile interiors, seats, consoles, tables, cabinets, maintenance access space, hatches and doors, tunnels, ladders. Includes any gross volume designed for human occupancy, for work, pleasure, hygiene, rest, treatment, or education.	Reach limits, body clearances, and clothing allowances, forces, torques, centres of mass, moments of inertia, mobility, volume, eye locations.	Assure operator/occupant has adequate volume, proper location of controls, displays, devices, tools. Maximize work efficiency, sales and profits, safety.
Clothing and personal equipment design and development — pressure suits, cooling and heating garments, fuel handler's suits and armour. Harness, life support, and temperature control packs. Emphasis on 'engineered' clothing, not on home or business dress.	Circumferences, surface lengths along body, contours, areas, volumes, diameters, limb movements and restrictions.	Proper fit to the wearer, minimize restriction of movement, define range of sizes and number of each required to prevent overstock. Assure proper work space interface.
Components and devices — electrical switches, knobs, levers, buttons, etc., hand-holds, latches, wheels, cranks, stick controls, small appliances, instruments.	Details of body parts in contact with product — fingertips, face contours, foot and shoe shape.	Assure proper interface with hand, foot, head, etc. to enhance operability, safety, convenience, comfort. Maximize sales, reduce rework costs.

Evaluation criteria and testing

Specify bases for determining if design drawing or product/work space is adequate for intended users. Perform comparative measurements and test operability.	As required by the case.	Evaluation to determine if design meets goals, or to develop limits for rework of design if required.
Measurement of sample subjects—select persons representative of users.	Per critical design limits.	
Population description—prepare drawings, tables, graphs, computerized data base.		
Evaluation device design—prepare reach envelopes, contour templates, articulated drafting manikins, anthropomorphic dummies, computer models.		
Testing—perform measurements on product, work space, clothing, and subject.		

Operator selection

Specify operator dimensions—prepare list of measurements to be taken and limits for acceptance for critical spaces or clothing, etc.	As required by the cases. Usually height, weight, sitting height, breadths, strength tests.	Assure personnel are of proper size range for equipment design limits (size or stress).
Personnel measurement—train and initiate programme of selection.		Assure correct methods and accuracy.

*Adapted from Roebuck, Kroemer, and Thomson (1975)

founder of the École d'Anthropologie in Paris, conducted theoretical research and devised many measurement techniques and devices. In 1914, Martin published the first edition of his *Lehrbuch der Anthropologie* which remained the standard textbook for decades.

Military personnel provided a captive data source for anthropometrists. Thus, large amounts of anthropometric data, taken with consistent techniques, provide reliable information on changing body dimensions. For example, in the U.S.A. very substantial anthropometric surveys were conducted between the Civil War and World War II. The military services are most interested in body dimensions, space requirements, reach, and strength capabilities. Hence, centres of military engineering anthropometry developed in several countries, such as in Farnborough, U.K., or Wright-Patterson AFB, U.S.A. (For more detail, see Roebuck, Kroemer, and Thomson, 1975; Hertzberg, 1979.) Triggered by the successes demonstrated by military man–machine systems, industry caught on and applied human factors engineering or ergonomic data to the design of products, and in the manufacturing process. With anthropometry as the basis, biomechanical, physiological and psychological inputs merged with engineering to create, as one should hope, best performing, safe, healthy, and satisfying manned work systems. Table 1 lists application areas and data requirements in engineering anthropometry. As this list indicates, engineering anthropometry provides information on the human body for three main ergonomic tasks:

(1) Establishment of criteria for the design of technical components (equipment, etc.) of systems in which the human is the prime mover, operator, or supervisor. For this, major demographic and anthropometric dimensions are needed, such as age and sex, and primary body dimensions such as height, eye height, reach capabilities, and muscular strength.

(2) Provision of anthropometric criteria for the evaluation and testing of proto-type or existing equipment. This task requires in essence the same information as just listed; however, often more detailed or specific data are needed, such as hand clearances, or the range of popliteal heights of the user population to provide adequate adjustability of a seat height. Both tasks often require the design and use of special devices, such as contour templates, articulated manikins, or computerized models of the human body in relation to the work space, for example, SAMMIE, or COMBIMAN — see later.

(3) Finally, existing work space requirements occasionally need the selection of operators to fit the equipment dimensions. While this may be an unavoidable task for very specialized equipment such as small experimental deep-sea diving machines, this would not be an advisable ergonomic procedure for often-used equipment meant for the general population: one of the primary axioms of ergonomics is to fit the equipment to the operator, and not vice versa.

Today's engineers use information on human dimensions and physical capabilities to design hand tools, work stations, equipment, and work tasks to fit them to the human operator. Thus, 'engineering anthropometry' is the application of anatomical and anthropological measurement methods to human subjects for the development of engineering design requirements. Therefore, engineering anthropometry is one of the backbones of 'ergonomics', or 'human factors' as it is often called in North America, which study human characteristics for the appropriate design of the living and working environment.

A separate branch of applied anthropometry developed in the late 1900s. Body structures, kinetics and kinematics of the human body, the mechanics of the musculoskeletal system, etc. were investigated. This field of scientific endeavour, called 'biomechanics', is the interdisciplinary science comprising mainly anthropometry, mechanics, physiology, and engineering studying mechanical structure and behaviour of biological materials. It concerns primarily dimensions, mobility, composition, and mass properties of body segments; mechanical reactions of the body to force fields, vibrations, and impacts; voluntary actions in bringing about controlled movements, and applying forces, torques, and energy and power to external objects such as controls and tools.

The relationships between engineering anthropometry and biomechanics are so close that it is difficult and probably useless to draw demarcation lines between them. Knowledge about the physical characteristics of the body is obviously basic to each, and designing the man-made environment from tools to tasks such as to suit human dimensions and to meet human capabilities is the common desired result.

SECULAR CHANGES IN BODY SIZE

Looking at medieval body armour one cannot help but notice that today's males would have a hard time fitting into these small shells. Such secular increase in body size is also apparent from the everyday experience of children being larger than their parents. While evidence for long-term gains in body size is only indirect, statistical comparison of anthropometric data taken by the military services on large samples with consistent techniques proves increases in stature in the neighbourhood of 1 centimetre per decade in this century. Figure 1 shows this development in the U.S.A. A gain in body weight of about 2 kg per decade has become apparent in the U.S.A. during the second half of this century.

Regarding the reasons for such secular changes in anthropometry, and the expected future development, one may assume that hereditary capabilities for the achievement of one's optimal body dimensions generally had not been fully utilized in the past, due to deficient living conditions. Recent improvements

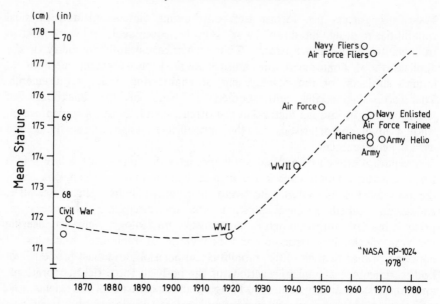

Figure 1. Secular trend in stature for young U.S. males: 1870–1980

in hygiene and nutrition facilitate achieving inherited growth potentials. Thus, body heights of families that have been well-off for generations no longer increase, while those families still improving their socioeconomic status show gains in stature. With favourable living conditions for most, the increase should diminish, and body height will probably reach a new statistical value asymptotically (Stoudt, 1978).

For most engineering applications, the relatively small changes in body dimensions are of little consequence—but should be considered for the design of manned systems that are meant to be used well into the future. For example, when the plans for the U.S. Space Shuttle were first developed in the 1960s, the question needed to be answered whether the shuttle crew would be significantly different in body dimensions from current pilots since the crew station was to be designed for use 20–30 years hence.

Secular changes of body dimensions are often intermingled with the variability of body data related to geographic or ethnic origin. There is, for example, considerable discussion regarding the possible change in body dimensions of the Japanese whose trunk length (sitting height) is comparable to European or North Americans, but whose legs used to be considerably shorter. Is indeed leg length, and thus the overall proportion of the Japanese, changing? Such changes are difficult to document within relatively short periods of time, such as decades.

Within a nation, differences related to ethnic origin or socioeconomic strata play only a minor role with respect to design of common equipment. For example, it is rather unlikely that in Great Britain kitchen ranges would be designed in different heights for, say, Scottish households as compared with families of Indian extraction; or, in the U.S.A., for households in New York as compared with households in Houston, Texas. Usually, either the design dimensions are generally acceptable, though perhaps not optimal for every person, or one is able to use built-in adjustments, such as screwing feet further in or out. However, for special industries such different dimensions of population subgroups, or of different populations, may play an important role. Consider in this context the garment industry.

For export businesses, consideration of different body dimensions of various user populations is often of major importance. Consider here, for example, the design of earth-moving equipment, of machine tools, or of military equipment to be used, say, by some relatively small-sized Asian populations as compared with Europeans. Such diverse populations may show very different body dimensions, and strength capabilities, in addition to starkly different population stereotypes, varying perception of technical components and their use, etc. (Chapanis, 1975; NASA, 1978).

Changes in civilian anthropometry are difficult to observe and to demonstrate given that the relative sparsity of reliable anthropometric data only cover recent decades. Thus, statements about expected changes in body dimensions are often speculative and may differ from researcher to researcher: for example, a French estimate of a 2.4 centimetre per decade increase in stature for the U.S. (Guillien and Rebiffé, in Oborne and Levis, 1980) is considerably larger than stated by U.S. authorities (NASA, 1978). Very clearly, interpretations of the same data and extrapolations of their expected changes into the future may differ quite considerably. Still, changes in stature of 1, 2, or 3 centimetres per decade would not make much difference for the design of most technical equipment which is most often designed for use periods in the range of a few to perhaps 10–15 years.

Altogether only a relatively small number of populations have been measured using consistent and modern techniques. On most developing nations, up-to-date, reliable, and complete information is simply not available. Attempts to establish worldwide anthropometric surveys have not succeeded for a variety of reasons including the cost involved. It may be hoped that standardized measurements proposed to the International Standardization Organization (ISO; see later) will help to provide such international information in the foreseeable future.

ANTHROPOMETRIC MEASUREMENT TECHNIQUES

Traditional standard anthropometry relies on a small set of instruments: anthropometer, several types of calipers, measuring tape, grip strength dynamometer, and a weight scale (Hertzberg, 1968; Roebuck, Kroemer, and Thomson, 1975). These are effective measurement tools if used by a skilled anthropometrist, but (with exception of the scale) represent obsolete technology with respect to the acquisition and recording of the data. They need a specially trained user, reading by eye, and recording by hand. They are error-prone and slow. Many attempts have been made to improve these standard instruments, such as adding potentiometers to anthropometer, caliper, and tape and to use their electric outputs as direct inputs to a computer recording the data (Snyder, 1981).

Photography does not need physical contact, but can record only surface contours of the body which are, with few exceptions, determined by compressible tissue and give little information about the underlying bony landmarks, traditionally preferred by the anthropologist. Standard photography, using either one camera and mirrors or several cameras, has been applied in one major survey (USAF, 1968). Stereometric photography, with its techniques derived from cartography, provides 3-D pictures of the surface contours of the human body. To overcome the difficulty of relating surface features to underlying bony structures, the use of 'point marks' has been proposed (Reynolds, 1981) which would allow locating limbs (represented by the point marks) with respect to each other in spatial coordinates. This technique has yet to be applied to living subjects in general surveys.

In fact, the relation of surface measurements to the underlying skeletal structures of the body is of major concern to the anthropometrist, biomechanist, and engineer. Usually, the human body is modelled as a basic system of rigid links connected by articulations with known degrees of freedom, covered by masses of given distribution and contours, powered by muscle action around the joints, etc. — very much in the tradition of Borelli's model described in his *De motu animalium* about 1680. Such models require knowledge of the relationships between the surface measurements, as traditionally provided by anthropometry, and the body structures representing links and articulations. Reynolds (1982) questioned whether current (often deterministic and overly simplistic) biomechanical models can represent the characteristics of the human body sufficiently, and if classical anthropometry can provide the information needed for state-of-the-art modelling.

Measurement of grip strength has often been part of anthropometric surveys. Usually a mechanical device was used that gave somewhat under force application (the amount depending on the special design features). The deflection of the device was calibrated and used as a measure of strength exhibited by the subject. For muscle strength assessment other than grip strength, a large number of measurement tools have been used (Roebuck, Kroemer, and Thomson, 1975). Non-recording devices, usually pointer instruments, are suitable for quick checks, but do not satisfy the need for yielding a true record of the strength exerted, as controlled strength tests require (Caldwell *et al.*, 1974; Kroemer and Marras, 1980). A very convenient means to attain an analogue record of the strength exertion is via strain-gauges, which transform a very small deflection of an elastic component of the dynamometer into an electrical signal that can be calibrated, recorded, and analysed easily. Such strain gauges can be applied to any suitable part in the measuring system which often allows modifications of actual work equipment to serve as a measuring tool; many commercially available load cells use strain-gauge technology.

In traditional anthropometry, the person to be measured is placed in a stiff erect position, with body joints usually at 0, 90, or 180 degrees, such as in the so-called anatomical position. Deviations from this posture, commonplace at work, are difficult to describe in the traditional medical–anatomical terminology. A comprehensive and unambiguous notation proposed by Roebuck (described in Roebuck, Kroemer, and Thomson, 1975) has yet to be applied commonly; thus, describing the continuously changing body segment positions of a person at the workplace, or in sports, is still a difficult task. Choreographic notation systems do not yet appeal to the human factors engineers (Badler and Smoliar, 1979); however, a technique called 'posture targeting' allows classification of body segment positions quickly (Corlett, Madeley, and Manenica, 1979).

Many persons and institutions are, at this time, working to develop better measuring techniques to assess human body characteristics, and to understand human biomechanics better so that one can describe realistically body dimensions, mechanics, and functional capabilities needed for workplace design. Results of such work were presented at a special symposium on anthropometry and biomechanics held in 1980 in Cambridge, England. The proceedings of this meeting provide detailed information (Easterby, Kroemer, and Chaffin, 1982).

Survey sampling

The selection of the subject sample to be measured is highly critical because it determines the validity of the data, and the cost of the procedure. Measuring every citizen of a nation is time-consuming but yields an exact anthropometric picture of that population. Counter-examples of highly selected samples would be visitors to automobile exhibitions (excluding those not interested in car shows, or living in remote areas), or telephone owners. On the other hand, if one is interested in, say, the weights of shoppers at supermarkets, exactly such persons should be sampled.

The most comprehensive, and most expensive, technique in sampling is to measure all subjects, such as is routinely done in military entrance exams. Thus, the whole population of concern is assessed. If the population group is not 'captive', random selection from a master file, such as the national census, is in order. While likely to yield a highly accurate picture of the population, this is certainly a very expensive method. However, sampling techniques stratified for age, sex, social status, region, etc., are feasible and have been proposed for nationwide surveys (Churchill and McConville, 1976). If the selection criteria are well defined, quasi-quota matching can be used, possibly specialized to the extent of using 'microcosm' subsamples. Many combinations of these techniques are feasible, such as measuring a rather large sample in selected key dimensions, and taking additional measurements on every third or tenth subject.

The more specialized the sample and the dimensions taken, the more this method resembles 'subgrouping', such as applied to pre-selected individuals usually representing the extreme ends of population distributions—for example, the tall–heavy, or short–light. As discussed later, such subgroups are often used by engineers to check their designs for fit to the extremes of the user population, assuming that the mid-ranges will be accommodated if the design fits the unusual persons. The ultimate is, of course, measuring individuals to fit equipment exactly to the person, such as in tailoring space suits for selected astronauts, or custom fitting face masks to champion deep-sea divers.

Measurements needed

The first question is: Who needs anthropometric data for what purpose? A manufacturer of loosely fitting garments is interested in different anthropometric data than a physical anthropologist. The manufacturer of face masks needs information very different from that used by an automobile designer. To determine the size and location of safe openings in equipment so that the operator cannot be caught in them requires information other than needed to determine leg room, and chair adjustments, for work-stations used by seated operators. Muscle strength data are used either to set control force requirements which a given percentage of all potential users can meet, or to determine design specifications so that nobody will break the equipment.

The needs are closely related to the question of the necessary exactness of the data. How much uncertainty can the anthropologist, manufacturer of face masks, or automotive engineer tolerate? This user requirement determines how much inaccuracy can be tolerated in the prediction of, say, civilian data from military information, or the exactness with which the initial measurer must take the data.

A problem probably more critical than the exactness of data (which seems to be satisfactory for most application purposes) is how to translate the traditional static anthropometric data into dynamic information which would depict reliably the functional dimensions of the human body in motion. Body dimensions are traditionally taken on subjects assuming a rigid, standardized posture in which the body segments are at 0, 90, or 180 degrees to each other.

These are not the conditions in which work is performed, and for which equipment must be designed. At this moment there is still no theoretically sound procedure for the systematic translation of the static standard data into functional measurements. Until detailed sound procedures are developed, the following 'rules of thumb' may be helpful:

Heights (stature, eye, shoulder, hip): reduce by 3 per cent.
Elbow height: no change, or increase by up to 5 per cent if elevated at work.
Knee or popliteal height, sitting: no change, except with high shoe heels.
Forward and lateral reaches: decrease by 30 per cent for convenience, increase by 20 per cent for extensive shoulder and trunk motions.

Obviously, these are only very rough estimates which can be quite different for certain body postures, working conditions, etc. Furthermore, it might be expected that small persons would not show much slumping at the workplace because the equipment is often designed to fit larger workers; conversely,tall persons might be used to bending over and crouching down. (This, incidentally, again gives reason to use adjustable workplaces.) Certainly, more research is needed to establish better founded procedures to translate static body position data into functional design recommendations.

The number of measurements to be taken from the subject depends on the three aspects mentioned, i.e., who needs the data, how exact the data must be, and how they translate from the static to the dynamic condition. Accordingly, and depending on other specific constraints, dimensions actually taken range from very few (twelve in the 1967 U.S. HANES survey) to very many (189 taken in the 1968 USAF survey). The ISO (International Organization for Standardization) through its Technical Committee 159, Ergonomics, is developing a key list of measurements to be taken. Draft standard 7250 provides a core of measurements in anthropometric surveys that, finally, could establish a common basis for comparative anthropometry. This core list proposes six measurements on the standing subject (including body weight; stature; eye, shoulder, and elbow height); eight measurements on the sitting subject. It also refers to thirteen measurements of specific body segments, plus eleven functional measurements, such as forward reach, forearm–hand length.

As discussed later, one might need just two or three dimensions to predict practically any others in which an engineer is interested. The two dimensions needed mostly are stature and weight which, combined, yield through regression equations good predictions of other body dimensions (see below for more details). Table 2 lists such body dimensions, calculated for the current civilian U.S. population. To carry it to the extreme: since it has shown that just asking subjects for their height and weight yields rather exact figures (with predictable overstatements for height and understatements for weight) it might suffice (and be very expedient) to use this simple technique, relying on predictive equations for the remainder of the data.

Table 2
U.S. Civilian body dimensions, female/male in cm or kg, for ages 20 to 60 years
(Courtesy of Dr J. T. McConville, Anthropology Research Project, Yellow Springs,
OH 45387 and Dr K. W. Kennedy, USAF-AMRL-HEG, WPAFB, OH 45433).

	Percentiles			
	5th	50th	95th	Std. Dev.
Stature (height)	149.5/161.8	160.5/173.6	171.3/184.4	6.6/6.9
Eye height	138.3/151.1	148.9/162.4	159.3/172.7	6.4/6.6*
Shoulder (acromion) height	121.1/132.3	131.1/142.8	141.9/152.4	6.3/6.1*
Elbow height	93.6/100.0	101.2/109.9	108.8/119.0	4.6/5.8*
Knuckle height	64.3/69.8	70.2/75.4	75.9/80.4	3.5/3.2*
Height, sitting	78.6/84.2	85.0/90.6	90.7/96.7	3.5/3.7
Eye height, sitting	67.5/72.6	73.3/78.6	78.5/84.4	3.3/3.6*
Shoulder height, sitting	49.2/52.7	55.7/59.4	61.7/65.8	3.8/4.0*
Elbow rest height, sitting	18.1/19.0	23.3/24.3	28.1/29.4	2.9/3.0
Knee height, sitting	45.2/49.3	49.8/54.3	54.4/59.3	2.7/2.9
Popliteal height, sitting	35.5/39.2	39.8/44.2	44.3/48.8	2.6/2.8
Thigh clearance height, sitting	10.6/11.4	13.7/14.4	17.5/17.7	1.8/1.7
Head breadth	13.6/14.4	14.5/15.4	15.5/16.4	0.57/0.59
Head circumference	52.2/53.8	54.9/56.8	57.7/59.3	1.63/1.68
Interpupillary distance	5.1/5.5	5.8/6.2	6.5/6.8	0.44/0.39
Forward reach, functional	64.0/76.3	71.0/82.5	79.0/88.3	4.5/3.6*
Elbow–fingertip length	38.5/44.1	42.1/47.9	46.0/51.4	2.2/2.2*
Hand length	16.4/17.6	17.95/19.05	19.8/20.6	1.04/0.93
Hand breadth, metacarpal	7.0/8.2	7.66/8.88	8.4/9.8	0.41/0.47
Hand circumference, metacarpal	16.9/19.9	18.36/21.55	19.9/23.5	0.80/1.09
Chest depth	21.4/21.4	24.2/24.2	29.7/27.6	2.5/1.9*
Elbow-to-elbow breadth	31.5/35.0	38.4/41.7	49.1/50.6	5.4/4.6
Hip breadth, sitting	31.2/30.8	36.4/35.4	43.7/40.6	3.7/2.8
Buttock-knee length, sitting	51.8/54.0	56.9/59.4	62.5/64.2	3.1/3.0
Foot length	22.3/24.8	24.1/26.9	26.2/29.0	1.19/1.28
Foot breadth	8.1/9.0	8.84/9.79	9.7/10.7	0.50/0.53
Weight (in kg)	46.2/56.2	61.1/74.0	89.9/97.1	13.8/12.6

*Std. Dev. estimated by Kroemer.

Unfortunately, body dimensions and muscle strength capabilities are only meagrely related with each other: the fact that body weight is the variable that correlates best with strength attests to this. Like the traditionally measured grip strength which is only weakly indicative of other body strengths, muscle strength measurements do not correlate well with each other (NASA, 1978; Roebuck, Kroemer, and Thomson, 1975); however, in certain cases, multiple-regression equations can be used to predict strength capabilities from several anthropometric variables measured (Ayoub, *et al.*, 1980).

MUSCLE STRENGTH ASSESSMENT

Borelli's 300-year-old model of the human body incorporated muscles as moving the body segments. Generally, a muscle connects two body segments rotatable about a common joint. If the muscle is under tension it applies torque to each segment. The magnitude of torque depends on the amount of internal muscle force, on the distance between the joint and the location of the muscle or tendon attachment to the bone, that is, the lever arm, and on the pull angle between the vector of muscle force and the limbs. Usually, neither pull angle nor lever arm are known, and for practical purposes the muscle is inaccessible. Therefore, internally developed muscle forces usually cannot easily be measured directly.

For engineering purposes, however, the force applied to an outside object is of primary interest. Since this force depends on the inherent strength of the muscles as well as on the prevailing mechanical advantages, the location of the force-measuring device must be specified with respect to the body, usually to the next joint, to make the measurement meaningful.

Human muscular strength is, for engineering purposes, expressed as the linear, or translational, force exerted at the interface with the measuring device in terms of a vector, having magnitude and direction. Torque measurements (force multiplied by the prevailing lever arm) or pressure measurements (force evenly distributed over a known surface area) can be conceived as modified assessments of linear force.

By definition, strength data refer to maximal efforts only. The relevance of such maximal data to submaximal, optimal, reasonable, or acceptable conditions is discussed in some detail by Roebuck, Kroemer, and Thomson, 1975.

Measurement of human voluntary muscular strength has been part of many anthropometric surveys. Design of work equipment and work tasks must take into account human strength capabilities, such as hand forces applied to tools and controls, or foot forces applied to pedals. While the human operator applies most forces in movement, that is dynamically, so far most strength assessments have been performed under static conditions. This is primarily due to the fact that the static case (in which all forces are in balance and where therefore no new movement occurs) constitutes simple mechanics, hence allowing use of simple mechanical measuring instruments under simple experimental conditions. With no displacement occurring, no time derivatives of displacement such as speed and acceleration must be considered.

In the static strength exertion, muscles do not change their length during their contraction. In physiological–anatomical terms, this is called an isometric contraction because the length of the muscle remains unchanged. For practical reasons (discussed by Kroemer, 1970) such an isometric contraction is often accompanied by an isotonic one, in which the tonus or tension of the muscle remains constant also. (The term isotonic is often misused, for instance by falsely assuming that moving a constant mass would load muscles isotonically.) If no isotonus is requested from the subject, then the muscular contraction is often quick and strains muscular and tendon tissues in an elastic manner; furthermore, some movement of the body segments involved might occur. Thus, testing muscle strength of a subject by allowing or requesting an instantaneous peak force might lead to rather unreliable and unrepeatable strength measurements. To achieve reliable and repeatable measurements, and in order to control motivational aspects of the strength exertion (which might also affect the result significantly) a technique has been introduced which allows the control and theoretical sound measurement of human strength capabilities (Caldwell *et al.*, 1974). In fact, some new research results indicate that utilization of this Caldwell Regimen might control or perhaps help to assess the motivational component of voluntary strength exertion (Kroemer and Marras, 1980).

Until recently only very little effort has been devoted to the assessment of human dynamic muscle strength capabilities in scientifically controlled laboratory experiments. While indeed dynamic exertion of strength is the essence of many sports events, no suitable measurement techniques were at hand to measure the dynamic strength exertions until so-called isokinetic instruments found increasing acceptance in recent years. Isokinetic equipment requires the subject to apply his/her muscular strength while maintaining a pre-selected constant angular speed. (This constant speed is, obviously, only one of the many possible dynamic ways to exert voluntary muscular strength.)

In essence, then, there are three approaches to measure human muscle strength:

(1) The individually selected, but not externally controlled, dynamic effort (such as in sports): no direct measures of the human strength exerted is usually attempted; hence, no derived design data are available.
(2) The isokinetic exertion, in which force is applied in a movement with constant speed: some strength data are available now in physiological journals.

(3) The traditional static (or isometric) strength exertion, with no motion: the currently available data fall almost exclusively into this category.

It is well to keep these considerations in mind while comparing the large number of strength data scattered in the literature. Unfortunately, even for the static strength information, caution must be applied in interpreting the published data. Experimental controls are often not reported together with the experimental results. It may be unclear under what conditions subjects exerted their strength, exactly what instructions were given to them, which instrumentation was used, and how the data were recorded and analysed. (There is evidence that differences in some reported strength data may reflect not so much variances in capabilities among subject samples, but rather in experimental procedures.) Nevertheless, the existing information on static muscle strength capability can be applied to the important design case of no or slow motion during strength exertion. If one must be assured that the equipment may not be broken by the user, a strength percentile value at or above 100 would be selected as the design criterion. If one wants to design the object or task so that 'weak' persons can do the job, then this subgroup of the population will determine the percentile strength datum to be selected. There is, finally, some speculation that isometric strength data may indeed be the largest forces or torque values that can be measured, whether statically or dynamically, in tests of voluntary muscle strength. Whether indeed this proves to be true needs to be seen.

The term 'endurance' signifies the ability to continue to work or, in the static case, to exert force in the presence of fatigue. It is common experience that small forces can be exerted over long periods of time while maximal efforts have to be terminated soon because of fatigue or exhaustion. A non-linear relationship exists between the fraction of strength required and length of time needed during which it can be maintained. Figure 2 shows this relationship schematically. If less than about 15 per cent of total strength is required, such a force can be maintained over periods of time 'indefinitely' longer than 10 minutes. With increasing force requirements, the endurance time decreases quickly; 'maximal strength' can be maintained for only a few seconds.

Age and sex are statistically related to strength. Muscular strength increases until approximately 30 years of age and thereafter tapers off. With both sexes being about equally strong at the age of 10, the strength of males increases more rapidly and to a higher amount. In men, strength reaches the maximum in the middle or late twenties. It remains on this level for 5 or 10 years and then drops slowly but increasingly. Only about 80 per cent of the maximum strength of the twenties is still available at age 60. However, not all muscle groups vary in strength in this way. For example, the strength of hand and arm shows a relatively strong ascent after the age of 20, and later declines less steeply with increasing age.

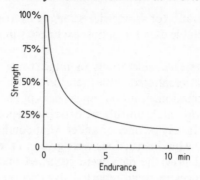

Figure 2. Endurance time as a function of available strength required.
(Schematic, from Kroemer, 1970)

Strength of women has been measured variously at 0 to 60 per cent weaker than that of men of the same age. A generally accepted overall estimate for the strength of women at age 30 is two-thirds of the men's strength at the same age. Following about ten years of rather constant strength, the strength of women decreases somewhat faster than that of men; at about 50 years, women are only about half as strong as their male contemporaries. (These are, of course, all 'averages', not indicative of individual scores.)

In right-handed persons (approximately 90 per cent of all), the right arm is slightly stronger than the left, though usually less than 10 per cent. Strength differences between the two legs are even less obvious. For most practical purposes, the slight differences in strength of the two sides of the body can be neglected.

EXCURSION INTO ANTHROPOMETRIC STATISTICS

The simplest and most often used (and misused) statistic in engineering anthropometry is the mean. It applies to normal data distributions only; if the median or mode are different from the mean, the data set is not bell-shaped, or normal, but skewed — see Table 3 for the appropriate formulae. Another false use of the mean stems from the misconception that one could add average values of 'stacked' body segments (such as forearm length and upper arm length) and thus arrive at the total length of both segments (for example, total arm length). As basic statistical considerations and practical experiences show, this is not true: people are simply not average in many or even all dimensions. Robinette and McConville (1981) demonstrated this fallacy both with statistical rigour, and by practical example. As early as 1952, Daniels tested the practicality of the 'average man' concept: he generously called the central 25 per cent of the data distribution average and counted how many of his more than 4000 subjects were 'average' in stature: 1055 subjects fell into this

Table 3

Measures of central tendency

Mean	$\bar{x} = \Sigma x/N$	(1st moment)
Median	Middle value (of values in numerical order), 50th percentile	
Mode	Most often found value	

Measures of variability

Range $\qquad\qquad x_{max} - x_{min}$

Standard deviation $\quad S = $ (Variance)$^{1/2}$

$\qquad\qquad\qquad\quad = [\Sigma(x - \bar{x})^2/N]^{1/2}$ (Use N–1 for N<15)   (2nd moment)

Coefficient of
variation $\qquad\qquad CV = S/\bar{x}$

Standard error of
the mean $\qquad\qquad SE = S/N^{1/2} = (S^2/N)^{1/2}$

Confidence limits
for mean $\qquad\qquad \bar{x} \pm k \cdot SE$ (see Table 5 for values of k)

Skewness $\qquad\qquad \Sigma(x - \bar{x})^3/N$ (3rd moment)

Measure of relationship between variables

Coefficient of
correlation $\qquad r = S_{xy}/(S_x \cdot S_y)^{1/2}$

$\qquad\qquad\qquad = \Sigma[(x - \bar{x})(y - \bar{y})]/[\Sigma(x - \bar{x})^2 \Sigma(y - \bar{y})^2]^{1/2}$

Technique of estimating the value of one variable from another

Regression $\qquad y = \alpha x + \beta \qquad\qquad \beta = \bar{y} - \alpha\bar{x}$

$\qquad\qquad\quad \alpha = r \cdot S_y/S_x \qquad\qquad SE_y = S_y(1 - r^2)^{1/2}$

---

category. Of these, 302 were also 'average' in chest circumference. Table 4 shows that only 1 per cent of his initial sample was 'average' in six dimensions. Obviously, had the true definition of average (i.e., 'mean ± 0 standard deviation') been applied, hardly any person would have been average in more than one dimension. Incidentally, the idea of persons being small in all dimensions (or large in all dimensions) is as fallacious as the phantom of the 'average person'.

Table 4. The 'average man' concept (Data from Daniels, 1952)

Of 1055 men with 'average' stature ('average' defined here as mean ±0.3S):

302	(29%)	also had 'average' chest girth
143	(14%)	also had 'average' sleeve length
73	(7%)	also had 'average' crotch height
28	(3%)	also had 'average' torso circumference
12	(1%)	also had 'average' hip circumference
6	(0.6%)	also had 'average' neck circumference, etc.

Daniel's selection of the central 25 per cent of his data sample could have been expressed as ranging from the 37.5th to the 62.5th percentile. For a normal distribution, percentiles can be calculated from mean and standard deviation as indicated in Table 5. The use of percentiles is very convenient for two reasons:

(1) one can easily see what sample portions are included, or excluded, if one selects certain percentiles; and
(2) one can simply arrange data in ascending or descending order and quickly determine given percentage values without having to assume normality of the data sample.

Table 5. Calculation of percentiles

If a random variable has a normal distribution with the mean $\bar{x}$ and the standard deviation S, percentiles p can be calculated as follows:

	Percentile p associated with x		Central percentage
k	$x = \bar{x} - kS$	$x = \bar{x} + kS$	included
2.576	0.5	99.5	99
2.326	1	99	98
2.06	2	98	96
1.96	2.5	97.5	95
1.88	3	97	94
1.65	5	95	90
1.28	10	90	80
1.04	15	85	70
1.00	16.5	83.5	67
0.84	20	80	60
0.67	25	75	50
0.32	37.5	62.5	25
0	50	50	0

Examples: to determine 20th percentile, use $k = 0.84 : \bar{x} - 0.84S \rightarrow P_{20}$
to determine 95th percentile, use $k = 1.65 : \bar{x} + 1.65S \rightarrow P_{95}$

Thus, one needs only to be able to count, with no further statistical skills required. Figure 3 presents, schematically, such a procedure. Here a distribution skewed towards the lower values of x is simply sectioned in discrete values of x which indicate 5th, 10th, 50th, 90th, and 95th percentiles. If the distribution is normal, which fortunately is the case in most anthropometric dimensions, one can simply calculate percentiles by using mean and standard deviation. Table 5 shows this procedure. Values for the standard deviation are multiplied with a specific factor k, and then added to or subtracted from the mean value. (For values of k not listed, see any table of the normal distribution function in a statistics book.)

This procedure can be put to good and easy use if one wants to determine, for example, what adjustment range one would need to 'fit' a given population. Knowing the statistics of the associated body dimension, one would decide on the smallest percentile to be accommodated (say, the 5th percentile) and on the largest percentile to be fitted (say, the 95th percentile; this then includes the central 90 per cent of the population dimension). The trade-off between population fit and design range, that is fit versus expense, can be determined quickly.

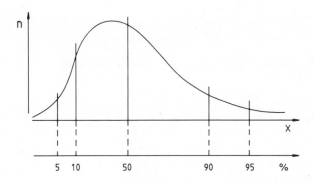

Figure 3. Skewed distribution sectioned into percentile portions

Another example would be the determination of descriptive statistics for a composite population. Often data for subsamples are at hand, while the population composed of these samples has not been measured. For example, one may know that a user population consists of 75 per cent males, and 25 per cent females. For both males and females the statistic in question (for example, functional reach forward) is known. What is the combined statistic which takes into account the given distribution of males and females? The use of the mean, standard deviation, and appropriate k values helps to answer such a question. In Table 6, two examples are given to determine values of composite populations. In each case, only mean, standard deviation, and the portions of the subsamples comprising the composite population need to be known. The first example uses two samples, the second example a population composed of three samples. Obviously, this procedure can be adapted to include more subsamples.

MODELS AS DATA 'MASSAGE' SYSTEMS

Before anthropometric measurements can be used as input for data storage and retrieval systems, they must be checked for errors. Errors used to be quite

Table 6. Percentile values of composite populations

Given: Two samples, a and b
Composite population: $a\% + b\% = 100\%$

You want to know: at what percentile of the composite population is a specific value of x (e.g., pertaining to strength, or a body dimension)

You need to know: $\bar{x}_a, S_b$ ⎫ Mean and Standard Deviation of distribution of the variable x for samples a and b.

$\bar{x}_b, S_b$ ⎭ (See page 129 in Roebuck, Kroemer, and Thomson, 1975, if you must estimate S)

Step 1: Determine factors k associated with x in the samples a and b
1.1 For sample a:

$$x_a = \bar{x} - k_a \cdot S_a \qquad \text{if } x_a < \bar{x}_a$$
$$x_a = x_a + k_a \cdot S_a \qquad \text{if } x_a > \bar{x}_a$$

$$k_a = \frac{|x_a - \bar{x}_a|}{S_a} \qquad (1.1)$$

1.2 Similarly, for sample b

$$k_b = \frac{|x_b - \bar{x}_b|}{S_b} \qquad (1.2)$$

Step 2: Multiply k values with proportion factors a and b; add results to obtain factor k that is associated with x in the combined population.

$$k = k_a \cdot a + k_b \cdot b \qquad (2)$$

Step 3: Determine percentile p associated with k from Table 5.

Step 4: Repeat for other x values of interest.

Step 5 (alternate): If percentile values for each x are known in each group, one may simply add the proportioned percentiles

$$p = p_a \cdot a + p_b \cdot b \qquad (3)$$

Step 6 (optional): Plot results.

Examples: (hypothetical)

Example 1. Finger strength of a population composed of two samples (in Newtons)

$$a: \bar{x}_a = 15N \qquad S_a = 2N \qquad a = 15\%$$
$$b: \bar{x}_b = 19N \qquad S_b = 3N \qquad b = 85\%$$

Table 6. *(continued)*

Finger strength x	k_a from (1.1)	k_b from (1.2)	k from (2)	Approximate percentile p from Table 5
10 N	2.50	3.00	2.93	< 0.5
12.5 N	1.25	2.17	2.03	2
15 N	0	1.33	1.13	13
17.5 N	1.25	0.83	0.89	21
20 N	2.50	0.33	0.66	75
22.5 N	3.75	1.17	1.56	94
25 N	5.00	2.00	2.45	>98

Example 2. Stature of a population composed of three samples

Three samples: $a = 30\%$; $b = 45\%$; $c = 25\%$.
(Example taken from Roebuck, Kroemer, and Thomson, 1975, page 158)

Using Step 5:

Stature x (cm)	k_a	k_b	k_c	p
155	0.03	0.3	12.5	3.3
162.5	1.4	6.0	59.0	17.9
170	18.0	36.0	94.6	45.3
178	64.0	80.0	99.9	80.2
185	94.6	98.0	100	97.5

frequent with traditional anthropometric surveys, in which data were written down manually and then transcribed into computer-readable information. However, even newer data-recording techniques suffer from a great number of possible errors in information input, and in computational routines. In fact, since often no human is involved who could apply judgement, grossly wrong data can be displayed by the computer. Two editing routines, designed by Kikta and Churchill (1978) to eliminate errors and outliers, have proven to be highly successful: the XVAL method sorts out extreme values (ten highest and ten lowest) for each data category; EDIT tests each selected actual data point against a predicted value based on other inputs contained in the sample. Numerous other checks can be performed, among them plotting of individual data points, or of frequency distributions, graphically displayed on the CRT.

One purpose of a model utilizing computerized calculating routines is to present data as predicted values for defined population samples. The simplest model is that of the 'average person' relying solely on mean values, accumulated over several data categories. This mythical person, having only average body dimensions, was proven to be nonexistent in the early 1950s and pronounced useless and dead repeatedly since — but some designers still believe in this ghostly figure (they should again check Table 4). Another concept assumes that a large female can be represented by the body dimensions of an average man; relatedly, that the dimensions of a small man are similar to that of an average female (small females are not included in this scheme). This concept has been scrutinized recently and found to be inappropriate and misleading in many anthropometric aspects (Robinette, Churchill, and McConville, 1979).

A more sophisticated and appropriate means to represent selected body dimensions utilizes the fact that given percentage values can be calculated from the mean by adding or subtracting certain multiples of the standard deviation. Clearly, the percentile approach is fully correct and very useful for one given dimension, provided the variable is distributed normally. However, it is fallible to add percentile values to derive, say, a 95th percentile phantom having 95th per cent body dimensions throughout. For statistical reasons, percentile values are not additive — the '50th percentile person' is the same ghost as the 'average person'.

Obviously, data on civilian populations are largely missing, while data on military personnel are rather amply available. Since the military sample is just part of the overall civilian population, it appears logical to use the military data to infer on the general civilian population. This approach was investigated by McConville, Robinette, and Churchill (1981). They selected the 1965 Health Examination Survey; for males, the U.S. Air Force 1967 and the U.S. Army 1966 surveys; for females, the 1958 U.S. Air Force and 1977 U.S. Army surveys. Their underlying assumption was that if a good height and weight match can be achieved between civilian and military individuals, then the means and standard deviations of other dimensions (measured in either survey) should be well matched also.

The procedure used was to match individuals from the civilian and military surveys on the basis of stature and weight. A new military sample was created which represents the civilians in height and weight. From this sample, dimensions other than height and weight were selected and compared to the equivalent data measured in the civilian survey.

For the males, an excellent fit was achieved: 99 per cent of all civilian subjects could be matched with a military subject, with negligible differences in stature and height with regard to means and standard deviations. A comparison of six linear dimensions measured both in the military and civilian surveys proved to be an excellent match both in means and standard deviations.

The authors also checked the use of regression equations in which body dimensions are predicted from height and weight. The predictions for the means of the six civilian dimensions from the military set were as good as the results achieved in matching. However, standard deviations predicted from regression equations turned out to be considerably larger than those obtained in the matched-pair procedure.

The same procedures were used in comparing female data. This attempt was less successful than for the males. Even after considering only certain age groups, only about 94 per cent of the civilians could be matched with military individuals, with reasonably good fit in stature but rather poor match in weight. A closer examination of the unmatched individuals indicated problems with very short/very heavy civilians, some weighing more than 200 or even 300 lb, for whom no military matches were found.

Stature and weight (and sitting height for seated samples) are the best single predictors of other body dimensions. This model has been checked recently by Robinette and Churchill (1979) and found to be fully valid. Regression equations have been developed that predict other body dimensions with high accuracy (Robinette and McConville, 1981): Table 2 presented such predicted body dimensions for U.S. civilians. Body dimensions calculated through regression equations are additive. Thus, regression equations provide currently the best model to massage stored anthropometric data for the prediction of any selected percentile values.

A sizeable number of computer models have been developed in order to interface human body dimensions with the geometry of the work station. Underlying all of them is the Borelli concept of rigid body lengths connected by joints. Most models are distinguished by the number of links and joints, degrees of freedom, and the methods used to drive the model, particularly to position body parts in space. Other major distinctions are the linking of the model to the work space, and the manner in which anthropometric data bases are incorporated in the model. At this time, most computer models of the human body are deterministic (for example, the SAE standard procedures used in automobile design), although some attempts have been made to include probabilistic techniques.

A short (and certainly incomplete) survey of the development since the early 1970s (Kroemer, 1972) indicates the rapid growth in numbers and complexity of computer models of the operator–work space interface. (For more details see, for example, Easterby, Kroemer, and Chaffin, 1982):

(1) Jenik developed, two decades ago, a somatographic representation of the human body either in the standing or sitting posture. Despite its many simplifying assumptions, this model was successfully employed.
(2) BOEMAN was one of the first complex models, developed in the early 1960s by Ryan and co-workers. It was meant to indicate the geometry of the crew station in relation to the pilot.
(3) COMBIMAN is 'a son of BOEMAN' employed by the U.S. Air Force to represent the operator–station interface in three-dimensional variable geometry. The model has 35 links, is anchored to the work space through the seat reference point, and displays dimensions, reach, vision, strength, and mass properties of the seat operator.

(4) CAPE is a more recent development by the U.S. Navy, designed to check how percentage representations of the operator can be accommodated by work station dimensions. Randomly generated 'linkmen' are among the basic features distinguishing CAPE from COMBIMAN; recently, however, specified percentiles have also been incorporated in this model.

(5) CAR is a 'simple relative' of CAPE, designed for assessment of reach capabilities, but neither employing graphics nor considering interference points in the reach movement.

(6) NASA has made significant progress in combining features of CAR, COMBIMAN and other models regarding anthropometry, strength, and the geometry of the work station and its details, such as display and control panels. This model allows real-time simulation of the operator and the work space, and direct interaction with the engineer. Many operator–equipment interfaces in the U.S. space shuttle were designed and tested using computerized models.

(7) SAMMIE, developed at the University of Nottingham, represents the standing or sitting body in relation to the geometry of the work station. This model has undergone much refinement in its anthropometric data contents and its underlying biomechanics since its initial role as part of a production-optimizing industrial engineering tool.

While these models have been rather successful as means to store, retrieve and massage anthropometric data (for example, COMBIMAN contains data for nearly 100,000 measured individuals), major problem areas still need improvement. These include: mode of operation; assumptions about underlying links and joint centres; representation of voluntary versus forced movement; mass distribution; contours; time-related strength and work capacities; transition from the seated to the standing or walking posture; representation of external constraints such as clothing or obstacles in the path of movement; the graphics to be employed; the internal computation times needed; ease of interaction with the user–designer. One solution may be to use rather simple models for gross statements and to employ more complex models only when there is a need for more detailed information. For simple design and evaluation tasks the use of basic tools is still very appropriate, efficient, and successful. For example, the templates and manikins recently developed by Jürgens in Germany and Kennedy in the U.S.A. representing different body dimensions, and combinations, have proven to be of high value for design engineering tasks (Easterby, Kroemer, and Chaffin, 1982).

INTERFACING THE OPERATOR WITH THE EQUIPMENT

As just discussed, a number of model approaches have been used for checking existing work station designs, or for designing new workplaces, to achieve optimal fit to the human operator. Among others, major differences among these models lie in the interfacing of the operator with the equipment, i.e., cockpit, cab, machine, bench or table, chair, work objects, tools, controls, visual displays, etc. Designated interface points connect defined body segments of the operator with components of the workplace or equipment. In the past, the following interface points have been used:

(1) *The eye*. Called eye design point, eye ellipse, line of vision, etc., in different industries, this point constitutes the geometrical link between targets and the eyes of the operator, usually assumed to be seated.

(2) *The hip*. Depending on industry usage, either an approximation of the hip joint is used for design purposes (H-point), or the intersection of the seat pan and the backrest planes (Seat Reference Point, SRP) is used to establish the link with the body of the seated operator.

(3) *The foot*. Often called heel-rest point, accelerator-heel point, or package-origin point, this reference location connects one or both feet of the sitting operator with the equipment.

(4) *The hand*. Despite its importance, and because of the difficulties in defining specialized activities, this interaction between the human body and the equipment is only loosely described either as reach envelope, as preferred manipulation area, or as work plane projected onto horizontal bench or table surfaces.

Confounding variables in these models would be obstacles in the line of sight, or within the motion envelope of the hands; extreme contours of voluminous or obese people; reduced mobility or strength due to physical disabilities of the handicapped; environmental conditions such as increased or decreased gravity in aeroplanes or space vehicles, etc. These confounding variables can make the rather straightforward approach of interfacing the operator with the equipment quite difficult. For example, an operator moving around, wearing protective motion-hindering garments, and experiencing reduced performance capabilities due to heat stress and fatigue, poses a design problem which, at this time, cannot be solved by employing a computerized man/equipment/environment model. Thus, the task of designing this interface still requires from the design engineer a combination of analytical skills, of routines, and of creativity based on knowledge and experience. This designer will produce less than optimal, if not deficient of dangerous, designs if an approach is not used that is based on analytical understanding and modelling of task, constraints, and data available, such as outlined above. Common sense and 'gut feeling' are not sufficient substitutes for ergonomic knowledge and systematic human engineering.

Several books on ergonomics, or human engineering, provide information on techniques to fit equipment to the human operator. Already classics, but still very useful, are Shackel's *Applied Ergonomics Handbook* (3rd edn., 1976) and *Ethnic Variables in Human Factors Engineering*, edited by Chapanis (1975). VanCott and Kinkade's *Human Engineering Guide to Equipment Design* (1972) consolidated earlier pioneering works (for example by Murrell, McFarland, Woodson) with the vast information gathered by the military. Though written for use in North America, its contents also apply to most European people. (Incidentally: the regularly updated military design handbooks, such as MIL-STD-1472, or MIL-HDBK-759 in the U.S.A., provide excellent although somewhat limited information and guidelines for the designer.) The monumental (1047 pages) *Human Factors Design Handbook* by Woodson (1981) is certainly a design thesaurus. Recent European books include *Human Factors in Transport Research* (edited by Oborne and Levis, 1980) and Grandjean's *Fitting the Task to the Man* (1980). The journal *Applied Ergonomics* provides continuous commentaries, and many examples, of ergonomic design problems and their solutions.

SOURCES OF ANTHROPOMETRIC DATA

Until recently, the designer and engineer were largely limited to checking anthropometric journals, and the publications in the human factors/ergonomics field for occasional reports of body dimensions that were applicable to the given case. Furthermore, a number of textbooks would display compilations of anthropometric data; however, these were usually quickly outdated. Outstanding among the newer printed sources is the *International Bulletin of Current Research in Anthropometry*, first edition published in 1981 (edited by D. Thompson, Department of Occupational Health and Safety, University of Aston, Birmingham, England). This Bulletin is designed to provide contact between generators and users of anthropometric data. It contains descriptions of about 70 research projects being conducted in all parts of the world. The next update of this Bulletin is planned for 1983. Table 7 presents an overview of published survey results of civilian populations in the U.K. since 1950.

Another major source of reasonably current anthropometric information is the NASA *Anthropometric Source Book* (1978). Its three volumes not only contain U.S. military and civilian anthropometric data but discuss, in considerable detail, their application to industrial populations having a wide range of strength and anthropometric configurations.

Two computer-based systems are available to the general public:

(1) The *USAF Anthropometric Data Bank* contains the results of more than 30 surveys with approximately 100,000 measured individuals. About one-third of the surveys concerns U.S. military male and female populations, another one-third relates to foreign military populations, while the remainder consists of U.S. civilian data (AMRL-HEG, Wright-Patterson

Table 7. Details of anthropometric surveys of civilian populations in the U.K.
(Based on information contained in Oborne, 1982)

Source	Year	Sample size	Sex	Age
Kemsley, *Annals of Eugenics*, **15**, 161–183	1950	27515 33562	male } female }	14 to 75
Roberts, *Ergonomics*, **3**, 21–37	1960	78	female	Average 72
Ward and Fleming, *Ergonomics*, **7**, 83–90	1964	70	male	?
Ward and Kirk, *Ergonomics*, **10**, 17–24	1967	100	female	? (elderly)
Lewin, *Ergonomics*, **12**, 883–902	1969	87 77	male } female }	25 to 49
Andrews and Manoy, *Applied Ergonomics*, **5**, 132–135	1972	323	male	24 to 65
McClelland and Ward, *Ergonomics*, **19**, 465–478	1976	140	male & } female }	18 to 30; 60 +
Haslegrave, *Ergonomics*, **22**, 145–153	1979	1548 416	male } female }	17 to 64
Wira Clothing Services ISBN 0-0900820	1980	?	male	18 to 45

AFB, Ohio 45433, U.S.A.). In the U.K., the Royal Aircraft Establishment at Farnborough is a good source of such information.

(2) *ERGODATA* is an international data source for European anthropometry primarily based on French anthropometric surveys but now also including other national data, such as from the U.K. The ERGODATA system is located at the Anthropology Laboratory, Université René Descartes, 45 rue de Saints Pères, Paris 6 (Professor A. Coblentz), with the U.K. office at the University of Birmingham (Professor K. B. Haley), and a U.S. office located at the State University of New York in Buffalo, N.Y. (Professor C. G. Drury).

INTERNATIONAL STANDARDIZATION

While the origins of what we today call ergonomics easily can be traced at least 100 years back (see for example the biomechanical studies by Braune and Fischer described in Roebuck, Kroemer, and Thomson, 1975), a first boom occurred in the 1920s and 1930s, when engineers became interested in certain applications of physiology and psychology. This carried over into the World War II era, when utmost performance was demanded from military man-machine systems. Often the human was the system component that limited the system output. For example, the radar operator was often overloaded or underloaded; some aeroplane cockpits and tanks were so small that only selected crew members could fit into them. Several transdisciplinary research and application areas came into existence, such as engineering anthropometry, engineering psychology, work physiology, bioengineering, etc. The manned space flights were in fact triumphs of scientific study and engineering application in human factors or ergonomics.

The 1970s marked the intensive application of ergonomics in industry, particularly in Europe and Japan. At this time, working conditions had come into the focus of employees and employers, according to the dictum of the World Health Organization that work should not only be free from health and injury hazards, but in fact should contribute to welfare and well-being. At this time, 'humanization of work' was seriously attempted to create the satisfactory design of work task and work place (including seats, tables, benches, equipment, tools, and the work environment with climate, sound, lighting, etc.). Depending on the philosophical background, ergonomics was seen primarily as a means either to achieve the high 'quality of life', or productivity— perhaps both.

A compromise between these two goals appears to have been reached in many highly industrialized countries. Here, both union representatives and management have accepted ergonomics as making work more human (that is less dangerous, less monotonous, more interesting, more challenging and satisfying) and at the same time, increasing the work output (in quantity and quality, and by reducing costs related to absenteeism, labour turnover, and accidents). Laws, regulations, and guidelines made the consideration of ergonomic principles and data mandatory and legally enforceable in many countries.

In 1979 the member countries of the International Organization for Standardization accepted by an overwhelming majority of votes the International Standard ISO/6385, 'Ergonomic Principles in the Design of Work Systems'. It establishes guidelines to adjust work space and work equipment to body dimensions and physiological capabilities of the individual operator. With respect to the work area, this standard requires that the height of the working surface be adapted to the body dimensions of the operator. The operator should be able to alternate between sitting and standing, if feasible, with provisions made that the operator can change his or her body posture during the course of the work. Seating arrangements shall be adjusted to the anatomical and physiological features of the individual. Sufficient space shall be provided for body movements. Controls shall be within functional reach with grips and handles fitted to the anatomy of the hand. The design of the work shall be such as to avoid unnecessary or excessive strain on muscles, joints, ligaments, and on central (respiratory, circulatory, metabolic) body systems.

Thus, for the first time in history, an international standard demands that in any manned system the human be considered the 'critical component'; that work task, work space, work equipment, and work conditions be designed to suit the human—for which task the engineer needs, as the most basic input, anthropometric data.

REFERENCES

Ayoub, M. M., Mital, A., Asfour, S. S., and Bethea, N. J. (1980). Review, evaluation, and comparison of models for predicting lifting capacity. *Human Factors*, **22**, 257-269.

Badler, N. I., and Smoliar, S. W. (1979). Digital representations of human movement. *Computing Surveys*, **11**, 19-38.

Caldwell, L. S., Chaffin, D. B., Dukes-Dobos, F. N., Kroemer, K. H. E., Laubach, L. L., Snook, S. H., and Wasserman, D. E. (1974). A proposed standard procedure for static muscle strength testing. *American Industrial Hygiene Association Journal*, **35**, 201-206.

Chapanis, A. (ed.) (1975). *Ethnic Variables in Human Factors Engineering* (Baltimore: The Johns Hopkins University Press).

Corlett, E. N., Madeley, S. J., and Manenica, I. (1979). Posture targeting: a technique for recording working postures. *Ergonomics*, **22**, 357-366.

Churchill, E., and McConville, J. T. (1976). *Sampling and Data Gathering Strategies of Future USAF Anthropometry*. Report AMRL-TR-74-102 (Wright-Patterson AFB, Ohio: Aerospace Medical Research Laboratory).

Daniels, G. S. (1952). *The 'Average Man'?* Technical Note No. WCRD 53-7 (Wright-Patterson AFB, Ohio: Wright Air Development Centre).

Easterby, R., Kroemer, K. H. E., and Chaffin, D. B. (eds.) (1982). *Anthropometry and Biomechanics*. Proceedings of the July 7-11, 1980 NATO Symposium in Cambridge, England (New York: Plenum).

Grandjean, E. (1980). *Fitting the Task to the Man* (3rd edn.) (New York: International Publications Service).

Hertzberg, H. T. E. (1968). The Conference on Standardization of Anthropometric Techniques and Terminology. *American Journal of Physical Anthropometry*, **28**, 1-16.

Hertzberg, H. T. E. (1979). Engineering anthropology: past, present, and potential. In *The Uses of Anthropology* (American Anthropological Association) No. **11**, 184-204.

Kennedy, K. W. (1982). Workspace evaluation and design: USAF drawing board mechanisms and development of cockpit geometry design guides. In Easterby, R., Kroemer, K. H. E., and Chaffin, D. B. (eds.) *Anthropometry and Biomechanics* (New York: Plenum).

Kikta, P., and Churchill, T. (1978). *Editing Procedure for Anthropometric Survey Data*. Report AMRL-TR-78-38 (Wright-Patterson AFB, Ohio: Aerospace Medical Research Laboratory).

Kroemer, K. H. E. (1970). Human strength: terminology, measurement and interpretation of data. *Human Factors*, **12**, 297-313.

Kroemer, K. H. E. (1972). *COMBIMAN—COMputerised BIomechanical MAN-model*. Report No. AMRL-TR-72-16 (Wright-Patterson AFB, Ohio: Aerospace Medical Research Laboratory). Reprinted in: *Proceedings of the IFU Colloquium Space Technology—A Model for Safety Techniques and Accident Prevention?* (1973). Cologne, Germany, April 1972 (Cologne: Verlag TUV Rheinland).

68   *The Physical Environment at Work*

Kroemer, K. H. E., and Marras, W. S. (1980). Towards an objective assessment of the 'maximal voluntary contraction' component in muscle strength measurements. *European Journal of Applied Physiology*, **45**, 1–9.

Martin, R. (1914). *Lehrbuch der Anthropologie* (Jena: Fischer Verlag).

McConville, J. T., Robinette, K. M., and Churchill, T. (1981). *An Anthropometric Data Base for Commercial Design Applications*. NSF Grant DAR-8009861, Final Report (Yellow Springs, Ohio: Anthropology Research Project).

NASA (1978). *Anthropometric Source Book* (3 volumes). NASA Reference Publication 1024 (Springfield, VA: National Technical Information Service).

Oborne, D. J. (1982). *Ergonomics at Work* (Chichester: John Wiley & Sons).

Oborne, D. J., and Levis, J. A. (eds.) (1980). *Human Factors in Transport Research* Volumes I and II (London: Academic Press).

Reynolds, H. M. (1982). The human machine in three dimensions. In Easterby, R., Kroemer, K. H. E., and Chaffin, D. B. (eds.) *Anthropometry and Biomechanics* (New York: Plenum).

Robinette, K. M., and Churchill, T. (1979). *Design Criteria for Characterising Individuals in the Extreme Upper and Lower Body Size Ranges*. Report No. AMRL-TR-79-33 (Wright-Patterson AFB, Ohio: Aerospace Medical Research Laboratory).

Robinette, K. M., and McConville, J. T. (1981). *An Alternative to Percentile Models*. SAE Technical Paper No. 810217 (Warrendale, PA: Society of Automotive Engineers).

Robinette, K. M., Churchill, T., and McConville, J. T. (1979). *A Comparison of Male and Female Body Sizes and Proportions*. Report No. AMRL-TR-76-69 (Wright-Patterson AFB, Ohio: Aerospace Medical Research Laboratory).

Roebuck, J. A., Kroemer, K. H. E., and Thomson, W. G. (1975). *Engineering Anthropometry Methods* (New York: John Wiley & Sons).

Shackel, B. (ed.) (1976). *Applied Ergonomics Handbook* (3rd edn.) (Guildford, Surrey: IPC Business Press).

Snyder, R. G. (1981). Fundamentals of anthropometric survey measurement techniques. In Easterby, R., Kroemer, K. H. E. and Chaffin, D. B. (eds.) *Anthropometry and Biomechanics* (New York: Plenum).

Stoudt, H. W. (1978). *Are People Still Getting Bigger— Who, Where, and How Much?* SAE Technical Paper No. 780280 (Warrendale, PA: Society of Automotive Engineers).

VanCott, H. P., and Kinkade, R. G. (1972). *Human Engineering Guide to Equipment Design* (rev. edn.) (Washington, D.C.: U.S. Government Printing Office).

Woodson, W. E. (1981). *Human Factors Design Handbook* (New York: McGraw-Hill).

The Physical Environment at Work
Edited by D. J. Oborne and M. M. Gruneberg
©1983 John Wiley & Sons Ltd.

Climate and Human Performance

John L. Kobrick and Bernard J. Fine
U.S. Army Research Institute of Environmental Medicine,
Natick, Massachusetts, USA

The natural climate has always been a major source of concern for human beings. From the cave person to the space person, survival has meant coping with extremes of temperature, humidity, and wind. Because of inherent physiological limitations and only relatively slight adaptive capability, we have had to deal with climate through the rational invention of protective devices such as clothing, shelter, and controllable sources of heating and cooling.

INDICES OF CLIMATIC EFFECTS

(a) Physical indices

Scientific attempts to analyse the effects of heat and cold on humans were made by Galen as early as A.D. 160. However, it was not possible to measure properly or to document effectively climatic conditions until Galileo invented the thermometer in the sixteenth century, followed later by the development of temperature scales by Fahrenheit and by Celsius (Centigrade) in the seventeenth century. Two hundred years later, de Sasaure devised the wet-bulb thermometer, and numerous other thermal measurement devices followed as still other components of man's thermal environment were identified. These included discovery of the differences between convective and radiant heat action, originally noted by Benjamin Franklin in 1729, and the realization of the role of air motion and moisture content in heat transfer.

Ellis first reported the greater discomfort of humid compared with dry heat in Georgia in 1758, but Fordyce in 1775 was the first to document heat and humidity effects on man in actual hot-room experiments. Understanding the effects of moisture in ambient air led ultimately to current concepts of relative humidity and the notion of a dynamic heat balance between man and his thermal environment. In 1826, Heberden studied the combined effects of air temperature and velocity, but it was not until 1914 that Hill combined these findings with the available knowledge of the role of humidity to develop the kata-thermometer, an early attempt to incorporate physiological effects of thermal conditions into temperature measurement. While dry-bulb and wet-bulb temperatures are still the most familiar indices of the thermal environment, a developing understanding of the interaction of temperature, humidity, and windspeed has led to more complex concepts, such as the wind chill index proposed by Siple and Passel in 1945 and the wet-bulb globe temperature (WBGT) developed by Yaglou and Minard in 1957. The wind chill index was devised to serve as an expression of the cooling effect of wind velocity in the thermal process and the WBGT was developed to guide U.S. Armed Forces in determining endurable limits of heat exposure during training and military operations. Determination of the WBGT requires the use of a wet-bulb thermometer inserted inside a 6-inch black sphere, and indicates the wet-bulb heat load influenced only by natural air convection at the respective temperature and humidity conditions.

A recent development based on the WBGT is the 'Botsball', devised by Botsford in 1971. This instrument consists of a dial thermometer enclosed in a black copper sphere with a black cloth cover and has the advantages of strength and durability not present in glass thermometers. It provides a measure of wet globe temperature (WGT), which Ciriello and Snook showed in 1977 to be highly correlated with WBGT values taken under the same radiation, humidity, and air movement conditions. The Botsball has a practical advantage for use by military troops in field operations and for similar situations involving hard usage.

A different approach to thermal measurement, called the operative temperature index, was originated at the J. B. Pierce Laboratory of Hygiene in the U.S.A. by Winslow, Herrington and Gagge in 1938. This index was developed to assess the thermal exchange between man and the environment and to reflect thermal stress through the amount of heat flow. The index was developed further in 1955 by Belding and Hatch to evaluate high levels of heat exposure in industrial settings.

(b) Subjective indices

The measures described so far relate only to the physical and physiological aspects of thermal response and do not involve the subjective appraisal of thermal conditions. Consideration of the more subjective aspects of thermal relationships prompted the development of another facet of research in the 1920s by the American Society of Heating and Ventilation Engineers (later renamed the American Society of Heating, Radiation, and Air Conditioning Engineers, or ASHRAE), to develop guidance data for the design of heating systems. Out of this came the development of the effective temperature scale (ETS) by Houghten and Yaglou in 1923, based on subjective matching by raters of various actually experienced combinations of ambient temperatures, humidity levels, and air motion rates, to determine those combinations which produced equivalent feelings of personal comfort. Two scales were derived from this procedure: one (basic) scale for men stripped to the waist, and another (normal) scale for men wearing light clothing. The original measurements were seriously limited in the absence of an allowance for radiation, which could not be assessed adequately at the time. However, the development of the blackened globe thermometer by Vernon in 1930 and by Bedford and Warner in 1933 subsequently led to a practical radiant temperature index which was used by Vernon and Warner in 1932 and by Bedford in 1946 to include an allowance for radiation in a corrected effective temperature scale.

Another useful thermal index which involves subjective response is the predicted four-hour sweat rate (P4SR) developed by McArdle *et al.* in 1947 to compensate for certain deficiencies of the effective temperature scale. This index, however, applies only to fully heat-acclimatized individuals and is inappropriate for short exposures to very high temperatures because it requires a 4-hour exposure.

The development of the study of thermal phenomena has been summarized in an excellent review by Fox (1965), and is the basis of the foregoing historical review.

THERMAL RECEPTION

Now let us consider the main features of the human neurosensory system for detecting and mediating thermal experience, and then briefly review the general process of human thermoregulation.

The thermal environment is detected through the action of specialized sensory nerve processes embedded in the skin, the adrenal medulla, the hypothalamus, and other internal tissues. Relatively little is known about the distribution of thermal receptors in the deep tissues. The density and distribution of the population of thermal receptors in the skin has not been established completely and has been the subject of some argument (Hensel, 1973). However, it is clear that both density and distribution of the thermal receptors vary for different skin areas of the body.

In terms of the specificity of the thermal receptors, using electrophysiological techniques, Hensel and Bowman (1960) found receptors for cold in human skin, but were unable to locate receptors for warmth. However, Iggo (1969) and Hensel (1970) reported that 'warm' receptors generate nerve potentials with positive coefficients whereas 'cold' receptors produce negative coefficients. They found also that both kinds of receptors show a relatively constant rate of potential discharge at static temperatures *within their thermal range of activity* and that they display an increased rate of discharge for changing temperatures proportionate to the rate of change.

Hensel and Iggo (1971), studying the skin of rhesus monkeys, identified different cutaneous receptors which they considered to be maximally responsive to warm or to cold temperature ranges, but not to both. On the basis of the general evidence, it is presumed that receptors for cold and warmth both exist in human skin and probably take the form of free nerve endings. Receptors for mechanical experience (tactual, pressure, etc.) are thought to produce essentially no thermal reaction, although Hahn (1974) has reported that some mechanoreceptors are responsive to cooling.

The neural discharges generated in response to thermal stimuli travel along their associated afferent nerve pathways and join with dorsal nerve trunks in the spinal cord which reach the anterior hypothalamus, a brain centre thought to be active in temperature monitoring and control (Chowers and Bligh, 1976). The mode of organization of the involved sensory coding is not well understood. Under steady-state temperature conditions, both warm and cold receptors habituate rapidly.

It was known as early as 1896 (Goltz and Edwards) that temperature sensation depends also on deep-body sensors outside of the nervous system. An account of the roles of deep-body sensors in thermoregulation would be too complex for use here, but a concise review of their operation is available in Elizondo (1977).

THERMOREGULATION

As stated by Mitchell (1977), the general process of thermoregulation can be considered to be based on the first law of thermodynamics in which:

$$S = M + W + K + R + C + E$$

In this equation, the rate of heat storage (S) includes the metabolic rate (M) combined with the physical work rate (W), and with the rate of heat exchange of the individual with his surroundings through conduction (K), radiation (R), convection (C) and evaporation (E). Humans possess a variety of physiological mechanisms which enable them to dissipate or conserve body heat. These mechanisms are controlled by the action of the anterior hypothalamus through its connection with the autonomic nervous system (Cabanac, 1975). Heat dissipation is accomplished by sweating and by dilation of the peripheral blood vessels which allows increased amounts of blood from the warmer core of the body to be shunted towards the body surface for cooling by radiation, convection, conduction and/or evaporation. Obviously, the rate of heat dissipation by these mechanisms is determined to a large extent by the temperature, humidity, and rate of air movement in the surrounding environment. Heat conservation is maintained by shivering, by the constriction of the peripheral blood vessels, which restricts the blood to the warmer core of the body, and, to a lesser extent, by the erection of hair follicles.

Recent discoveries in neuroendocrinology have led to a greater understanding of the complex interactive roles of the anterior hypothalamus and the adrenal medulla in thermoregulation. On the basis of this new information, Robertshaw (1977) has proposed a hypothetical model of thermoregulatory action in which the anterior hypothalamus is assumed to have two primary modes of control: one through its influence on the sympathetic pathways of the autonomic nervous system, and the other through its ability to control secretion of catecholamines (epinephrine and norepinephrine), by the adrenal medulla, directly into the circulating blood stream. These adrenal medullary hormones are known to have profound effects on metabolism, and to cause increases in circulating free fatty acids and glucose, which are directly involved in mechanisms of thermal adjustment. The catecholamines also have some effect on thermal receptor mechanisms at their local tissue sites, but these effects are considered to be only slight to moderate.

An alternative to the currently accepted concept of a single central neural integrator of body temperature in the anterior hypothalamus has also been proposed (Satinoff, 1978). In this conception it is assumed that there are multiple integrators; as many as there are thermoregulatory responses. These are presumed to be located at various levels of the nervous system, rather than at a single location. They are assumed also to have an interactive function, such that facilitation and inhibition of certain levels by other levels can be achieved. This model provides for system-oriented and much more sensitive thermoregulatory action, and is more in keeping with recent physiological research findings.

A related aspect of physiological thermoregulation is the general adaptive reaction which has been observed to follow chronic exposure to heat or cold and has been termed 'acclimatization'. The processes involved in adaptation to heat differ considerably from those involved in adaptation to cold; both are too complex to be reviewed in detail here. However, excellent analyses of physiological adaptation have been prepared by Fox (1965, pp.64–76) for heat, and by Carlson and Hsieh (1965, pp.34–47) for cold. In essence, acclimatization to heat has been observed to produce in most individuals a reduced increase in heart rate during physical work, lowered skin and core temperature, a higher rate of sweat production, and a gradual reduction of subjective feelings of discomfort. The adaptive responses involved in acclimatization to cold are less clear-cut. Some changes which have been observed include: elevated resting metabolic rate, an increase in the ratio of lean body ('active tissue') mass to total body weight, and increases in both overall skin temperature and temperature of the extremities, although these latter may be related to the rate of metabolic heat production. Other research suggests an increase in time of onset of shivering and lowered metabolic heat production in winter compared to summer (Davis, 1961a,b; Davis and Johnston, 1961).

CLIMATE AND PERFORMANCE

Up to this point we have dealt only with the physical, biological, and physiological aspects of human responses to climate. An ever-increasing ability to measure the physical environment precisely and to portray accurately the functioning of human physiological and neurosensory systems has been noted. However, as we shall see, similar progress has not been made towards understanding the psychological and performance-oriented aspects of the person–climate interface. Well-defined relationships between climatic conditions and human performance have not been established; it is impossible to predict, with a high degree of accuracy, the capabilities of *groups* of people, let alone specific individuals, to perform their jobs under a given set of climatic conditions.

There are a number of reasons for this state of affairs. Some of the reasons are centred around the philosophy of, and the commonly used approaches to, the study of human behaviour. Other reasons are related to the technical and scientific aspects of the subject matter being studied. Before discussing these matters further, we will present a general overview of the relationship between climate and performance in order to provide a suitable perspective.

For many years, scientists have used several research approaches to study the effects of climatic variables on human performance. In retrospect, it seems apparent that these approaches are related and probably would have been pursued best in an integrated manner. However, there is little indication of any such organization over the years. This has been due partly to differing scientific orientations and partly to parochial rather than eclectic viewpoints.

We have already discussed the development of one research approach which focused on the structure and function of the neurosensory system. A second approach deals primarily with the effects of extreme climates on performance, and a third approach with the effects of more moderate conditions. Extreme climates are those occurring naturally in certain geographic regions, or are man-made conditions, such as the heat of boiler rooms and steel mills or the cold of refrigeration plants and high-altitude flight. Study of the effects of extreme climates generally has been referred to as 'thermal stress' research, whereas that devoted to more moderate conditions has been called 'subjective comfort'. A major difficulty in distinguishing between 'thermal stress' and 'subjective comfort' is that both involve combinations of different levels of temperature, humidity, wind speed, and duration of exposure. Thus, a 2-hour exposure to temperatures generally considered to be thermal stress may neither be more arduous nor deleterious to performance than a 6-hour exposure to more moderate temperatures lying in the subjective comfort range.

THERMAL STRESS

Research on the effects of climate on human performance has been going on for only about 70 years, a comparatively short period of time in the history of science. As noted by Auliciems (1973), much of the early research concerned the effects of conditions which were more like those occurring in real life than was the case in later research. The very early studies in the thermal stress category were field studies, usually carried out by industrial organizations, to determine the effects of very severe temperature and humidity conditions on workers; for example, studies by Orenstein and Ireland (1922) and Bedford and Warner (1931) of effects of climatic conditions on mine workers' performance. Auliciem's (1973, p.3) brief review suggests the flavour of those early studies: 'Accident rates in ammunition factories appeared to increase by some 30% in temperatures above 24°C (75°F) and below 10°C (50°F) . . . .

'In coal mines, absences due to accidents showed a substantially higher incidence in hot seams . . . and at 27°C (81°F) ET less coal tubs were filled and more frequent rest pauses taken than at 19°C (66°F) ET, . . . Production in heavy glass and metallurgical industries . . . showed a marked decrease during the hottest months of the year, and in textile industries . . . linen and cotton weaving production decreased above wet-bulb temperatures of 21–23°C (70–73°F).'

Most of these early studies primarily were observational and descriptive, and simply were chronicles of changes in behaviour or differences in production. Techniques had not yet been developed for establishing true scientific controls and for ruling out extraneous factors which could have contributed to the changes which were observed. With the continuing development of scientific knowledge and experience came a growing appreciation of the need for better control of confounding factors in research studies. This led to a growing realization that decrements in psychological performance and critical changes in physiological states do not necessarily occur together and, in fact, that psychological changes often precede physiological deterioration. This insight resulted in a period of 'thermal stress' type of research designed to identify characteristic psychological 'breaking points' in performance, rather than to study changes in physiological processes. This era began in the 1940s with the work of Mackworth (1945, 1946a,b), Pepler (1953a–g), and Viteles and Smith (1946), and since then has changed very little in emphasis and approach.

PERFORMANCE AND COMFORT

The earliest scientifically controlled studies of performance in the area of subjective comfort were conducted in 1914, and were reported in 1923 by the

New York State Commission on Ventilation. These studies involved the performance of school children in classrooms at several different moderate temperatures, using arithmetic and typewriting tasks. No differences in performance between temperature conditions of 68°F and 75°F were found. However, Wyon (1974) reanalysed the data using modern statistical techniques and found that these relatively moderate temperatures did have an effect on the typewriting task.

Although there have been gradual improvements in instrumentation and statistical techniques, research on subjective comfort, like that on thermal stress, has continued relatively unchanged in focus and emphasis over the years. Much of this work has been reviewed by Auliciems (1973).

OTHER RESEARCH APPROACHES

Diurnal Rhythms

While the aforementioned areas of research were developing, each primarily independent of the others, yet another area of research had begun. In retrospect, it seems surprising that this one was not readily integrated into the areas of thermal stress and subjective comfort, but it was not. This research area seems to have grown out of two different perspectives. One of these came from a study published by Marsh (1906) in which he noted that human performance varied diurnally; i.e. in daily cycles of change. He observed that diurnal performance profiles take many forms; for example, a continuous rise, a continuous fall, a morning rise and an afternoon fall, a morning fall and an afternoon rise, or no variation at all. Some years later, Kleitman and his associates (Kleitman, 1933; Kleitman and Doktorsky, 1933; Kleitman, Teitelbaum, and Feiveson, 1938) measured body temperatures of people while they were being tested on various performance tasks and noted that task performance covaried with body temperature. Increases in body temperature were found to be associated with improved performance. Furthermore, the changes of body temperature showed diurnal patterns: increases in the morning and decreases in the afternoon in speed and accuracy on tasks such as code transcription, arithmetic operation, mirror-drawing, and reaction time.

Kleitman speculated that the observable effects of temperature on performance indicated that he was dealing with a chemical phenomenon. He offered two interpretations. One was that mental processes represent chemical reactions themselves. The second was that speed of thinking depends on the level of metabolic activity of cells of the cerebral cortex. He theorized that an increase in body temperature indicates an increase in metabolic activity which, in turn, leads to a speeding up of thought processes.

Time perception

Research from another perspective began in 1927, when François noted a relationship between body temperature and time perception. He measured body temperature at the high and low points in diurnal rhythms and before and after body heating with diathermy apparatus, and found that subjective impressions of the passage of time were such that time passed more quickly at the higher temperature. From these findings he conceived the notion of an internal 'clock', the timing of which would vary with changes of internal body temperature. A few years later, Hoagland (1933) studied one diathermy patient and two others with fevers and found the same effect. He plotted the log speed of counting versus the reciprocal of absolute temperature (the so-called Arrhenius equation) and found that speed of counting increased with higher temperatures. On the basis of this, Hoagland proposed the existence of a chemical clock which he conceived to be integrally related to the respiratory processes of certain parts of the brain. Subsequent studies by others (Bell, 1965, 1966; Fox *et al.*, 1967; Kleber, Lhamon, and Goldstone, 1963) have tended to support this early work, but large individual differences have been found in changes in time judgements with increased body temperatures, making overall generalizations difficult.

A major factor which influenced the evolution of these areas of research is the milieu in which they developed. While much of the work in most areas was done in the traditional manner by scientists in universities, research on the effects of thermal stress evolved primarily out of the need to meet military requirements, especially by the Americans and British during the World War II. This burgeoning need made the thermal stress area the most prolific of all of the research areas we have mentioned. Most of this research was conducted in government-sponsored laboratories, was designed to answer specific problems, and had a practical rather than a theoretical emphasis. It was aimed mainly towards performance tasks of military relevance such as vigilance, reaction time, tracking, cognition, and perception. Furthermore, since the military, especially the American forces, characteristically consider all men to be capable of functioning equally well in all environments, it is not surprising that almost all of this research was focused on the average performance of groups of soldiers rather than being concerned with the performance of individuals. Because of this focus, it was almost inevitable that the early observations and work of Marsh, Kleitman, Hoagland and others, which focused on underlying mechanisms and in which individual differences were of paramount importance, were neglected or, if considered, were minimized.

STUDIES OF THE EFFECT OF CLIMATE ON PERFORMANCE

Let us now turn to a consideration of what is known about the effects of climate on performance. An organized overview of the valid results contained in the published literature is a very complex undertaking. This is due partly to the many differences among the testing conditions, performance tasks, types of test subjects, and pre-training regimens that were used in the various studies, as well as to frank deficiencies in the nature of some of the research itself. Rather than present this extensive material narratively, we have summarized it in tabular form so that the interested reader can inquire further into studies which may be of specific interest.

We have focused only on the thermal stress area for reasons discussed below. Each article included in the review was evaluated on the basis of the following criteria: (1) number of test subjects, (2) adequacy of pre-training in performance of the experimental tasks, (3) validity and appropriateness of the study design, (4) appropriateness of the statistical analyses, (5) clarity of presentation, and (6) apparatus or equipment problems. The outcome of this review is summarized in Table 1, which includes the articles judged to be deficient as well as those judged to be acceptable.

The table is subdivided into sections for heat and cold research. Studies are grouped according to performance tasks employed. Studies involving more than one task are reported under each task heading, except that tasks performed simultaneously appear under the heading of 'Concurrent tasks'. Climatic conditions are delineated by both temperature (in degrees Fahrenheit) and percentage relative humidity. Duration of exposure in minutes is also shown. Studies that are acceptable are denoted by an × in that column, and are accompanied by a short descriptive statement of results in the 'Comments' column. Deficient studies are indicated by the numbers of the criteria listed above according to which they were judged to be lacking. A few studies (denoted by ×? in the 'Accept' column) were included because they appeared to be exceptionally well carried out, even though they were deficient in numbers of test subjects.

It is clear from Table 1 that generalizations about the effects of heat or cold on performance are almost impossible to make on the basis of the available data. With respect to heat, there is some indication of impairment in vigilance tasks above and below 85 to 90°F (29 to 32°C). A number of studies which measured various types of cognitive performance indicated impairments at exposure above 100°F (38°C). However, other studies of cognitive tasks found no differences, or even improvements, in performance. Manual tracking also shows some degradation at or above 80°F (27°C) in a number of instances but different periods of exposure create a further complication. The effects of heat on reaction time, psychomotor performance, and on concurrent tasks are equivocal, since both improvements and decrements have been noted for similar exposure conditions. Furthermore, one should not ignore the numerous instances of unchanged performance reported in all of the categories of tasks.

Much less research has been done on the effects of cold. Here, impairments generally seem to be related to losses in manipulative abilities. Psychomotor tasks tend to be affected significantly at temperatures below 20°F (−7°C). Sensory sensitivity becomes impaired at somewhat higher temperatures, around 32°F (0°C), but this conclusion is based on one study. Although not stated in terms of ambient temperatures, the repeated observations of impaired manual dexterity at hand-skin temperatures around 55°F (16°C) doubtless are significant findings.

The two accepted studies of visual reaction time show no effects, but the one accepted vigilance study and the only sensory study show decrements below 32°F (0°C). Thus, no conclusions can be drawn about the effects of cold on categories of tasks other than manual dexterity.

Given the great amount of research effort reflected in Table 1, it is unfortunate that so little of general significance can be concluded. The fact that 42 out of 96 studies were found to be deficient for various reasons may have some bearing on this situation. The most common reasons for rejection were inadequate training of participants and faulty study design, with inadequate numbers of subjects and inappropriate statistical analyses also being of major concern.

As mentioned above, Table 1 is limited to studies which are defined as 'thermal stress'. Other research areas related to climate and performance were not included for a variety of reasons. While considerable research has been conducted in the area of subjective comfort (for example, Griffiths and Boyce, 1971; Langkilde *et al.*, 1973; Wyon, 1973, 1974; Wyon *et al.*, 1975; Wyon, Anderson, and Lundquist, 1979), it generally is difficult to interpret the results for a number of reasons. For example, while the performance data usually were samples of real-life working situations, such as school children performing class-work, the control of environmental conditions typically was quite poor. There also are notable instances of mismatches in 'comparison' groups which render the groups non-comparable. Numerous other extraneous factors which cannot be assessed also are evident, and contribute to the difficulty of interpreting the soundness of the research. Despite all of these inconsistencies, one gains an impression of possible impaired performance with increased discomfort.

Research on subjective comfort may have even wider-reaching ramifications than thermal stress research because it involves climatic conditions similar to those encountered by most people in daily living. A need certainly exists for more information in this important area. It must be emphasized, however, that comfort is a highly personal issue which varies greatly among individuals; thus, one should not expect optimum performance and feelings of subjective comfort to be achieved by all people under the same environmental conditions.

Another group of articles concerns both heat and cold effects, but involves artificial manipulation of core temperatures by thermal suits, water immersion, and other techniques. These articles are included as supplementary references,

Table 1. Summary of articles reviewed

A. Heat research

Author(s)	Temp. (°F)	Rel. Humid. %	Exposure (min.)	Accept	Deficient*	Comments
Variable: Reaction time						
Benor and Shvartz (1971)	86	—	Up to 120		1, 3, 4	N = 7
	95	—				
	105	—				
	115	—				
	120	—				
Grether et al. (1971)	72	ambient	95	×		Possible decrement in choice reaction time at 120°F
	120	ambient	95			
Lovingood et al. (1967)	74	30	60, 120, 180	×		Improvement in simple RT 126°F
	126	30	60, 120, 180			
Ramsey et al. (1975)	99	42	120	×		Possible increase in simple reaction time at 120°F
	110	44	90			
	120	47	45			
Variable: Concurrent tasks						
Azer et al. (1972)	95	50	125		3, 4	
	95	75	125			
	100	50	125			
Bell (1978)	72	45	33	×		Primary task = pursuit rotor; subsidiary task = number processing. Decrement only in subsidiary task at 95°F
	84	45	33			
	95	45	33			

Study			Tolerance time			
Blockley and Lyman (1951)	80	—			1	N = 4
	160	<10				
	200	<10				
	235	<10				
Bursill (1958)	70	55	80		1, 3, 4, 5	N = 18
	105	69	80			(3 groups of 6)
Chiles et al. (1972)	75	14	30		3, 4, 5	
	140	12	30			
Dean and McGlothlen (1965)	70	40	20	×		Very short exposures; no differences in tracking and radar/meter monitoring
	80	41	20			
	90	44	20			
	100	48	20			
	110	50	20			
Iampietro et al. (1969)	75	12	30		2, 3, 5	
	140	9	30			
	160	8.5	30			
Iampietro et al. (1972)	77	45	50	×		Decrements in some segments of simulated flight at both 110°F and 140°F
	110	22	50			
	140	11	50			
Mackie and O'Hanlon (1976)	66 (WBGT)		540	×		More steering adjustments, poorer brightness discrimination, more driver errors at 90°F
	90		540			
Poulton and Kerslake (1965)	77	—	20		1, 2, 5	N = 12
	113	—	20			(2 groups of 6)
Provins and Bell (1970)	68	59	175	×?		Training unspecified; initial improvement then no change in serial RT at 104°; no difference in vigilance performance
	104	72	175			

*Deficient studies: 1 = Insufficient number of test subjects; 2 = Inadequate pre-training in the performance of the experimental tasks; 3 = Questionable validity and appropriateness of the study design; 4 = Inappropriate statistical analysis; 5 = Clarity of presentation; 6 = Apparatus or equipment problems

Table 1 *(continued)*

Author(s)	Temp. (°F)	Rel. Humid. %	Exposure (min.)	Accept	Deficient	Comments
Variable: Vigilance						
Arees (1963)	55	40	80	×		Visual vigilance; different temperature/performance relationships among different subjects
	75	40	80			
	105	40	80			
Bell *et al.* (1964)	85	67	varied		1, 2, 3, 4	N = 8
	109	60				
	124	41				
	124	61				
	145	41				
Benor and Schvartz (1971)	86	—	up to 120		1, 3, 4	N = 7
	95	—				
	105	—				
	115	—				
	120	—				
Colquhoun (1969)	75	59	120	×		No difference in visual vigilance performance
	90	65	120			
	120	24	120			
Colquhoun and Goldman (1972)	75	41	120	×		Involved 0, 10, 20, or 30 minutes walking before visual vigilance test. No difference in performance
	103	68	120			
Loeb and Jeantheau (1958)	65–75	4–24	225		2	
	110–125	—	225			
Mackworth (1946a)	75	59	120	×		Decrements in visual search performance above and below 85°F; acclimatized subjects
	85	63	120			
	95	66	120			
	105	69	120			

Study	Temp (°F)		Duration	Effect	Refs	Comments
Mortagy and Ramsey (1973)	80	50	180	×?		visual vigilance, training may have been inadequate; decrements at 102°F increasing with work level and work–rest ratio
	92	50	180			
	102	50	180			
Pepler (1958)	75	59	120	×		Decrements in visual vigilance performance above and below 90°F
	90	65	120			
	120	24	120			
Poulton and Edwards (1974b)	68	72	90	×	1, 2, 3, 4	Visual vigilance; fewer correct detections at 100°F
	100	74	90			
Poulton and Edwards (1974b)	68	72	30, 60, 90			N = 3 per cell
	100	74	30, 60, 90			
Poulton et al. (1974)	68	72	90	×		Auditory vigilance; fewer correct detections at 100°F
	100	74	90			

Variable: Memory, cognition, and perception

Study	Temp (°F)		Duration	Effect	Refs	Comments
Allen and Fischer (1978)	52	57	17		3, 4	
	62	45	17			
	72	34	17			
	82	25	17			
	92	21	17			
Bartlett and Gronow (1953)	60–70	—	60	×		No difference in performance on a cognitive game
	80	61	60			
	90	65	60			
	100	68	60			
Bell (1980)	72	40	Not stated		5	
	94	40	Not stated			
Blockley and Lyman (1950)	160	<10	Tolerance time		1, 2	N = 8
	200	<10				
	235	<10				

Table 1 *(continued)*

Author(s)	Temp. (°F)	Rel. Humid. %	Exposure (min.)	Accept	Deficient	Comments
Chiles (1958)	85	63	60		2	
	90	65	60			
	95	66	60			
	100	68	60			
	110	46	60			
	120	31	60			
Fine and Kobrick (1978a)	70	35	420	×		Improved performance at 3rd hour; significant decrements thereafter; field artillery tasks
	95	88	420			
Fine *et al.* (1960)	70	30	390	×		No difference in performance of anagram and auditory discrimination tasks
	70	90	390			
	95	28	390			
	95	89	390			
Givoni and Rim (1962)	77	40	120		1, 3	N = 4
	109	40	120			
Grether *et al.* (1971)	72	ambient	95	×		No difference in performance; short-term memory
	120	ambient	95			
Leibowitz *et al.* (1972)	Not stated	Not stated	Not stated		1, 2, 5	N = 8
Lovingood *et al.* (1967)	74	30	60, 120, 180	×		Improvement in mental arithmetic at 126°F
	126	30	60, 120, 180			
Mackworth (1946a)	85	63	180	×		Decrements in morse code reception above 90°F; acclimatized subjects
	90	65	180			
	95	66	180			
	100	68	180			
	105	69	180			

Study				X		Comments
Nunneley *et al.* (1978)	77	—	30		2, 3, 5	
	95	50	120			
	104	48	120			
Pepler (1958)	85	63	80		2	
	90	65	80			
	95	67	80			
	100	68	80			
Pepler (1959b)	69	77	50	×		Decrement on serial choice task at 100°F
	100	68	50			
Pepler and Warner (1968)	62	45	180	×		Increased effort, greater errors and faster performance on programmed learning task above and below 80°F
	68	45	180			
	74	45	180			
	80	45	180			
	86	45	180			
	92	45	180			
Poulton and Edwards (1974a)	68	72	60	×		No difference in performance on 5-choice discrimination task
	100	74				
Poulton and Edwards (1974b)	68	72	30, 60, 90		1, 2, 3, 4	*N* = 3 per cell
	100	74	30, 60, 90			
Poulton *et al.* (1974)	68	72	60	×		Increase in gaps and errors on 5-choice task at 100°F
	100	74	60			
Ramsey *et al.* (1975)	99	42	120	×		Possible decrements on arithmetic task in heat
	110	44	90			
	120	47	45			
Reilly and Parker (1968)	75	40	360	×		Of 16 tasks, 6 improved, 2 impaired, 8 unchanged at 100°F
	100	42	360			
Viteles and Smith (1946)	79	45	240		1, 2	*N* = 6
	88	49	240			
	98	48	240			
	108.5	50	240			

Table 1 *(continued)*

Author(s)	Temp. (°F)	Rel. Humid. %	Exposure (min.)	Accept	Deficient	Comments
Wing and Touchstone (1965)	80	38	60	X		Decrements in short-term memory at 120°F
	110	30	60			
	120	28	60			
Variable: Tracking						
Carpenter (1950)	85	64	54		2	
	90	65	54			
	95	67	54			
	100	68	54			
Epstein *et al.* (1980)	75	70	120		4, 5	
	98.6	50	120			
	122	40				
Grether *et al.* (1971)	72	ambient	95	X		No difference in performance on compensatory tracking task
	120	ambient	95			
Nunneley *et al.* (1979)	77	—	30		4	
	95	50	120			
	104	48	120			
Pepler (1953a)	75	59	160	X		Decrements in pointer alignment task at 85°F, increasing in various aspects with increased temperature; acclimatized subjects
	85	63	160			
	93	66	160			
	100	68	160			
Pepler (1953b)	79	79	160		6	
	85	80	160			
	89	24	160			
	90	81	160			
	97	83	160			
	100	21	160			

Study				×	N	Comments
Pepler (1958) (1)	75, 85, 93, 100	59, 63, 65, 68	160, 160, 160, 160		2	
(2)	79, 85, 89, 90, 97, 100, 110, 120	79, 80, 24, 81, 83, 21, 19, 24	100, 100, 100, 100, 100, 100, 100, 100		2	
(3)	85, 90, 95, 100	63, 65, 67, 68	150, 150, 150, 150	×		Decrements in manual tracking task above and below 90°F; acclimatized subjects
Pepler (1959a)	116	70	30	×		Obvious error increase in pointer alignment at 116°F, but no statistical analysis
Pepler (1959b)	69, 100	77, 68	30, 30	×		Decrements in pointer alignment at 100°F
Pepler (1960)	69, 100	77, 68	40, 40	×		Decrements in pointer alignment at 100°F
Poulton and Edwards (1974a)	68, 100	72, 74				
Poulton and Edwards (1974b)	68, 100	72, 74	30, 60, 90 / 30, 60, 90		1, 2, 3, 4 N = 3 per cell	
Poulton et al. (1974)	68, 100	72, 74	30, 30		2	
Ramsey et al. (1975)	99, 110, 120	42, 44, 47	120, 90, 45		2	

Table 1 *(continued)*

Author(s)	Temp. (°F)	Rel. Humid. %	Exposure (min.)	Accept	Deficient	Comments
Russell (1957)	68 85 103	47 33 30	73 73 73	×		No differences in movement and pressure tracking tasks
Variable: Psychomotor						
Kuusinen and Heinonen (1972)	146 174	25 —	20 20		2, 3	
Lovingood et al. (1967)	74 126	30 30	60, 120, 180 60, 120, 180	×		Improvement in aptitude classification test and hand and arm steadiness at 126°F
Mackworth (1945)	85 90 95 100 105	63 65 66 68 69	180 180 180 180 180	×		Decrements in pointer alignment above 90°F
Peacock (1956)	75 96.1 to 111.2	—	Not stated		2, 3, 5	
Ramsey et al. (1975)	99 110 120	42 44 47	120 90 45		2	
Teichner and Wehrkamp (1954)	70 85 100	— — —	28 28 28		1, 2	N = 20 (1 group of 10, 2 groups of 5)

	Temp. (°F)	Rel. Humid. %*	Exposure (min.)	Accept	Deficient	Comments
Vaughan et al. (1968)	50	50	130		2, 3, 5	
	80	50	130			
	115	40	130			
Viteles and Smith (1946)	79	45	240		1, 2	N = 6
	88	49	240			
	98	48	240			
	108.5	50	240			
Weiner and Hutchinson (1945)	65	50	100		1, 3, 4	N = 6
	95	82	100			
Variable: Sensory						
Russell (1957)	68	47	73	×		Tactile sensitivity best at 85°F
	85	33	73			
	103	30	73			

B. Cold research

Author(s)	Temp. (°F)	Rel. Humid. %*	Exposure (min.)	Accept	Deficient	Comments
Variable: Vigilance						
Angus et al. (1979)	32–41		45	×?		Decrements in vigilance task following outdoor sleeping at −5 to −35°F. Questionable results due to low number of subjects
Teichner (1966)	55	40	40		1, 2	N = 13 (1 group of 5, 1 group of 8)
	80	40	40			

*Relative humidities generally are not specified in cold studies.

Table 1 *(continued)*

Author(s)	Temp. (°F)	Rel. Humid. %*	Exposure (min.)	Accept	Deficient	Comments
Variable: Psychomotor						
Aiken (1956)	14 41 'neutral'		Not stated		1, 2, 3, 5	$N = 40$ (8 groups of 5)
Allan *et al.* (1974)	−22 −4 +14 +50		Varied with hand skin temperature	×?		Performance decrements (egress from aircraft seat harness) at +14°F and below, related to duration of exposure and hand-skin temperature. Questionable results due to low number of subjects
Bensel and Lockhart (1974)	20 60		180 180	×		Decrements in variety of manual tasks at 20°F
Clark (1961)	10 70		Up to 60	×		Dexterity (knot-tying) impaired at hand-skin temperature of 55°F, only hands exposed to low temperatures
Gaydos (1958)	45 75		Varied according to skin temperature	×		Dexterity (knot-tying/block stringing) impaired at hand-skin temperature between 50 and 55°F
Gaydos and Dusek (1958)	15 75		Varied according to skin temperature	×		Dexterity (knot-tying/block stringing) impaired at low temperature; effect related to hand-skin temperatures
Horvath and Freedman (1947)	−20 −10 to −14 72		8–14 days 180 4 days	×		Gear assembly and transcription both affected by temperatures
Marshall (1972)						

Study	°F				Exposure	Results
Variable: Sensory						
Russell (1957)	−35				60	
	−25				60	
	−15				60	
	0				60	Decrements in kinaesthetic and tactile sensitivity at 32°F or lower
	+30				60	
	+60				60	
	14	X			73	
	32				73	
	50				73	
	68				73	
Variable: Visual reaction time						
Aiken (1957)	−4	X			36	No effects of cold on learning multiple RT task
	70				36	
Horvath and Freedman (1947)	−20	X			8–14 days	No difference in discrimination RT
	−10 to −14				180	
	72				4 days	
Teichner (1958)	+ wind			2, 4	60	
	−35				60	
	−25				60	
	−15				60	
	0				60	
	+30				60	
	+60				60	
Variable: Tracking						
Payne (1959)	40			4	200	
	55				200	
	70				200	
Russell (1957)	14	X			73	Decrements in tracking at 32°F or lower
	32				73	
	50				73	
	68				73	

*Relative humidities generally are not specified in cold studies.

but they will not be discussed because interpretation of the performances involved was based on criteria related to the internal core temperatures of the subjects. These cannot be interpreted directly into equivalent natural ambient environmental conditions.

In addition to the research articles included in the 'Cold' section of Table 1, there are numerous other reports concerned with the effects of cold combined with isolation over various periods of time; for example, accounts of sojourns in the Antarctic and at isolated military duty stations. Some examples of this type of research are included in the supplementary references (for example, Gunderson and Nelson, 1963; Nelson and Gunderson, 1963; Gunderson, 1966). However, this literature will not be discussed because the direct effects of cold alone on performance could not be separated from the concurrent effects of isolation which prevailed in those situations.

RESEARCH CONSIDERATIONS

Let us turn now to a number of considerations which are of special importance for carrying out and understanding research on the effects of climate on performance. They are not presented in any particular order, and their importance may be different for each set of circumstances.

Acclimatization

The extent to which participants in research studies are acclimatized should be a fundamental consideration. Acclimatization, by definition, means a better physiological tolerance or adaptation to extreme climates and implies that an acclimatized person should perform better on psychological tasks than a non-acclimatized person under environmental stress. This assumption has never been tested.

Some investigators attempt to minimize differences between individuals in levels of acclimatization by conducting heat studies in winter and spring and cold studies in summer and fall. However, investigators who wish to study the performance of *acclimatized* people should establish an acclimatization regimen instead of assuming that summer or winter will automatically accomplish that end. Most research involves the use of unacclimatized persons and the season in which the research took place is rarely stated. Some inter-individual variability in performance undoubtedly is due to different states of acclimatization. Many investigators seem to be unaware of this problem.

Choice of climatic conditions

The choice of conditions is sometimes determined by the specific problems to be solved or the questions to be answered. In most instances, however, choice of conditions seems to be quite arbitrary and is reflected in the literature we have reviewed. Each investigator uses a set of conditions which, typically, are unlike those of other investigators. These discrepancies make generalization of results very difficult.

Both temperature and humidity should be taken into account in any study, although the effect of humidity on performance is not clearly understood. Only a few studies have been designed specifically to isolate the effect of humidity on performance at high temperatures (Pepler, 1953; Chiles, 1958; Fine, Cohen, and Crist, 1960), and have produced equivocal results. Investigators seem to be unaware that two environmental conditions which are comparable in relative humidity may not be comparable in terms of the amount of moisture in the air. *Relative* humidity indicates the proportional relationship of the amount of aqueous vapour actually present in the air at a given temperature to the maximum amount of vapour possible at that temperature. *Absolute* humidity expresses the actual weight of the vapour present in the air in terms of grains per cubic foot. As an example, environments of 110/100°F (DB/WB) and 90/82°F each have relative humidities of approximately 70 per cent. However, 1 cubic foot of air in the former case weighs about 18.3 grains, but only about 10.4 grains in the latter. Thus, the 110/100°F environment is more saturated with moisture per given volume of air. This relationship should be taken into consideration in tests of the effect of the moisture content of air on performance.

The effect of humidity on performance in the cold has not been studied. People typically seem to feel that wet-cold is much more uncomfortable, 'penetrating' and, hence, more debilitating than dry-cold; but the question has not been addressed systematically.

Duration of exposure

Very few studies have used exposures of more than 2 hours duration. Obviously, physiological tolerance limits determine the endurable durations of exposure for climatic conditions. However, the conditions in most studies are well below those limits. Few studies extend beyond 5 hours, yet many people spend at least 8 hours a day working in hot or cold man-made environments; for example, boiler rooms, steel mills and refrigeration plants. Residents of polar or tropical regions spend entire seasons there and, of particular importance, so do other individuals who, out of necessity, visit these extreme climates; for example, military personnel and business people.

Furthermore, combinations of temperature and humidity are rarely constant over periods as long as 24 hours. Performance under realistically changing temperature/humidity conditions 'around-the-clock' has not been studied.

Performance tasks and training

The choice of tasks and the amount of training are both critical for a valid assessment of the effects of climate on performance. By consciously manipulating either or both variables, an experienced investigator can strongly influence the outcome of research. Therefore, in order for the body of research to be valid, tasks should be selected carefully and subjects should be trained thoroughly.

Other problems arise out of the widespread tendency to use new and/or different tasks with each experiment, rather than to replicate tasks which other investigators have used. This practice severely limits the generalizability of results from one study to another.

However, in those instances where the intention *was* to replicate previous research, the original tasks typically have been *modified*, very often substantially. We have noticed that subsequently, when the results have not turned out as expected, the differences between the tasks then were used to explain the discrepancies.

Motivation

Some investigators feel that poorly motivated people do not perform well and, consequently, are more susceptible than highly motivated people to the effects of stress. Although we agree that poorly motivated people generally are poor performers, it does not necessarily follow that their performance under stress will be poorer than that of highly motivated people. On the contrary, we have found highly motivated subjects to be quite susceptible to the effects of stress when working at or near the limits of their abilities (Fine and Kobrick, 1978a). This probably is true only for severe stress conditions; under minimal or even moderate stress, motivation probably can compensate for impairments due to the stress. However, there is no way at present to specify precise points at which motivation can override stress, since individual responses to stress vary widely.

There is no systematic knowledge available about combinations of motivation and training that produce the best performance under stress. In the absence of such knowledge, the following practices are suggested to minimize the impact of acute stress on performance: (1) insure that the tasks are over-learned, (2) provide that they do not tax the performers to their limits when over-learned, (3) establish a baseline working situation in which the task(s) can be accomplished by *moderately* motivated people, (4) select people who have the capacity to increase their motivation, and (5) be able to provide the impetus for the increase.

Effective temperature

The effective temperature index was devised as a measure of subjective *comfort*. Ratings of personal comfort were obtained from different individuals who were exposed to a variety of moderate temperatures at different humidities.

In some inexplicable way, this index of *comfort* has become a measure of the *stressfulness* of extreme environmental conditions. This is a questionable practice. For example, conditions of 110/84°F (DB/WB) and 93/91°F both yield effective temperatures of 90°F. Yet, in the former condition, the relative humidity is 34 per cent whereas in the latter it is 92 per cent. These two conditions may have different effects on performance, since the effects of humidity on performance have not been determined. If it is true that 'it isn't the heat, it's the humidity', then one should be very cautious about relying upon the effective temperature index to equate experimental conditions in hot environments, particularly where humidities are greatly different.

Differences among individuals

Most of the research we have reviewed is based on the use of 'normative concepts'. These concepts are oriented around a view of human behaviour which focuses on group averages. In our experience, conclusions drawn from group averages very often have been misapplied to the individual members of the group so that the individuals have been improperly labelled with a hypothetical 'average' quality which, in fact, does not exist.

The normative approach and its opposite, the individual differences approach, both use many of the same experimental and statistical procedures. However, they differ significantly in the assumptions made about human behaviour and, consequently, in research emphasis.

In the normative approach, similarities among people in structure and function of mind and body are emphasized. This approach assumes that 'a body is a body is a body'; behaviour must be of the same substance from person to person and, therefore, people are interchangeable. While obvious inter-individual differences, such as size or sex, are taken into consideration, the implicit assumption is made that the basic processes underlying behaviour must be the same for everyone. The experiment now becomes a device to determine that performance which, once known, is assumed to be standard under the given circumstances for all individuals. Differences between individuals are assumed to average out. In statistical terms, the variance due to subjects is considered to be irrelevant random error, or 'noise', in the system; i.e., it corrupts the picture of the 'true' behaviour.

In the individual differences approach it is assumed that while people in general are similar in some respects, they still may differ from one another in the basic processes underlying their behaviour. For example, some may have more sensitive or stronger nervous systems than others, some may respond to stress with increased and others with decreased excretions of the same hormones, and some may be left-hemisphere dominant and some right-hemisphere dominant in brain activity. It is assumed that these kinds of differences can be categorized; in other words, that people can be classified into 'types' on the basis of these and most other characteristics. Experiments are designed so as to maximize the possibilities of studying the differences between people, and an awareness of the characteristics or 'types' of individuals is critical. In the climate–performance area, these kinds of studies have been all too rare.

One should not conclude from this discussion that all individuals perform consistently with a variety of tasks or stressors. We have found the converse more likely to be true (Fine and Kobrick, 1978a,b; Fine and Sweeney, 1968). Individuals who perform well on a task in the cold may be poorer performers on the same task in the heat, at altitude, or under normal conditions. Those who excel at high altitude may be poorer in the heat, and so on. The problem of sorting out which kinds of individuals can perform specific kinds of tasks best in various climates is a critical issue which should be pursued.

Experimental design and controls

In the formulation of studies of the effects of climate on performance, one has the option of choosing between two types of experimental designs: *between-groups* or *within-groups*. In a between-groups design, comparisons are made between the performances of different groups of individuals, each group having been assigned to a different experimental treatment. In a within-groups design, comparisons are made between the relative performances of one group of people who have been exposed to *all* of the experimental treatments. The majority of studies we have examined were of the between-groups type.

There are advantages and disadvantages in each type of design. For example, Poulton (1973) has noted a 'range-effect' associated with within-groups designs. The effect arises from the standard procedure of assigning different treatment orders to different test subjects so that the orders of treatment are equalized statistically across the group of subjects. Poulton recommends the use of between-groups designs.

The use of between-groups designs has even greater problems associated with it. There is an implicit assumption in such designs that personnel in the different groups are alike in all salient characteristics. Our experience indicates that the likelihood of this being true is of low probability, even when group members are selected 'at random' from the same general population (Fine and Kobrick, 1978b). Furthermore, the between-groups design does not lend itself readily to the study of individual differences. Thus, in view of the potential importance of these differences to an integrated understanding of the effects of climate on performance, this type of design has serious shortcomings.

In the final analysis, however, the best approach to building a useful body of scientific knowledge in this area is to demonstrate that the results are replicable, irrespective of type of research design, and are relevant to real-life situations. This can be done only by the systematic use of appropriate climatic conditions; the employment of reliable, valid, and realistic tasks; and the judicious selection and training of test subjects. By these standards, some investigators have made significant contributions, but there is still *much* to be done.

ACKNOWLEDGEMENT

We wish to express our deep appreciation to Miss Ann Marie Antico for her invaluable assistance in the background and preparation work, and to Mrs Elaine O'Toole for typing and organization of the manuscript.

NOTE

The views, opinions, and/or findings contained in this report are those of the author(s) and should not be construed as an official Department of the Army position, policy, or decision, unless so designated by other official documentation.

REFERENCES

(Articles denoted R are reviews.)

Aiken, E. G. (1956). *Combined Environmental Stresses and Manual Dexterity.* U.S. Army Medical Research Laboratory Report 225 (Fort Knox, KY).

Aiken, E. G. (1957). *Response Acquisition and Reversal under Cold Stress.* U.K. Army Medical Research Laboratory Report 227 (Fort Knox, KY).

Allan, J. R., Marcus, P., and Saxton, C. (1974). Effect of cold hands on an emergency egress procedure. *Aerospace Medicine*, **45**, 479–481.

Allen, M. A., and Fischer, G. J. (1978). Ambient temperature effects on paired associate learning. *Ergonomics*, **21**, 95–101.

Angus, R. G., Pearce, D. G., Buguet, A. G., and Olsen, L. (1979). Vigilance performance of men sleeping under arctic conditions. *Aviation, Space and Environmental Medicine*, **50**, 692–696.

Arees, E. A. (1963). *The Effects of Environmental Temperature and Alerting Stimuli on Prolonged Search.* Institute of Environmental Psychophysiology, Technical Note 2 (Amherst: University Massachusetts).

Auliciems, A. (1973). *Thermal Environments and Performance. Review for Division of Health Effects Research NAPCA.* (Washington: U.S. Dept. of Health, Education, & Welfare) (R).

Azer, N. Z., McNall, P. E., and Leung, H. C. (1972). Effects of heat stress on performance. *Ergonomics*, **15**, 681–691.

Bartlett, D. J., and Gronow, D. G. C. (1953). *The Effects of Heat Stress on Mental Performance.* Institute of Aviation Medicine Research Report 846 (Farnborough).

Bedford, T. (1946). *Environmental Warmth and its Measurement.* M.R.C. (War) Memo. No. 17 (London: HMSO).

Bedford, T., and Warner, C. G. (1931). Observations on the working capacity of coal miners in relation to atmospheric conditions. *Journal of Industrial Hygiene*, **13**, 252–260.

Bedford, T., and Warner, C. G. (1933). Influence of radiant heat and air movement on cooling of kata-thermometer. *Journal of Hygiene*, 33, 330–348.

Belding, H. S., and Hatch, T. F. (1955). Index for evaluating heat stress in terms of resulting physiological strains. *Heating, Piping and Air Conditioning*, 27, 129–136.

Bell, C. R. (1965). Time estimation and increases in body temperature. *Journal of Experimental Psychology*, 70, 232–234.

Bell, C. R. (1966). Control of time estimation by a chemical clock. *Nature*, 210, 1189–1190.

Bell, C. R., Provins, K. A., and Hiorns, R. W. (1964). Visual and auditory vigilance during exposure to hot and humid conditions. *Ergonomics*, 7, 279–288.

Bell, P. A. (1978). Effects of noise and heat stress on primary and subsidiary task performance. *Human Factors*, 20, 749–752.

Bell, P. A. (1980). Effects of heat, noise and provocation on retaliatory evaluative behaviour. *Journal of Social Psychology*, 110, 97–100.

Benor, D., and Shvartz, E. (1971). Effect of body cooling on vigilance in hot environments. *Aerospace Medicine*, 42, 727–730.

Bensel, C. K., and Lockhart, J. M. (1974). Cold induced vasodilation onset and manual performance in the cold. *Ergonomics*, 17, 717–730.

Blockley, W. V., and Lyman, J. (1950). *Studies of human tolerance for extreme heat: 3. Mental performance under heat stress as indicated by addition and number checking tests.* USAF Technical Report 6022 (Wright Patterson AFB, Dayton, Ohio).

Blockley, W. V., and Lyman, J. (1951). *Studies of human tolerance for extreme heat: 4. Psychomotor performance of pilots as indicated by a task simulating aircraft flight.* USAF Technical Report No. 6521 (Wright-Patterson AFB, Dayton, Ohio).

Botsford, J. H. (1971). A wet globe thermometer for environmental heat-measurement. *American Industrial Hygiene Association Journal*, 32, 1.

Bursill, A. E. (1958). The restriction of peripheral vision during exposure to hot and humid conditions. *Quarterly Journal of Experimental Psychology*, 10, 113–129.

Cabanac, M. (1975). Temperature regulation. *Annual Review of Physiology*, 37, 415.

Carlson, L. D., and Hsieh, A. C. L. (1965). Cold. In Edholm, O. G. and Bacharach, A. L. (eds.) *Physiology and Human Survival* (London: Academic Press).

Carpenter, A. (1950). A comparison of the influence of handle load and of unfavourable atmosphere conditions on a tracking task. *Quarterly Journal of Experimental Psychology*, 2, 1–6.

Chiles, W. D. (1958). Effects of elevated temperatures on performance of a complex mental task. *Ergonomics*, 2, 89–96.

Chiles, W. D., Iampietro, P. F., and Higgins, E. A. (1972). Combined effects of altitude and high temperature on complex performance. *Human Factors*, 314, 161–172.

Chowers, I., and Bligh, J. (eds.) (1976). Proceedings of the Jerusalem symposium on temperature regulation. *Israel Journal of Medical Science*, 12, 905.

Ciriello, V. M., and Snook, S. H. (1977). The prediction of WBGT from the Botsball. *American Industrial Hygiene Association Journal*, 38, 6.

Clark, R. E. (1961). The limiting hand-skin temperature for unaffected manual performance in the cold. *Journal of Applied Psychology*, 45, 193–194.

Colquhoun, W. P. (1969). Effects of raised ambient temperature and event rate on vigilance performance. *Aerospace Medicine*, 40, 413–417.

Colquhoun, W. P., and Goldman, R. F. (1972). Vigilance under induced hyperthermia. *Ergonomics*, 15, 621–632.

Davis, T. R. A. (1961a). *Chamber cold acclimatization in man.* U.S. Army Medical Research Lab. Report No. 475 (Ft. Knox, KY).

Davis, T. R. A. (1961b). *The effect of heat acclimatization on artificial and natural cold acclimatization in man.* U.S. Army Medical Research Lab. Rept. No. 95 (FT. Knox, KY).

Davis, T. R. A., and Johnston, D. R. (1961). Seasonal acclimatization to cold in man. *Journal of Applied Physiology*, **16**, 231-234.

Dean, R. D., and McGlothlen, C. L. (1965). Effects of combined heat and noise on human performance, physiology, and subjective estimates of comfort and performance. *Institute of Environmental Science, Annual Technical Meeting Proceedings*, 55-64.

Elizondo, R. (1977). Temperature regulation in primates. In Robertshaw, D. (ed.) *Environmental Physiology*, II, Vol. 15, *International Review of Physiology* (Baltimore: University Park Press).

Epstein, Y., Keren, G., Moisseiev, J., Gasko, O., and Yachin, S. (1980). Psychomotor deterioration during exposure to heat. *Aviation, Space and Environmental Medicine*, **51**, 607-610.

Fine, B. J., and Kobrick, J. L. (1978a). Effects of altitude and heat on complex cognitive tasks. *Human Factors*, **20**, 115-122.

Fine, B. J., and Kobrick, J. L. (1978b). Human performance under climatic stress and the fallacy of the 'average' soldier: potentially serious implications for military operations in extreme climates. *Proceedings of U.S. Army Science Conference*, West Point, NY, AD A056400.

Fine, B. J., and Sweeney, D. R. (1968). Personality traits and situational factors and catecholamine excretion. *Journal of Experimental Research in Personality*, **3**, 15-27.

Fine, B. J., Cohen, A., and Crist, B. (1960). Effect of exposure to high humidity at high and moderate ambient temperature on anagram solution and auditory discrimination. *Psychological Reports*, **7**, 171-181.

Fox, R. H. (1965). Heat. In Edholm, O. G., and Bacharach, A. L. (eds.) *The Physiology of Human Survival* (London: Academic Press).

Fox, R. H., Bradbury, P. A., Hampton, I. F. G., and Legg, C. F. (1967). Time judgment and body temperature. *Journal of Experimental Psychology*, **75**, 88-96.

François, M. (1927). Contribution à l'étude du sens du temps: la température interne comme facteur du variation de l'appréciation subjective des durées. *L'Année Psychologie*, **27**, 186-204.

Gaydos, H. F. (1958). Effect on complex manual performance of cooling the body while maintaining the hands at normal temperature. *Journal of Applied Physiology*, **12**, 373-376.

Gaydos, H. F., and Dusek, E. R. (1958). Effects of localised hand cooling versus total body cooling on manual performance. *Journal of Applied Physiology*, **12**, 377-380.

Givoni, B., and Rim, Y. (1962). Effects of the thermal environment and psychological factors upon subjects' responses and performance of mental work. *Ergonomics*, **5**, 99-114.

Goltz, F., and Edwards, I. R. (1896). Der hund mit verkürztem rückenmark. *Pfleugers Arch.*, **63**, 362.

Grether, W. F., Harris, C. S., Mohr, G. C., Nixon, C. W., Ohlbaum, M., Sommer, H. C., Thaler, V. H., and Veghte, J. H. (1971). Effects of combined heat, noise and vibration stress on human performance and physiological functions. *Aerospace Medicine*, **42**, 1092-1097.

Griffiths, I. D., and Boyce, P. R. (1971). Performance and thermal comfort. *Ergonomics*, **14**, 457-468.

Gunderson, E. K. E. (1966). *Selection for Antarctic service.* U.S. Navy Medical Neuropsychiatric Research Unit, Report No. 66-15 (San Diego, CA).

Gunderson, E. K. E., and Nelson, P. D. (1963). Adaptation of small groups to extreme environments. *Aerospace Medicine*, **34**, 1111-1115.

Hahn, J. F. (1974). Somesthesis. *Annual Review of Psychology*, 25, 237-240.

Heberden, W. (1826). An account of the heat of July 1825: together with some remarks on sensible cold. *Philosophical Transactions*, 116, 69-74.

Hensel, H. (1970). Temperature receptors in the skin. In Hardy, J. D., Gagge, A. P., and Stolwijk, A. J. (eds.) *Physiological and Behavioral Temperature Regulation* (Illinois: Thomas).

Hensel, H. (1973). Cutaneous thermoreceptors. In Iggo, A. (ed.) *Handbook of Sensory Physiology*, Vol. II (Berlin: Springer-Verlag).

Hensel, H., and Bowman, K. (1960). Afferent impulses in cutaneous sensory nerves in human subjects. *Journal of Neurophysiology*, 23, 564-578.

Hensel, H., and Iggo, A. (1971). Analysis of cutaneous warm and cold fibres in primates. *Pfleugers Arch.*, 329, 1-8.

Hill, L., Black, M., McIntosh, J., Rowlands, R. A., and Walker, H. B. (1913). *The influence of the atmosphere on our health and comfort in continued and crowded places.* Smithson. Misc. Coll., 60, Publication No. 2170 (Washington, D.C.: Smithsonian Institution).

Hoagland, H. (1933). The physiological control of judgments of duration: evidence for a chemical clock. *Journal of General Psychology*, 9, 267-287.

Horvath, S. M., and Freedman, A. (1947). The influence of cold upon the efficiency of man. *Journal of Aviation Medicine*, 18, 158-164.

Houghten, F. C., and Yaglou, C. P. (1923). Determination of the comfort zone. *Transactions of the American Society of Heating and Ventilation Engineers*, 29, 361.

Iampietro, P. F., Chiles, W. D., Higgins, E. A., and Gibbons, H. L. (1969). Complex performance during exposure to high temperatures. *Aerospace Medicine*, 40, 1331-1335.

Iampietro, P. F., Melton, C. E. Jr., Higgins, E. A., Vaughan, J. A., Hoffman, S. M., Funkhouser, G. E., and Saldivar, J. T. (1972). High temperature and performance in a flight task simulator. *Aerospace Medicine*, 43, 1215-1218.

Iggo, A. (1969). Cutaneous thermoreceptors in primates and subprimates. *Journal of Physiology*, 200, 403.

Kleber, R. J., Lhamon, W. T., and Goldstone, S. (1963). Hyperthermia, hyperthyroidism and time judgment. *Journal of Comparative and Physiological Psychology*, 56, 362-365.

Kleitman, N. (1933). Studies on physiology of sleep: diurnal variation in performance. *American Journal of Physiology*, 104, 449-456.

Kleitman, N., and Doktorsky, A. (1933). Studies on physiology of sleep: effect of position of body and of sleep on rectal temperature in man. *American Journal of Physiology*, 104, 340-343.

Kleitman, N., Teitelbaum, S., and Feiveson, P. (1938). Effect of body temperature on reaction time. *American Journal of Physiology*, 121, 495-501.

Kuusinen, J., and Heinonen, M. (1972). Immediate aftereffects of the Finnish sauna on psychomotor performance and mood. *Journal of Applied Psychology*, 56, 336-340.

Langkilde, G., Alexandersen, K., Wyon, D. P., and Fanger, P. O. (1973). Mental performance during slight cool or warm discomfort. *Archives of Science and Physiology*, 27, 511-518.

Leibowitz, H. W., Abernethy, O. N., Buskirk, E. R., Bar-or, O., and Hennessy, R. T. (1972). The effect of heat stress on reaction time to centrally and peripherally presented stimuli. *Human Factors*, 14, 155-160.

Loeb, M., and Jeantheau, G. (1958). The influence of noxious environmental stimuli on vigilance. *Journal of Applied Psychology*, 42, 47-49.

Lovingood, B. W., Blyth, C. S., Peacock, W. H., and Lindsay, R. B. (1967). Effects of D-amphetamine sulfate, caffeine, and high temperature on human performance. *Research Quarterly of the American Association of Health and Physical Education*, **38**, 64–71.

Mackie, R. R., and O'Hanlon, J. F. (1976). A study of the combined effects of extended driving and heat stress on driver arousal and performance. In Mackie, R. R. (ed.) *Vigilance: Theory, Operational Performance, and Physiological Correlates* (New York: Plenum Press).

Mackworth, N. H. (1945). *Effects of heat and high humidity on pursuitmeter rotor scores.* Medical Research Council, RNPRC Habitability Sub-comm. Report RNP 45/199, H.S. 54 (London).

Mackworth, N. H. (1946a). *Effects of heat and high humidity on prolonged visual search as measured by the Clock Test.* Medical Research Council, RNPRC, Habitability Sub-comm. Report RNP 46/278, H.S. 124 (London).

Mackworth, N. H. (1946b). Effects of heat on wireless telegraphy operators hearing and recording Morse messages. *British Journal of Industrial Medicine*, **3**, 143–158.

Marsh, H. D. (1906). *The Diurnal Course of Efficiency* (New York: The Science Press).

Marshall, H. C. (1972). The effects of cold exposure and exercise upon peripheral function. *Archives of Environmental Health*, **24**, 325–330.

McArdle, B., Dunham, W., Holling, H. E., Ladell, W. S. S., Scott, J. W., Thomson, M. L., and Weiner, J. S. (1947). *M.R.C. (War) Memo. R.N.P. Report No. 47/381.* (London).

Mitchell, D. (1977). Physical basis of thermoregulation. In Robertshaw, D. (ed.) *Environmental Physiology.* II, Vol. 15, *International Review of Physiology* (Baltimore: University Park Press).

Mortagy, A. K., and Ramsey, J. D. (1973). Monitoring performance as a function of work-rest schedule and thermal stress. *American Industrial Hygiene Association Journal*, **34**, 474–480.

Nelson, P. D., and Gunderson, E. K. E. (1963). *Effective individual performance in small Antarctic stations: a summary of criterion studies.* U.S. Navy Med. Neuro-psychiatric Res. Unit, Report No. 63–8 (San Diego, CA).

Nunneley, S. A., Dowd, P. J., Myhre, L. G., and Stribley, R. F. (1978). Physiological and psychological effects of heat stress simulating cockpit conditions. *Aviation, Space and Environmental Medicine*, **49**, 763–767.

Nunneley, S. A., Dowd, P. J., Myhre, L. G., Stribley, R. F., and McNee, R. C. (1979). Tracking-task performance during heat stress simulating cockpit conditions in high-performance aircraft. *Ergonomics*, **22**, 549–555.

Orenstein, A. J., and Ireland, H. J. (1922). Experimental observations on the relation between atmospheric conditions and the prevention of fatigue in mine labourers. *Journal of Industrial Hygiene*, **4**, 30–46 and 70–91.

Payne, R. B. (1959). Tracking proficiency as a function of thermal balance. *Journal of Applied Physiology*, **14**, 387–389.

Peacock, L. J. (1956). *A field study of rifle aiming steadiness and serial reaction performance as affected by thermal stress and activity.* U.S. Army Medical Research Lab. Report No. 231/56 (Ft. Knox, KY).

Pepler, R. D. (1953a–g). The effect of climatic factors on the performance of skilled tasks by young European men living in the tropics:

——(1953a). A task of continuous pointer alignment—Exp. one. *RNPRC, TRU, 3/51* (London).

——(1953b). A task of continuous pointer alignment—Exp. two. *RNPRC, TRU, 4/51* (London).

——(1953c). A task of Morse Code reception. *RNPRC, TRU, 12/51* (London).

——(1953d). A task of prolonged visual vigilance. *RNPRC, TRU, 15/51* (London).

——(1953e). A complex mental task with varying speed stress. *RNPRC, TRU, 21/52* (London).

——(1953f). A task of continuous pointer alignment at two levels of incentive. *RNPRC, TRU, 28/52* (London).

——(1953g). A complex mental task with varying speed stress at two levels of incentive. *RNPRC, TRU, 33/52* (London).

Pepler, R. D. (1958). Warmth and performance: an investigation in the tropics. *Ergonomics*, **2**, 63–88.

Pepler, R. D. (1959a). Extreme warmth and sensorimotor coordination. *Journal of Applied Physiology*, **14**, 383–386.

Pepler, R. D. (1959b). Warmth and lack of sleep: accuracy or activity reduced. *Journal of Comparative Physiological Psychology*, **52**, 446–450.

Pepler, R. D. (1960). Warmth, glare, and a background of quiet speech: a comparison of their effects on performance. *Ergonomics*, **3**, 68–73.

Pepler, R. D., and Warner, R. E. (1968). Temperature and learning: an experimental study. *ASHRAE Trans*, **74**, 211–219.

Poulton, E. C. (1973). Unwanted range effects from using within-subject experimental designs. *Psychological Bulletin*, **80**, 113–121.

Poulton, E. C., and Edwards, R. S. (1974a). Interactions and range effects in experiments on pairs of stresses: mild heat and low frequency noise. *Journal of Experimental Psychology*, **102**, 621–628.

Poulton, E. C., and Edwards, R. S. (1974b). Interactions, range effects, and comparisons between tasks in experiments measuring performance with pairs of stresses: mild heat and 1 mg of L hyoscine hydrobromide. *Aerospace Medicine*, **45**, 735–741.

Poulton, E. C., and Kerslake, D. McK. (1965). Initial stimulating effect of warmth upon perceptual efficiency. *Aerospace Medicine*, **36**, 29–32.

Poulton, E. C., Edwards, R. S., and Colquhoun, W. P. (1974). The interaction of the loss of a night's sleep with mild heat: task variables. *Ergonomics*, **17**, 59–73.

Provins, K. A., and Bell, C. R. (1970). Effects of heat stress on the performance of two tasks running concurrently. *Journal of Experimental Psychology*, **85**, 40–44.

Ramsey, J. D., Dayal, D., and Ghahramani, B. (1975). Heat stress limits for the sedentary worker. *American Industrial Hygiene Journal*, **36**, 259–265.

Reilly, R. E., and Parker, J. F., Jr. (1968). *Effect of heat stress and prolonged activity on perceptual-motor performance.* NASA CR-1153 (Contr. NASA-1329) (Arlington, VA: Biotechnology Inc.).

Robertshaw, D. (1977). Role of the adrenal medulla in thermoregulation. In Robertshaw, D. (ed.) *Environmental Physiology.* II, Vol. 15, *International Review of Physiology* (Baltimore: University Park Press).

Russell, R. W. (1957). *Effects of variations in ambient temperature on certain measures of tracking skill and sensory sensitivity.* U.S. Army Medical Research Lab., Report No. 300 (Ft. Knox, KY).

Satinoff, E. (1978). Neural organization and evolution of thermal regulation in mammals. *Science*, **201**, 16–22.

Siple, P. A., and Passell, C. F. (1945). Measurements of dry atmospheric cooling in subfreezing temperatures. *Proceedings of the American Philosophical Society*, **89**, 177–199.

Teichner, W. H. (1957). Manual dexterity in the cold. *Journal of Applied Physiology*, **11**, 333–338.

Teichner, W. H. (1958). Reaction time in the cold. *Journal of Applied Psychology*, **42**, 54–59.

Teichner, W. H. (1966). Individual thermal and behavioral factors in cold-induced vasodilation. *Psychophysiology*, **2**, 295–304.

Teichner, W. H., and Wehrkamp, R. F. (1954). Visual-motor performance as a function of short-duration ambient temperature. *Journal of Experimental Psychology*, **47**, 447–450.

Vaughan, J. A., Higgins, E. A., and Funkhouser, G. E. (1968). Effects of body thermal state on manual performance. *Aerospace Medicine*, **39**, 1310–1315.

Vernon, H. M. (1930). The measurement of radiant heat in relation to human comfort. *Journal of Physiology*, **52**, XV–XVII.

Vernon, H. M., and Warner, C. G. (1932). Influence of humidity of air on capacity for work at high temperatures. *Journal of Hygiene (Camb)*, **32**, 431–463.

Viteles, M. S., and Smith, K. R. (1946). An experimental investigation of the effect of change in atmospheric conditions and noise upon performance. *Transactions of the American Society of Heating and Ventilation Engineers*, **52**, 167–182.

Weiner, J. S., and Hutchinson, J. C. D. (1945). Hot humid environment: its effect on the performance of a motor coordination test. *British Journal of Industrial Medicine*, **2**, 154–157.

Wing, J. F., and Touchstone, R. M. (1965). *The effects of high ambient temperature on short-term memory*. AMRL-TR-65-103 (Wright-Patterson AFB, OH: Aerospace Medical Research Laboratory).

Winslow, C. E. A., Herrington, L. P., and Gagge, A. P. (1938). Reactions of clothed human body to variations in atmospheric humidity. *American Journal of Physiology*, **124**, 692–703.

Wyon, D. P. (1973). The effects of ambient temperature swings on comfort, performance and behaviour. *Archives of Science and Physiology*, **27**, 441–458.

Wyon, D. P. (1974). The effects of moderate heat stress on typewriting performance. *Ergonomics*, **17**, 309–318.

Wyon, D. P., Andersen, J. B., and Lundquist, G. R. (1979). The effects of moderate heat stress on mental performance. *Scandinavian Journal of Work Environment and Health*, **5**, 352–361.

Wyon, D. P., Fanger, P. O., Olesen, B. W., and Pedersen, C. J. K. (1975). The mental performance of subjects clothed for comfort at two different air temperatures. *Ergonomics*, **18**, 359–374.

Yaglou, C. P., and Minard, D. (1957). Control of heat casualties at military training centers. *Archives of Industrial Health*, **16**, 302–316.

SUPPLEMENTARY REFERENCES

Allan, J. R., and Gibson, T. M. (1979). Separation of the effects of raised skin and core temperature on performance of a pursuit rotor task. *Aviation, Space and Environmental Medicine*, **50**, 678–682.

Auliciems, A. (1981). Toward a psycho-physiological model of thermal perception. *International Journal of Biometeorology*, **25**, 109–122 (R).

Baddeley, A. D. (1966). Time-estimation at reduced body-temperature. *American Journal of Psychology*, **79**, 475–479.

Baddeley, A. D., Cuccaro, W. J., Edstrom, G. H., Weltman, G., and Willis, M. A. (1975). Cognitive efficiency of divers working in cold water. *Human Factors*, **17**, 446–454.

Bell, P. A. (1981). Physiological, comfort, performance and social effects of heat stress. *Journal of Social Issues*, **37**, 71–94 (R).

Biersner, R. J. (1976). Motor and cognitive effects of cold water immersion under hyperbaric conditions. *Human Factors*, **18**, 299–304.

Bowen, H. M. (1968). Diver performance and the effects of cold. *Human Factors*, **10**, 445–464.

Braun, J. R. (1961). *The relation of isolation, cold and stress to behaviour at remote sites*. USAF Contract No. AF41(657)-323 (Texas Christian Univ., TX) (R).

Carlson, L. D. (1961). *Human performance under different thermal loads*. School of Aviation Medicine Report No. 61–43 (Brooks AFB, TX).

Clark, R. E. (1959). *The calculation of mean hand-skin temperature in studies of manual performance in the cold*. EPRD Rept. No. PB-29, U.S. Army QMR & E Comd. Natick, MA).

Clark, R. E., and Flaherty, C. F. (1963). Contralateral effects of thermal stimuli on manual performance capability. *Journal of Applied Physiology*, **18**, 769–771.

Clark, R. E., and Jones, C. E. (1962). Manual performance during cold exposure as a function of practice level and the thermal conditions of training. *Journal of Applied Psychology*, **46**, 276–280.

Dusek, E. R. (1957a). Effect of temperature on manual performance. In Fisher, F. R. (ed.) *Protection and Functioning of the Hands in Cold Climates* (Washington, D.C.: NAS-NRC) (R).

Dusek, E. R. (1957b). *Manual performance and finger temperatures as a function of ambient temperature*. U.S. Army R & E Center. EPRD Report No. EP-68 (Natick, MA).

Ellis, H. (1758). An account of the heat of the weather in Georgia in a letter from his Excellency Henry Ellis, Esq. *Philosophical Transactions*, **50**, 755.

Enander, A., Skoldstrom, B., and Holmer, I. (1980). Reactions to hand cooling in workers occupationally exposed to cold. *Scandinavian Journal of Work, Environment and Health*, **6**, 58–65.

Findikyan, N., and Sells, S. B. (1965). *Coldstress: parameters, effects, mitigation*. Arctic Aeromedical Laboratory Report No. AAL-TR-65-5 (Ft. Wainwright, AK) (R).

Fine, B. J. (1958). The comparative effectiveness of some psychological and physiological measures in ranking the impact of diverse environmental conditions. *Journal of Applied Psychology*, **42**, 353–356.

Fine, B. J. (1961). The effect of exposure to an extreme stimulus on judgments of some stimulus-related words. *Journal of Applied Psychology*, **45**, 41–44.

Fine, B. J., and Gaydos, H. F. (1959). Relationship between individual personality variables and body temperature response patterns in the cold. *Psychological Reports*, **5**, 71–78.

Fisher, F. R. (ed.) (1957). *Protection and Functioning of the Hands in Cold Climates* (Washington, D.C.: NAS-NRC).

Fox, W. F. (1967). Human performance in the cold. *Human Factors*, **9**, 203–220 (R).

Fraser, D. C., and Jackson, K. F. (1955). Effect of heat stress on serial reaction time in man. *Nature*, **176**, 976–977.

Gibson, T. M., and Allan, J. R. (1979). Effect on performance of cycling deep body temperature between 37.0 and 37.6 degrees C. *Aviation, Space and Environmental Medicine*, **50**, 935–938.

Gibson, T. M., Allan, J. R., Lawson, C. J., and Green, R. G. (1980). Effect of induced cyclic changes of deep body temperature on performance in a flight simulator. *Aviation, Space and Environmental Medicine*, **51**, 356–360.

Gibson, T. M., Redman, P. J., and Allan, J. R. (1980). Effect of direction and rate of change of deep body and skin temperatures on performance of a rotary pursuit task. *Aviation, Space and Environmental Medicine*, **51**, 445–447.

Goldman, R. F. (1948). *Assessment of thermal comfort in flight and its effect on performance.* Aeromedical Aspects of Troop Transport and Combat Readiness, Agard Conference Proceedings No. 40, NATO, France.

Grether, W. F. (1973). Human performance at elevated environmental temperatures. *Aerospace Medicine*, **44**, 747–755 (R).

Grether, W. F., Harris, C. S., Ohlbaum, M., Sampson, P. A., and Guignard, J. C. (1972). Further study of combined heat, noise and vibration stress. *Aerospace Medicine*, **43**, 641–645.

Groth, H., and Lyman, J. (1963). *Measuring performance changes in highly transient extreme heat stress: rationale, problem and experimental procedure.* AMRL-TDR-631-1 (Wright-Patterson AFB, Ohio).

Hancock, P. A. (1981). Heat-stress impairment of mental performance—a revision of tolerance limits. *Aviation, Space and Environmental Medicine*, **52**, 117–180 (R).

Hendler, E. (1963). Temperature effects on operator performance. In Burns, N. M., Chambers, R. M., and Hendler, E. (eds.) *Unusual Environments and Human Behavior: Physiological and Psychological Problems of Man in Space* (New York: Free Press of Glencoe).

Jones, R. D. (1970). *Effects of thermal stress on human performance: a review and critique of existing methodology.* Human Engineering Labs., Tech. Memo. 11–70, U.S. Army Aberdeen R & D Ctr., MD.

Kiess, H. O., and Lockhart, J. M. (1970). Effects of level and rate of body surface cooling on psychomotor performance. *Journal of Applied Psychology*, **54**, 386–392.

Kleitman, N., and Jackson, D. P. (1951). Body temperature and performance under different routines. *Journal of Applied Physiology*, **3**, 309–328.

Le Blanc, J. S. (1956). Impairment of manual dexterity in the cold. *Journal of Applied Physiology*, **9**, 62–64.

Lifson, K. A. (1958). Production welding in extreme heat. *Ergonomics*, **1**, 345–347.

Lockhart, J. M. (1968). Extreme body cooling and psychomotor performance. *Ergonomics*, **11**, 249–260.

Lockhart, J. M., and Kiess, H. O. (1971). Auxiliary heating of the hands during cold exposure and manual performance. *Human Factors*, **13**, 457–465.

Lockhart, J. M., Kiess, H. O., and Clegg, T. J. (1975). Effect of rate and level of lowered finger surface temperature on manual performance. *Journal of Applied Psychology*, **60**, 106–113.

Mills, A. W. (1957). Tactile sensitivity in the cold. In Fisher, F. R. (ed.) *Protection and Functioning of the Hands in Cold Climates* (Washington, D.C.: NAS-NRC).

Morton, G. M., and Dennis, J. P. (1960). *The effect of environmental heat on performance, measured under laboratory conditions.* Directorate of Physiological and Biological Research. Clothing and Stores Experimental Establishment, Report No. 99 (London).

Newton, J. M. (1957). *An investigation of tracking performance in the cold with two types of controls.* U.S. Army Medical Research Lab. Report No. 324 (Ft Knox, KY).

Newton, J. M., and Peacock, L. J. (1956). *The effects of auxiliary topical heat on manual dexterity in the cold.* U.S. Army Medical Research Lab. Report No. 285 (Ft. Knox, KY).

Pepler, R. D. (1963). Performance and well-being in heat. In Hardy, J. D. (ed.) *Temperature: Its Measurement and Control in Science and Industry* (New York: Reinhold).

Pepler, R. D. (1964). Psychological effects of heat. In Leithead, C. S., and Lind, A. R. (eds.) *Heat Stress and Heat Disorders* (PA: Davis) (R).

Poulton, E. C. (1970). *Environment and Human Efficiency* (Illinois: Thomas) (R).

Poulton, E. C., Hitchings, R. N., and Brooke, R. B. (1965). Effect of cold and rain upon the vigilance of lookouts. *Ergonomics*, **8**, 163–167.

Provins, K. A. (1958). Environmental conditions and driving efficiency: a review. *Ergonomics*, 2, 97–107 (R).

Provins, K. A., and Bell, C. R. (1961). The effects of heat on human performance. *Proceedings of the International Biochemistry Congress, London 1960* (London: Pergamon) (R).

Provins, K. A., and Bell, C. R. (1962). Effects of high temperature environmental conditions on human performance. *Journal of Occupational Medicine*, 4, 202–211 (R).

Provins, K. A., and Clarke, R. S. J. (1960). The effect of cold on manual performance. *Journal of Occupational Medicine*, 2, 169–176.

Provins, K. A., and Morton, R. (1960). Tactile discrimination and skin temperature. *Journal of Applied Physiology*, 15, 155–160.

Ramsey, J. D., and Morrissey, S. J. (1978). Isodecrement curves for task performance in hot environments. *Applied Ergonomics*, 9, 66–72.

Revesman, S. L., Hollis, J. R., and Mattson, J. B. (1953). *A literary survey of human performance under Arctic environment.* U.S. Army Ordnance Human Engineering Lab. Tech. Memo. No. 6 (Aberdeen, MD) (R).

Rim, Y. (1975). Psychological test performance during climatic heat stress from desert winds. *International Journal of Biomedicine*, 19, 37–40.

Romansky, M. L. (1979). Stress and fatigue in the driving environment. *Dissertation Abstracts International*, 39, 5461.

Rubin, L. S. (1957). Manual dexterity of the gloved and bare hand as a function of the ambient temperature and duration of exposure. *Journal of Applied Psychology*, 41, 377–383.

Snook, S. H., and Ciriello, V. M. (1974). The effects of heat stress on manual handling tasks. *American Industrial Hygiene Association Journal*, 35, 681–685.

Stang, P. R., and Weiner, E. L. (1970). Diver performance in cold water. *Human Factors*, 12, 391–399.

Teichner, W. H., and Kobrick, J. L. (1954). *Effects of prolonged exposure to low temperature on visual-motor performance, flicker fusion, and pain sensitivity.* U.S. Army QMR & D Cmd., EPRD Report No. 230 (Natick, MA).

Teichner, W. H., and Kobrick, J. L. (1955). Effects of prolonged exposure to low temperature on visual-motor performance. *Journal of Experimental Psychology*, 49, 122–126.

Vaughan, W. S., Jr. (1975). Diver temperature and performance changes during long duration, cold water exposure. *Undersea Biomedical Research*, 2, 75–88.

Vaughan, W. S., Jr. (1977). Distraction effect of cold water on performance of higher-order tasks. *Undersea Biomedical Research*, 4, 103–116.

Vaughan, W. S., Jr. and Mavor, A. S. (1972). Diver performance in controlling a wet submersible during four-hour exposure to cold water. *Human Factors*, 14, 173–180.

Webster, A. J. F. (1974). Physiological effects of cold exposure. In Robertshaw, D. (ed.) *MTP International Review of Science, Physiology Series 1*, Vol. 7, *Environmental Physiology* (London: Butterworth).

Wilkinson, R. T. (1969). Some factors influencing the effect of environmental stressors upon performance. *Psychological Bulletin*, 72, 260–272 (R).

Wilkinson, R. T., Fox, R. H., Goldsmith, R., Hampton, I. F. G., and Lewis, H. E. (1964). Psychological and physiological responses to raised body temperature. *Journal of Applied Physiology*, 19, 287–291.

Wing, J. F. (1965a). *A review of the effects of high ambient temperature on mental performance.* AMRL-TR-65-102 (Wright-Patterson AFB, OH) (R).

Wing, J. F. (1965b). Upper thermal tolerance limits for unimproved mental perform-
ance. *Aerospace Medicine*, **36**, 960–964 (R).
Wyndham, C. H. (1973). The effects of heat stress upon human productivity. *Archives
of Science and Physiology*, **27**, 491–497.
Wyon, D. P. (1970). Studies of children under imposed noise and heat stress.
Ergonomics, **13**, 598–612.

The Physical Environment at Work
Edited by D. J. Oborne and M. M. Gruneberg
©1983 John Wiley & Sons Ltd.

Illumination at Work

E. D. MEGAW
Department of Engineering Production,
University of Birmingham, Birmingham, UK
and
L. J. BELLAMY
Department of Applied Psychology,
University of Aston, Birmingham, UK

The fundamental principle of good lighting practice is to provide optimum visual conditions at the minimum cost. Because it is not simply the quantity of light that is important for visual performance, a number of lighting factors must be explored. These factors, however, cannot be considered without examining the nature of the task itself in terms of its physical properties as well as the performance demands specific to that task.

An introduction to light units and some relevant properties of the visual system preludes a detailed analysis of methods for evaluating the effects of lighting on performance. Selected specific tasks are considered in order to illustrate some of the difficulties encountered in applying lighting principles to real-life situations. Finally, some adverse effects of lighting are described and these show up the need to perform more long-term investigations of the way lighting can affect performance indirectly by causing distraction, discomfort, and fatigue. Such aspects are often ignored in attempts to model the effects of light on work and in empirical studies. Throughout the chapter individual differences are introduced where appropriate; probably the most significant and most ignored in practice is the effect of ageing.

It could be concluded that, in terms of providing guidance for lighting specific tasks, no single approach is appropriate. In some cases, the provision of reasonable lighting conditions could almost be described as a matter of trial and error. However, knowledge of some of the relationships between lighting and performance can help to confine investigations to areas of relevance for a particular task and to enable the identification or elimination of lighting as a cause of sub-optimal performance.

Since reference is frequently made to publications of the Commission Internationale de l'Éclairage and the Illuminating Engineering Society, these will be abbreviated to CIE and IES respectively.

LIGHT UNITS

In lighting there are two principal related concepts: illuminance and luminance. In general terms these concepts refer respectively to the light received by a surface and the light emitted from a surface.

Illuminance

Illuminance is defined as the density of luminous flux per unit area. Luminous flux refers to the amount of light flowing in the space around the source and its capacity to produce visual sensation. It is measured in lumens (lm) and is the product of radiant flux (the power of a light source measured in Watts) and a constant which represents the spectral sensitivity of the visual system for an internationally agreed standard observer. Since illuminance is the concentration of luminous flux it is measured in lm m^{-2} or lux (lx).

Illuminance cannot be used to specify the total output of a light source. The quantity of illuminance depends not only on the distance of the source from the point of measurement but also, in any practical working interior, on the sum of the illuminances received from secondary sources, such as room surfaces, by direct reflection and inter-reflection. Although the total light output of a source is generally specified by the manufacturer in terms of lumens, when describing the distribution of light from a source luminous intensity is used. This is the power of a source to emit light in a given direction and is measured as the luminous flux emitted per unit solid angle in a specified direction. The unit of measurement is the candela (cd), equivalent to a lumen steradian^{-1}. Diffusers and reflectors for fluorescent tubes, for example, will affect the intensity distribution of a source such that the quantity of light emitted will vary depending on the angle from which the source is viewed. For this reason the distribution of light from a source is often represented in the form of a graph called a polar curve where intensity is represented in candelas according to direction.

In any environment, the quantity of light received by a surface will therefore depend on a number of factors. These can be summarized as the luminous intensity of the source(s) at the angle from which light is received, the distance of the working plane from the source(s), and the reflectances of room surfaces acting as secondary sources.

Luminance

The luminous appearance of a surface is referred to as its brightness while

Table 1. Conversion tables for photometric units

Illuminance

		Lux	Foot-candle
One lux (1m m^{-2})	equals	1	0.093
One foot-candle (1m ft^{-2})	equals	10.76	1

Luminance

		Apostilb	Foot-lambert	Lambert	cd m^{-2}	cd in^{-2}	Stilb
One apostilb (1m m^{-2})	equals	1	0.0929	0.0001	0.318	0.000205	0.0000318
One foot-lambert (1m ft^{-2})	equals	10.76	1	0.001076	3.426	0.00221	0.0003426
One lambert (1m cm^{-2})	equals	10,000	929	1	3183	2.054	0.318
One candela per sq metre (cd m^{-2})	equals	3.14	0.292	0.000314	1	0.000645	0.0001
One candela per sq inch (cd in^{-2})	equals	4869	452	0.487	1500	1	0.155
One stilb (cd cm^{-2})	equals	31,416	2929	3.14	10,000	6.452	1

Multiply a unit in column 1 by the factor shown to convert to units along the top line.

The Physical Environment at Work

luminance is a measure of its physical brightness. Both depend on reflectance which is defined as the ratio of luminous flux reflected from a surface to the flux incident on it. Luminance can be defined as the luminous flux emitted from a point on a surface in a given direction per unit solid angle per unit area and is measured in cd m^{-2}. The same units are used to express the luminance of a primary light source. A perfectly uniformly diffusing surface having a luminance of 1 cd m^{-2} would emit π lumens and its intensity per unit projected area would be the same from all directions of view. Thus for a perfectly diffusely reflecting surface the relationship between illuminance and luminance would be:

$$\text{Luminance (cd m}^{-2}) = \frac{\text{Illuminance (lx)} \times \text{Reflectance}}{\pi}$$

The relationship between illuminance and luminance can be illustrated by considering a sphere of radius 1 m with a uniform point source of 1 cd at its centre. The total number of lumens emitted in the space around the source is equal to the number of times an area of one square metre could be fitted on to the sphere's surface. This value is 4π, hence the source is emitting 4π lm. Taking one of the 4π steradians of the sphere, the luminous flux within this cone would be 1 lm and the light incident on 1 m^2 of the surface would be 1 lx. The luminance (assuming a reflectance of unity and a perfectly uniformly diffusing surface) would be 1 lm m^{-2}, the photometric unit being 1 apostilb or, in SI units, $1/\pi$ cd m^{-2}.

Due to the long history of photometry, many text books and meters do not use the approved SI units. A conversion table is therefore given in Table 1.

Retinal illuminance

It is sometimes necessary to talk about retinal illuminance when considering the response of the visual system to light. This is because the brightness of any image depends upon the diameter of the limiting aperture of the image-forming device. In the eye this limit is set by pupillary diameter. Retinal illuminance is measured in trolands (td). One troland is equal to the retinal illuminance obtained by looking through an artificial pupil of area 1 mm^2 at a matt surface whose luminance is 1 cd m^{-2}.

THE VISUAL RESPONSE TO LIGHT

Spectral sensitivity

The shift in the efficiency of different wavelengths of light to produce visual sensation in daylight (photopic conditions) compared to when little light is available (scotopic conditions) was first described by Purkinje in 1825 (Pirenne, 1967). A transition from photopic to scotopic conditions results in a shift in spectral sensitivity to light of shorter wavelengths (towards the blue end of the spectrum). This is illustrated in Figure 1 where it is shown that within the visible spectrum of 400 to 700 nm the peak sensitivity is at about 555 nm (green-yellow) under photopic conditions and at about 505 nm (blue-green) under scotopic conditions. The shift reflects the operation of two types of photoreceptors in the retina — the cones for day vision and the rods for night vision. Colour vision is mediated solely by cones. The cone receptors are mainly concentrated in a central region of the retina known as the fovea while the rods predominate in the peripheral regions.

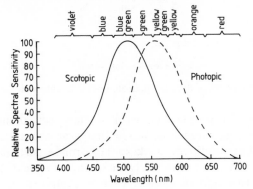

Figure 1. Relative spectral sensitivity curves for photopic and scotopic vision

Adaptation

The visual system can discriminate signals over a luminance range of 10^{-6} cd m^{-2} to 10^5 cd m^{-2} (Ditchburn, 1973). This capacity is made possible by the process of adaptation whereby the eye adjusts its sensitivity in accordance with prevailing light conditions. Changes in sensitivity can be observed as the eye adapts to darkness after being exposed to bright light. These changes are classically measured by the fall in the threshold (just perceptible) luminance of flashes of light over time (Hecht, Haig, and Chase, 1937). The resulting dark adaptation curve reveals a two-stage process as shown in Figure 2. The first, associated with the cone system (photopic vision), takes about 10 minutes and the second stage, associated with the rod system (scotopic vision), takes about 20 minutes. On the other hand, adaptation from scotopic to photopic vision takes about 2 minutes. Broadly it can be said that when the eye is adapted to luminances above 3 cd m^{-2} only the cone system operates, while below 0.001 cd m^{-2} only the rod system operates.

In measuring dark adaptation, if the test flash is red, the rod branch of the curve fails to appear since the rods are insensitive to red light (see Figure 1).

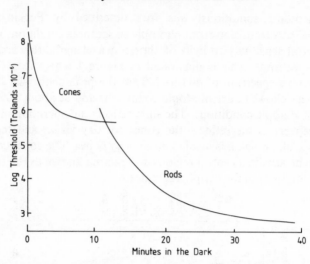

Figure 2. The temporal course of dark adaptation. (After Hecht, Haig, and Chase, 1937)

This is the reason why people who work in dark environments, such as photographic processing rooms, are advised to wear glasses fitted with red filters when they take intermittent breaks in the normal environment. By doing this the visual system remains in the fully dark adapted state. Currently, work is being carried out to determine whether a similar result can be achieved using neutral density filters (Cushman, 1980).

Visual acuity

Visual acuity is defined as the visual angle (or more frequently its reciprocal), in minutes of arc, subtended at the eye by the smallest detail that the eye can just resolve. The most familiar measure of acuity is the Snellen letter chart which is still used by opticians. This is composed of rows of high-contrast black letters on a white background which are graded in size. The British Standard (BS 4274, 1968) recommends that, at an illuminance of 45 lx and with a viewing distance of 6 m, an observer should be able to recognize letters whose line width is equal to a visual angle of 1 ′, equivalent to an acuity value of 1.

Values of acuity vary as a function of the nature of the task and the characteristics of the observer's visual system. In addition to letter recognition, measures of acuity involve identifying the position of a gap in a so-called Landolt ring, resolving a grating made up of alternating bands of light and dark, and detecting a single bar on a uniform background. In all cases the definition of acuity remains the same. For the grating, acuity values of around 2 are obtained (equivalent to a band width of 0.5′) and for the single bar, values as high as 100 (equivalent to a bar width of 0.01′). These differences can be appreciated when it is realized that in order to resolve detail, the visual system must discriminate between different luminances within the stimulus. The distribution of illuminance arising from the stimulus at the retina depends on several optical features of the eye such as the degree of blurring of the retinal image. On the other hand, the ability to resolve the brightness pattern of the retinal image is a function of the characteristics of the receptors and the associated neural networks. An example of the importance of the optical features is reflected in the well-known conditions of myopia (near sightedness) and hyperopia (far sightedness). In both conditions the ability to focus the image of the stimulus on the retina is impaired. A further case of the importance of optical features is demonstrated by the decrease in acuity accompanying ageing. This is primarily due to a hardening, yellowing, and increasing opacity of the lens and to a reduction in pupil diameter which result in increased blurring of the retinal image and decreased retinal illumination. These effects can only be partially offset by increasing task illuminance (Weale, 1961, 1963).

The influence of retinal factors on acuity can be illustrated by considering the effects of the retinal location of the test stimulus material. This is demonstrated by the results of Kerr (1971) shown in Figure 3. The task required observers to resolve a square wave grating. It is clear that the further out towards the periphery of the retina the target is presented the lower are the acuity values, particularly under the higher levels of target luminance. The extent of the fall-off in acuity with eccentricity

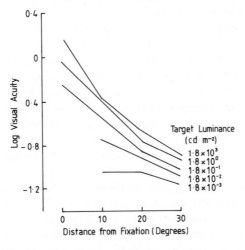

Figure 3. Visual acuity for a square wave grating as a function of retinal location and target luminance where acuity is expressed as the reciprocal of the band width in minutes of arc. (After Kerr, 1971)

is a function of the test material, being greater for tasks involving cognition than for those only requiring detection (Johnson, Keltner, and Balestrery, 1978).

The reason for specifying standard conditions of illuminance when sight-testing is apparent in the results shown in Figure 3. In a much earlier study, Hecht (1931) reported that for the Snellen chart, a maximum acuity of 1.7 (0.6′ of arc) is reached when the adaptation luminance is 300 cd m^{-2} and falls to around 0.1 (10′ of arc) at 0.003 cd m^{-2}. In addition to the task luminance, acuity is dependent upon the range of luminances within the visual field of view of the observer. One way of examining this has been to vary independently the luminances of the task and the surround to the task. Stevens and Foxell (1955) took this approach when they used a Landolt ring as the test target surrounded by a uniform background subtending 120°. They found that the maximum acuity was achieved when the surround luminance was equal to or slightly lower than the target luminance. The practical significance of this is discussed later.

When sight-testing it is assumed that the target contrast is maximum. Returning to the point made earlier that tests of acuity reflect the ability of the observer to make luminance discriminations, it should not be surprising to learn that acuity is greatly affected by target contrast. In fact, an alternative way of defining acuity is to consider the minimum (threshold) contrast at which a target can be resolved. Contrast refers to the relative luminances of the target and the background. The relationships between threshold target contrast and various target parameters will be described later since they form the basis of the CIE model (CIE, 1980) for measuring task visibility and for establishing optimum lighting conditions.

An additional application of the relationship between threshold contrast and target features is found in obtaining the so-called spatial modulation transfer function of the visual system. This function describes the sensitivity of the visual system to variations in luminance. By presenting an observer with a series of gratings of various spatial frequencies (expressed as the number of darker or lighter bars subtended per degree of visual angle) one can measure the contrast sensitivity of the observer where sensitivity is defined as the reciprocal of the threshold contrast values. Typically, under photopic conditions the maximum sensitivity is found at 3 cycles degree^{-1} (Campbell and Maffei, 1974). The importance of this approach to acuity is not only that it reflects a possible model of how the visual system operates but also that it may provide an important clue to designing the features of characters for optical displays (Ross, 1979). A further use of the transfer function has been to demonstrate that the reduced visual acuity experienced by divers under water can be predicted from performance on land if the contrast reduction due to the water is taken into account (Muntz, Baddeley, and Lythgoe, 1974).

Temporal resolution

When a light source is repeatedly switched on and off it appears to flicker. As the frequency of oscillations is increased there comes a point when the flicker is no longer perceived. The frequency at which this happens is called the critical fusion frequency (CFF). Of the numerous factors affecting CFF, two are of particular relevance. CFF values rise with an increase in the luminance of the flashing source and with an increase in the area subtended by the source (Hecht and Smith, 1936). Under certain circumstances CFF values can be as high as 75 Hz. Because observers find flicker annoying and possibly fatiguing it is, for example, important to ensure that the refresh rate of a screen for a visual display terminal (VDT) is above the conventional mains frequency of 50 or 60 Hz.

The most important characteristics of the visual system can be summarized as follows. At high luminances (photopic vision) spatial resolution is good, colour vision is present, but sensitivity to low luminance stimuli is poor. Under low luminances (scotopic vision) the eye can detect weak stimuli at the expense of good spatial resolution. Colour vision is lost.

METHODS OF ESTABLISHING LIGHTING FOR PERFORMANCE

Examples of guidance for 'good' lighting practice can be found in the British IES code (IES, 1977) and the CIE guide on interior lighting (CIE, 1975). Examples of IES recommended illuminances for different tasks are shown in Table 2.

Table 2. Recommended illuminances for a sample of tasks (After IES, 1977)

Task	Illuminance (lx)
Living rooms in the home — general lighting	50
Furnace rooms in glass works	150
General office work with mainly clerical tasks and occasional typing	500
Motor vehicle assembly	500
Proof reading in printing works	750
Colour matching in paint works	1000
Fine assembly work, e.g. electronic assembly	1000
Inspection of hosiery and knitwear	1500
Inspection and testing shops (engineering) — minute work, e.g. very small instruments	3000
Jewellery and watchmaking — minute processes	3000
Operating theatres in hospitals — local lighting	10,000–50,000

As well as taking into account economic factors, such as the cost of electricity and the lighting equipment available, recommendations and standards must consider task and observer factors irrespective of whether evidence is derived from research or practical experience. The aims of providing reasonable lighting for any visual task can be specified in terms of (1) the level of task visibility, (2) the speed and accuracy with which the task can be performed, (3) observer comfort, and (4) the subjective impression of the quality of the illuminated environment. Lighting can directly affect performance by changing the physical characteristics of the task or by affecting the state of the visual system.

Two major approaches to designing lighting for optimum performance will be considered: the analytic and the empirical. In the analytic approach, measurements are made of the operational characteristics of processes occurring during visual work such that a quantitative model of overall performance as a function of lighting parameters can be derived. This approach relies on using very simple basic tasks. In the empirical approach the speed and accuracy with which a task is performed is measured under real or simulated conditions of visual work.

A. The analytic approach

Beuttell (1934) suggested that the illuminance required for any task depends on certain conditions adversely affecting its performance. He argued that, providing one could define these conditions as well as the relationship between them and the lighting required to compensate for their adverse effects, it should be possible to calculate the illuminance suitable for performance of the task. This could be done by exhaustively investigating the effects of lighting on a standard task and determining the illuminance for any desired level of performance. Then the illuminance required for any other task could be obtained by introducing multiplying factors that take into account differences between the standard task and the task of interest.

Two of the major contributors to the analytic approach are Weston (1935, 1945) and Blackwell (1959). Their work, particularly that of Blackwell, has been instrumental in the development of the analytic model of the CIE (1980). In the analytic models the size and contrast of task detail are considered to be critical parameters in determining task difficulty. In order to perceive a visual stimulus there must be sufficient contrast to render it visible and it must be within the resolution capabilities of the eye. The amount of brightness contrast (C) can be expressed as a ratio of the difference in luminance between the target and the background $| L_t - L_b |$ to the background luminance value (L_b). Thus $C = | L_t - L_b | / L_b$.

The reason for expressing contrast as a ratio is that the visual system determines stimulus differences on a relative rather than an absolute basis. The contrast sensitivity of the eye depends on its level of adaptation. The eye can detect lower contrasts when adapted to moderate and high luminances than when it is adapted to low luminances. Depending on the reflectances of the contrasting areas, an increase in task illuminance will increase the mean luminance level of the task, and should therefore improve contrast sensitivity. The contrast value should be unaffected by illuminance changes because it is determined by the reflectances of task detail and background. However, in practical situations, perfectly matt surfaces are rare and the luminance of a surface having any degree of specularity (gloss) depends to some extent on the way it is illuminated (direction and polarization) as well as on the illuminance.

Weston's experiments

Weston (1935) used a simple paper and pencil task consisting of rows of high-contrast Landolt rings with gaps at different orientations. The speed and accuracy with which rings of specific orientations could be cancelled out by the subjects were used to evaluate the effects of different gap sizes (1–10′ arc) over a range of illuminance (2–5382 lx). After calculating and subtracting the time required for the purely manual aspect of the task (ring cancellation without the gap discrimination) performance was found to be directly proportional to the logarithm of the gap size for the range 1–4′ arc but for larger sizes the performance increment diminished and was relatively small. The results are shown in Figure 4 where performance is measured as the reciprocal of discrimination time per ring multiplied by an accuracy factor.

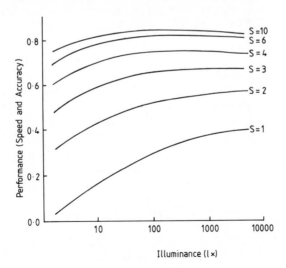

Figure 4. The effects of gap size (*S*, in minutes of arc) on the performance on a Landolt ring cancellation task at different illuminances. (After Weston, 1935)

The inter-relationship between contrast, size, and illuminance was also investigated (Weston, 1945). The effect of illuminance on performance for different contrasts depended very much on gap size. For intermediate and high contrast targets which were large (6′ arc) illuminance had very little effect over the range 9–5382 lx. However, for a 1′ target performance was considerably affected by illuminance and contrast. Weston's results are shown in Figure 5. In these experiments it was evident that, however high the illuminance, performance with a small size and poor contrast target can never reach the level of maximum performance obtained with a large size or good contrast. The importance of these findings is that, in terms of efficiency, there is an optimum illuminance for a task having a particular contrast. As illuminance increases, the payoff in terms of improvement in performance decreases. Also low contrasts will have more of an adverse effect on performance if the work involves discrimination of fine detail. This means that in practice a greater improvement in performance can generally be achieved by changing task factors than by increasing illuminance.

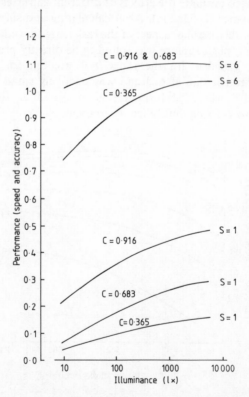

Figure 5. The effects of contrast (C) and gap size (S, in minutes of arc) on performance at different illuminances. (After Weston, 1945)

The Blackwell and CIE approach

Blackwell's work originated in an examination of the problems of establishing the visibility of Morse code light signals used by naval signalmen during the Second World War (Crouch and Cornell, 1977). This led to the development of a general method by which illuminance could be determined for various practical tasks, based upon visual performance criteria (Blackwell, 1959). In the laboratory the task required subjects to discriminate a luminous disc from a background of uniform luminance. The luminous disc was intended to represent the standard task from which standard performance data could be derived for different illuminance values, the basic philosophy being that lighting levels could be specified by determining the standard disc target equivalent in visual difficulty to each practical task of interest.

The development of standard performance data involved a great deal of tedious work. Between 1950 and 1952 two observers made a total of 81,000 observations and in 1956 and 1957 additional verifying experiments were performed. In these experiments the size and contrast of the disc was varied under different conditions of background luminance and exposure times. By determining the probability of correct responses to the presence of the disc target, threshold contrast ($\dot{C}$) was determined. The value of $\dot{C}$ was larger for shorter exposure times and smaller disc sizes. Provided disc size and exposure duration were constant it was possible to obtain smooth curves of log $\dot{C}$ plotted against log background luminance. Some examples of standard performance curves are shown in Figure 6 where the expected decrease in contrast threshold with increasing background luminance is evident.

In order to equate the difficulty of the task of interest with that of a standard disc, an optical device was developed. This is known as a visibility

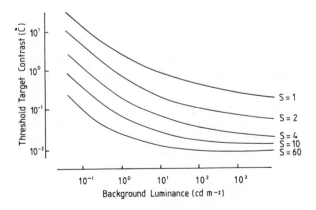

Figure 6. Threshold contrast ($\dot{C}$) as a function of background luminance and disc size (S, in minutes of arc) when discs are exposed for 100 ms. (After Blackwell, 1959)

meter (Blackwell, 1970; Eastman, 1971) which operates on the principle of contrast reduction achieved by superimposing a veil of light over the task. This principle is illustrated in Figure 7. The visibility meter allows the fractions of task and veiling luminances reaching the eye to be varied. Initially, the veiling luminance (V) is set equal to the task luminance (L), both unattenuated. The fractions of task luminance (f_1) and veiling luminance (f_2) are then simultaneously altered such that $f_1 + f_2$ remains constant at 1. This ensures that the level of adaptation of the eye remains constant. Increasing the fraction of veiling luminance will decrease the visibility of the task by decreasing its contrast and a value can be obtained at which the task is at threshold. The visibility of the task of interest can then be expressed in terms of its equivalent contrast ($\tilde{C}$). This is the initial luminance contrast of a reference task (having the same background luminance as the average luminance of the task of interest) which requires the same amount of veiling luminance as the target of interest to reduce it to its contrast threshold ($\bar{C}$).

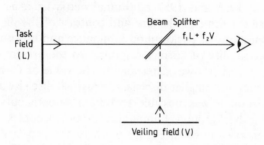

Figure 7. The operating principle of a contrast-reducing visibility meter where f_1 is the fraction of task luminance received by the eye and f_2 is the fraction of the veiling luminance. (After CIE, 1972)

The CIE reference task is a luminous 4′ disc exposed against a uniform luminance background field for 0.2 s glimpses. Reference curves of threshold disc contrast as a function of luminance are obtained under reference lighting conditions (unpolarized illumination at a colour temperature of 2856°K) using a reference population (observers aged between 20 and 30 with no visual, motor, or cognitive defects).

In the CIE model (1980) the effects of task luminance and task demand on visual performance are represented in terms of two sets of relationships. The first is between task luminance and task visibility level (VL), where VL $= \tilde{C}/\bar{C}$. Both $\tilde{C}$ and $\bar{C}$ are expressed in terms of contrast values for the reference task. Values of $\bar{C}$ can be obtained from the appropriate reference curve similar to those shown in Figure 6. Increases in luminance fail to produce proportional increases in VL due to the non-linear relationship between adaptation luminance and contrast sensitivity, an effect already demonstrated by the results of Weston and Blackwell.

The second relationship in the model is that between VL and relative visual performance (RVP). RVP is a measure of the visual performance potential in a task involving eye movements. It is expressed as a proportion of the maximum value achievable and is a composite of the relative performance obtained with each of three separate visual processes, one involving recognition of task detail and two concerned with oculomotor control. For different visual tasks the relative contribution of each process to overall performance will vary.

Performance curves relating RVP to different values of VL were obtained using a visual performance reference task. This task was required to take account of the fact that observers make use of off-axis information when searching and scanning a visual display. Measurements of VL were made under on-axis viewing conditions. The performance reference task consists of an array of five 4′ Landolt rings, one in the centre and the other four at the cardinal points of the compass. The observer has to specify which of the four rings has a gap in the same orientation as the centre ring. VL can be changed by altering the contrast of the rings or the adaptation luminance. Task demand is a function of exposure duration, the separation between rings and the type of information required. The relationship between RVP and VL can be fitted by log ogives and some examples are illustrated in Figure 8 for different levels of task demand.

During the course of the development of the model, the age of observers was found to affect VL. Older people have higher contrast thresholds and consequently have lower VLs than the reference population. This means that in practical situations older workers will require higher task luminances than younger workers to achieve the same level of relative visual performance.

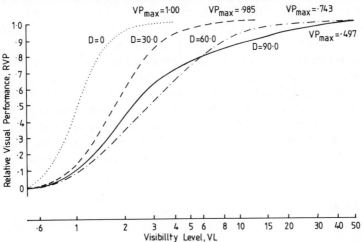

Figure 8. Relative visual performance as a function of visibility level for different levels of task demand (*D*). The curve for $D = 0$ represents on-axis performance and VP_{max} refers to the maximum level of performance that can be achieved. (After CIE 1980)

To summarize, it can be said that the level of visual performance efficiency provided by a given task illuminance or luminance is influenced by three major parameters. These are the difficulty of the discrimination as measured by $\tilde{C}$, the level of task demand and the age of the observer population. In calculating the luminance required to achieve a criterion level of performance, values of luminance for different values of $\tilde{C}$ must be provided for various levels of task demand and observer age.

The application of measures of VL cannot be achieved without taking into account the properties of practical lighting installations since these do not produce reference lighting conditions. A measure of the effectiveness of a given lighting installation in rendering a task visible in relation to task visibility under reference conditions is given by its contrast rendering factor (CRF), where:

$$CRF = \frac{\text{Relative visibility under actual lighting conditions}}{\text{Relative visibility under reference conditions}}$$

Relative visibility is measured by using the visibility meter and is defined as the reciprocal of the value f_1 when the target is at threshold level (see Figure 7). Clearly, the smaller the value of f_1, the easier the target was to see originally. CRF will have a value greater or less than 1 depending on whether the lighting under investigation is better or worse than reference conditions and as such quantifies the effect of veiling reflections on the task. Veiling reflections occur whenever images of bright sources are reflected into the eyes of the observer from surfaces within the task. The more specular the surfaces the greater these reflections are. How effective a particular lighting installation is in rendering a particular task visible can be given by VL × CRF, sometimes referred to as the effective visibility level. Similar weightings can be found for the effects of disability glare (DGF) and transient adaptation (TAF).

Not surprisingly several problems exist with using the CIE model. Although it has been shown to fit real and simulated work situations fairly successfully (Smith and Rea, 1978) it tends to be retrodictive rather than predictive. That is, it is only possible to fit the model by *post hoc* manipulation. This is a serious criticism of the model although future developments may reverse this situation. At present the model represents the most significant attempt to quantify the complex interaction of task, lighting, and individual effects on performance.

B. Empirical studies

Reading

To image successive parts of the text on to the fovea, the eyes execute a series of rapid eye movements called saccades. These last between 25 and 80 ms depending on the angular distance moved. Between the saccades the eyes remain relatively stationary for between 100 and 500 ms. This is the fixation time and it is generally agreed that this is when visual input occurs. Although the average saccade length is equivalent to 8 character positions for an experienced adult reader, it can range from 2 to 18 positions. In considering the effects of lighting on reading, it is reasonable to assume that they will be associated with the ease with which information can be extracted from the foveal and peripheral fields of view although some fatiguing effects due to poor lighting may be located at higher levels of processing.

Despite the high proportion of time that many people spend reading, there is little research into the effects of lighting on performance. In an early study, Tinker (1939) compared performance on the Chapman-Cook Speed of Reading Test at six different illuminances. The test required subjects to cross out words that spoilt the meaning of the text printed in 10-point type. There was no improvement in performance above 8 lx. This value is considerably less than the value of 300 lx recommended for reading surfaces in libraries (IES, 1977). More recently Smith and Rea (1978) have indicated that performance at different illuminances interacts with the age of the subject and the quality of the reading material. The material was selected from a 'well-written book of general interest'. The print quality was expressed in terms of VLs, although there were broadly three levels of quality. The task required subjects to cross out words which were incorrectly spelt. An *ad hoc* measure of performance was used which took into account both speed, hits, and false alarms. Generally, little improvement in performance was found for illuminances above 120 lx. The improvements that were observed up to 120 lx were most pronounced for the older subjects and for the poorest quality of print. For the younger subjects and the best print quality, there was no difference in performance between the 10 lx and 120 lx conditions.

Another factor to consider is the extent of veiling reflections. Such reflections could reduce the contrast of glossy text printed on matt paper because the luminance of the text would be increased to a greater extent than the luminance of the paper. Conditions of veiling reflections were simulated in a study by Ronchi and Neri (1974) who reduced the contrast by directly adding a veiling luminance and, at the same time, reducing the background luminance to give a constant adaptation luminance of $50 \, \text{cd m}^{-2}$. This method parallels the main principle of the visibility meter approach to the measurement of task difficulty (Figure 7). The results showed that as the print contrast is effectively reduced there is a marked increase in reading times. These results are in contrast to a more realistic study by Boyce (1979). His tasks involved copy typing and searching for telephone numbers. Veiling reflections were introduced by varying the specularity of the surfaces on which the material was printed and by varying the arrangement of the luminaires in relation to the task position. The extent of the veiling reflections was expressed in terms of the range of luminances and the CRFs for the various combinations of surface specularity and lighting arrangement. The lowest value of CRF that was achieved was 0.39. This was accompanied by task luminances in the range of 159 to 290 cd m^{-2} and involved the glossy task material. In all conditions the illuminance was constant at 560 lx. No detrimental effects of veiling reflections were found for either task in relation to both speed and errors. Boyce suggests that this is because the original contrast of the task was high and because subjects were able to move their heads about in order to avoid the glaring reflections. It is therefore possible that the increases in discomfort and subjective task difficulty experienced by the subjects under the conditions of higher veiling luminances were due to the awkward posture the subjects consequently adopted. In an earlier study by Petherbridge and Hopkinson (1955), glare was introduced by using a glossy table surface. It was reported that subjects complained primarily of distraction rather than a sense of pain–discomfort, a result confirmed later by De Boer (1977).

The text contrast can be manipulated directly, in the absence of veiling reflections, by varying the reflectances of the background and the text. Spencer, Reynolds, and Coe (1977) used a task where subjects had to search short paragraphs of text printed in 9-point type for six target words. They found that the number of words successfully found during 1 minute of reading only decreased significantly when the contrast was reduced to around 0.05. Using a proof reading task, Stone, Clarke, and Slater (1980) found that, although performance improved as the contrast was increased from 0.12 to 0.75, the only significant improvement was between contrasts of 0.12 and higher values.

Two further sets of results should be mentioned. Despite there being some evidence that people have a preference for light sources with certain colour rendering properties (Cochram, Collins, and Langdon, 1970; Bellchambers and Godby, 1972) no significant differences in performance under sources with different spectral emissions were obtained by Smith and Rea (1979). Their study required subjects to check lists of digits. The light sources included high-pressure sodium, metal halide, and cool white fluorescent. These results confirm those of Rowlands *et al.* (1973) who used searching through charts of Landolt rings as their experimental task. The other results concern the effects of lamp flicker on performance. Poulton, Kendall, and Thomas (1966) evaluated performance by giving subjects a comprehension test after they had read some text. While no significant effects were observed, 16 per cent of the subjects reported that they felt very uncomfortable with the highest level of flicker.

Overall, these studies have demonstrated that performance on reading text with the conventional black-on-white print is relatively insensitive to lighting conditions. Only when the quality of the text is poor, the contrast very low, the print size small, or the subject relatively old will increasing the illuminance cause an improvement in performance. To some extent these conclusions are predicted by the findings of Weston and Blackwell where ceiling levels in performance are observed. Because of the large amount of redundancy present in written text, these ceiling levels may be reached at lower illuminances and values of contrast than with the simulated tasks. The extent to which increases in illuminance decrease the thresholds for peripheral targets (Figure 3) and thereby increase the distance from the fovea at which relevant information can be extracted remains unclear.

It should be remembered that these studies have only required subjects to perform over short durations. It is open to question whether the results would have been different had more prolonged tests been used. The results on the subjective reports from subjects on matters of discomfort and fatigue indicate that lighting is possibly a more critical factor than the results from the performance studies suggest. This applies particularly to the possible adverse effects of veiling reflections which can be reduced by the use of non-specular materials for the table surface, the writing paper, and the ink; by the suitable positioning of the primary light sources and, in some cases, by fitting the luminaires with polarizing diffusers.

Inspection

In industry, product quality is largely dependent on the ability of inspectors to distinguish faulty items from acceptable ones not only by removing the faulty items but also by providing feedback to production and other interested departments. The inspection task typically requires the inspector to search for different fault types simultaneously. Each fault type can exhibit a wide range of severity. This means that in addition to detecting faults, inspectors must judge whether or not the faults are severe enough for them to be rejected. Despite the current increase in the automation of production processes, the relative unit costs attributable to visual inspection labour have risen sharply. Unfortunately, human error rates are notoriously high so that miss rates of 15 per cent are not uncommon (Sinclair, 1979). One approach to reducing these high error rates is based on a consideration of the numerous factors that are known to affect inspection performance (Megaw, 1979). Although it is generally considered that lighting is one of the most important of these factors, it is extremely difficult to specify lighting requirements. The effects of lighting are determined by the particular task characteristics such as the relative reflective properties of the defects and their immediate backgrounds. Because the main role of lighting is to increase the conspicuity of a defect from levels below or around threshold to those above threshold, many investigators have felt it unnecessary to carry out extensive performance studies.

As in reading, scanning of the stimulus material involves saccadic eye movements. While individual inspectors adopt their own overall scanning strategies, the role of peripheral vision in guiding the fine features of the search remains an important one. An element of most models of visual search is an estimate of the visual lobe area which reflects how far out in peripheral vision a target or fault can be detected. The size of the area depends upon the conspicuity of a target and this reflects the interaction of target and background features. As conspicuity is increased, search times are decreased by reducing the number of eye fixations required to give visual coverage to the stimulus material and by increasing the amount of control of the search strategy exerted by peripheral information. It follows that benefits should be gained from designing lighting conditions which increase fault conspicuity as far above threshold as possible, particularly where speed of performance is a critical consideration.

The IES code (1977) recommends illuminances for inspection tasks of between 500 and 3000 lx depending upon task difficulty. These values should only be taken as guidelines since the chosen illuminance should take account of the reflectance of the stimulus material. In fact, two studies have shown that increasing illuminance can lead to a decrement in performance. Wyatt and Langdon (1932) compared the rate of working in the periods immediately before and after the introduction of artificial lighting during a winter afternoon

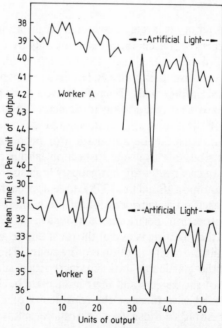

Figure 9. The effect of the introduction of artificial light on the performance of two operators. (After Wyatt and Langdon, 1932.) Reproduced by permission of the Controller of Her Majesty's Stationery Office

period. The task involved the inspection and packing of metal cartridges. The results for the two operators are shown in Figure 9 where the decline in the working rate immediately following the onset of the artificial lighting is evident. The operators commented that the artificial lighting produced a dazzling glare reflected from the components in addition to an uneven illuminance. In a more recent study, Saito and Tanaka (1977) reported that the detection of faults in empty glass bottles progressively decreased as the illuminance increased from 1000 lx to 10,000 lx. The bottles, which were inspected on a conveyor, had a complex shape and were not completely transparent. The higher illuminances led to reflected glare and disturbing flickering effects.

More important than illuminance are the qualitative aspects of the lighting conditions. These relate to the characteristics of the primary lighting sources and to the relative positioning of the task, the lighting source, and the observer. A comprehensive survey of these relationships can be found in the American National Standards Institute publication (1973). Because inspectors normally search simultaneously for several fault types with different characteristics, one should ideally provide more than one lighting method for any one inspection task. However, this is often impossible so that a compromise has to be reached. Some of the lighting techniques used for some common inspection tasks will now be described.

Inspection of fabric

Defects which result in small protuberances above the surface can be made more conspicuous by directing a concentrated beam of light at a very low angle to the surface of the fabric. This technique, known as surface grazing, produces a dark shadow and at the same time effectively magnifies the size of the fault. Feinstein (1970) introduced this method for the inspection of worsted cloth. While he found this marginally increased the overall fault detection probability, there was no evidence that the improvement was for any particular type of fault. Apparently there was difficulty in obtaining a source intensity high enough to overcome the effects of the general overhead fluorescent lighting, particularly on the side of the cloth furthest away from the grazing source. There were also problems with the radiant heat from the grazing source. Depending on how much light the cloth transmits, it is possible to increase the effects of the grazing source by replacing the overhead lamps with a source positioned underneath the fabric (transillumination). However, this could make it difficult to detect certain surface faults such as dirt marks or dyeing faults.

Inspection of sheet steel

A comparison between the benefits of directional and diffuse lighting for the inspection of sheet metal was made by Deroker and Frier (1969). Throughout the study the task illuminance was kept constant at 1100 lx and the proportions of directional and diffuse lighting varied. The diffuse lighting was provided by ten fluorescent lamps fixed above a diffusing ceiling. The directional lighting was provided either by other fluorescent lamps or by a series of 500 W incandescent lamps positioned immediately below the diffusing ceiling. An additional variable was the position of the task in relation to the light sources. Three classes of defects were established: (1) those that had a reflectance different from the background; (2) those that had a different specularity; and (3) those where there was a distortion of the surface.

The effects of changing the lighting conditions were assessed by measuring the visibility of the various faults using an Eastman visibility meter rather than by conducting lengthy experiments on inspection performance. The defects which increased in visibility as the light became more diffuse were those whose specularity was different from the background. As the light became more directional the visibility increased mainly for those defects where surface distortion had occurred. Defects which had different reflectances were only slightly affected by the proportions of directional and diffuse light. Certain fault types only became visible with additional lighting techniques. Most of the defects had their highest visibility when the task was positioned so that the light source was imaged directly in the task. Not only did the arrangement give the highest task luminance, it also produced a marked variation in the reflected brightness over the surface of the steel sheet. This arrangement is frequently used for the inspection of specular panels where defects are detected as distortions in the reflected brightness patterns. An interesting observation is that this is the arrangement which provides the highest veiling reflections in office-type tasks.

Inspection of glass

Gillies (1975) describes a technique, known as shadow-graphing, for the inspection of a ribbon of flat glass. The inspector is seated above the glass which is continually moving towards the inspector. A very intense monochromatic divergent light is directed downwards through the glass and falls on a white screen below. Body and surface defects are detected as dark shadows on the screen and are magnified by an amount depending on the distance separating the screen from the glass.

A task which has been the subject of numerous investigations is the inspection of glass bottles as they pass along on a conveyor in front of the inspector. Inspection rates of 200 bottles per minute are not uncommon. A study of the lighting requirements for the detection of faults known as crizzles (hairline cracks) was made by Dickens et al. (1967). The lighting was provided by two sources. One of these was a fluorescent lamp placed 30 cm directly above the conveyor belt and the other was a transilluminated opal diffusing screen positioned perpendicular to the belt on the side furthest away from the inspector. Inspection performance was assessed with each source separately and with the combined sources. Other variables included the inspection rate and the viewing angle. At the slow rate of inspection neither the lighting conditions nor the viewing angle were critical. At the faster rate, the best performance was obtained with the combined lighting and the worst performance with only the overhead lighting. The lower angle of viewing (25°) improved fault detection but had no effect on false alarms.

It is apparent that, apart from some guidelines on illuminance and lighting methods, the most suitable lighting conditions for a particular inspection task is often obtained by a process of trial and error. Some of the more common methods have been described and they include shadow graphing, surface grazing, diffuse lighting, reflected brightness patterns, and transillumination. By consulting Faulkner and Murphy (1973), one can appreciate that other methods are available. All these lighting methods are equally applicable to the design of automatic visual inspection devices.

Colour judgement

While the appreciation of colour is the basis of several inspection tasks, it also plays an important role in other tasks. A person's state of health can be inferred from skin colour. Similarly, the colours of foodstuffs reveal their freshness. There are two different, though closely related, aspects to colour judgement. One involves the ability to match colours and, therefore, to detect small differences between them. The other involves the ability to make an absolute judgement of a colour. Both are influenced by the colour properties of the primary light sources illuminating the coloured surfaces. The extent of the complex interaction between these properties and the reflecting characteristics of coloured surfaces is illustrated by the finding that the colour of a surface can appear different under a variety of primary sources even if the sources have the same colour appearance. In addition, two coloured surfaces which match under one light source do not necessarily match under another source. Such colours are referred to as metameric and the implications of them for practical colour matching tasks are obvious.

To establish the extent to which colour matching is influenced by the colour properties of primary sources, Boyce and Simons (1977) had subjects completing the Farnsworth-Munsell 100-Hue test (Farnsworth, 1943) under different fluorescent lamps. This required subjects to order 85 small coloured discs which differed only in hue. Accuracy of discrimination improved as the colour fidelity of the lamps (quantified by their colour rendering indices) increased, the most accurate performance being achieved under the artificial daylight fluorescent lamp.

In addition to the colour properties of the primary light sources, the least perceptible difference between two colours depends on their luminances, their size, and the colour of the background against which they are viewed. Because the perception of hue varies with the adaptation luminance there is a need to establish a standard illuminance for colour judgement tasks. Recommended values range from 1000 to 2200 lx. There is, however, little evidence to suggest that such high values are essential for all tasks. Brown (1951) concluded that no loss of accuracy of colour matching occurs until adaptation falls below $3 \, cd \, m^{-2}$. Cornu and Harlay (1969) and Boyce (1976) used the Farnsworth-Munsell 100-Hue test where the test fields are larger than those used by Brown. Both studies showed that with a fluorescent lamp performance was just as accurate with an illuminance of 300 lx as at higher levels. With an incandescent lamp Cornu and Harlay showed that performance was more accurate with a very high illuminance but that the improvement was due to the results at the extremes of the visible spectrum.

The studies that have been quoted have employed small stimulus fields with a dark surround. Such conditions are rarely met in practice, which is fortunate since colour judgement is impaired if very small stimulus fields are used (Weitzman and Kinney, 1969). A further investigation by Brown (1952) compared colour matching performance with test fields subtending either 2° or 12°. Red, green, blue, and white were used as the matching fields and these, with the addition of black, were used for the surrounding fields to give 20 combinations of field and surround colour for each size of test field. Matching was more accurate with larger test fields where performance was also largely unaffected by the colour of the surround. For the small test fields, accuracy was reduced if the surround colour was different from the test colour. The best matching occurred when the surround and test field colours were the same, although a white surround yielded satisfactory performance. More complex effects of field size and surround properties have been examined by Troscianko (1977).

Lyons (1970a) makes some general recommendations for the optimum conditions under which to perform colour matching tasks. Bright and colourful areas in the vicinity of the task should be avoided since they will act as secondary light sources and consequently interfere with the colour rendering by the primary source. In addition, the eye will become selectively adapted to the colour of the secondary source so that the appearance of the task takes on the complementary colour. Hunter (1975) recommends that neutral grey is the most suitable background colour. Finally, the angle at which the surface is viewed must take account of the material of the object. For example, in the case of metallic objects colour is seen by specular reflection while in non-metallic objects it is seen by diffuse reflection.

Colour anomalies

A majority of the population can match any colour of the visible spectrum by mixing, in relatively consistent proportions, three basic monochromatic lights: red, green, and blue. People who can do this are referred to as normal trichromats. However, approximately 8 per cent of the male and 0.5 per cent of the female population require different proportions and, as a result, show some kind of defective colour vision which is commonly, although misleadingly, called colour blindness. The imbalance between the sexes in the incidence of colour blindness is the result of the effects of a sex-linked recessive gene. There are cases of acquired colour blindness from pathological conditions such as diabetes mellitus and possibly from exposure to certain toxic substances such as carbon monoxide, but these cases are comparatively rare. In addition, small changes in colour vision can result from yellowing of the lens of the eye as part of the ageing process (Weale, 1963). This causes a filtering out of blue and violet light and a reduction in blue–green discrimination.

There is an enormous variation in the range and severity of colour blindness. A majority of those with defective colour vision are referred to as anomalous trichromats and these people require the three primary colours to match a colour but in different proportions from normal trichromats. Others, referred to as dichromats, can match any colour with a mixture of just two of the primary colours, while an extremely exclusive group of people called monochromats require only one primary colour. They, therefore, are truly colour blind.

It is extremely difficult to describe the effects of colour blindness on a person's appreciation of colour, although errors and hesitation in naming colours as well as errors in matching colours are the usual symptoms. For example, a dichromat who is insensitive to green (deuteranope) will confuse green with brown or red, while an anomalous trichromat, who is only relatively insensitive to green (deuteranomalous) will confuse greenish-yellow with yellow. Naturally, the effects can most easily be identified by those tests designed to screen people for colour vision. Of the many tests currently available, the most suitable for indicating a person's suitability for industrial and other jobs are the Farnsworth-Munsell 100-Hue test (Farnsworth, 1943) and the City University Colour Vision Test (Voke, 1979).

ADVERSE EFFECTS OF LIGHTING

Glare

When there is a range of luminances within the visual field of view subjects frequently report that they experience sensations of glare. An obvious example of the conditions producing glare is the dazzling effect of oncoming car

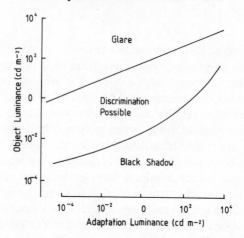

Figure 10. Diagram illustrating the range of object luminances within which discrimination of detail is possible for different adaptation luminances. (After Hopkinson and Collins, 1970.) Reproduced by permission of MacDonald Publishers

headlights when driving at night. Figure 10 indicates the luminances of objects that will give rise to glare depending on the state of adaptation of the eye. A distinction is usually made between disability and discomfort glare. *Disability glare* causes a reduction in task visibility while *discomfort glare* refers to a sense of discomfort experienced by the subject. Measures to control discomfort glare will normally take care of disability glare (CIE, 1975). Glare can occur directly from primary sources or indirectly by reflection from secondary sources.

Disability glare

Disability glare occurs as a result of light in the task surround reaching the observer's eyes and reducing task contrast because of the interocular scatter of light by the cornea and lens of the eye (Cole, 1978). This should be distinguished from those effects of veiling reflections which reduce contrast at the task before the light reaches the eye. Spectacles, visors, and windscreens can contribute to disability glare. As the eye's lens undergoes changes with age, resulting in a steady and then rapid increase in light scatter, it is not surprising to find that older observers are more subject to disability glare. Cole reports that disability for a 60-year-old can be up to three times that experienced by a 20-year-old.

Disability glare is quantified in terms of equivalent veiling luminance and is a function of the illuminance produced by the source at the eye and the reciprocal of the angular distance between the line of sight and the direction of the glare source (Holladay, 1926). In the CIE model (1980) the reduction in task visibility is quantified by the DGF.

Disability glare is only of major significance when there is an excessive range of luminances in the visual field, particularly when viewing under scotopic conditions as in night driving. The scattered light tends to fall obliquely on the retina and because the cones show a much greater reduction in sensitivity to light falling obliquely than do the rods (Stiles and Crawford, 1933) they are, therefore, less susceptible to disability glare.

Discomfort glare

Both veiling reflections and disability glare can cause discomfort. In addition, discomfort glare can result from lighting conditions which do not cause a loss of task contrast. The magnitude of discomfort glare is measured by subjective evaluation and is related to the luminance of the source (L_s), the luminance of the background to the source (L_b), the angle of the source relative to the line of sight (Θ) and to the solid angle subtended by the source at the eye (W). One formula developed in Britain by Petherbridge and Hopkinson (1950) is used by the IES (1967) to express the discomfort produced by one or more sources and can be expressed as:

$$\text{Glare index} = 10 \log_{10} (\Sigma\, G)$$

where G = glare constant for a single source

$$= \frac{0.48 L_s^{1.6}\ W^{0.8}}{L_b\, \Theta^{1.6}}$$

Although the values of the exponents in the formula depend to some extent on the experimental conditions, one can see that increasing the size and luminance of the source (L_s) would increase glare, while increasing the background luminance (L_b) would decrease it. Note, however, that in practice increasing source luminance could also increase background luminance. Increasing the deviation from the line of sight also decreases glare and, to control for this factor, glare sources should not be in the glare zone, that is within 45° above the line of sight (CIE, 1975). As a rough guide Hopkinson and Collins (1970) state that a glare index of less than 10 is rated as 'barely perceptible' while a value over 28 is rated as 'intolerable'. When setting limits to glare indices for field installations it is necessary to take account of the task demands. Based upon these demands glare index limits have been recommended by the IES (1977) for various tasks. One should stress that people show an enormous variation in the extent of reported glare sensation (Boyce, 1981).

The question of whether discomfort glare alone has an effect on performance has been studied by Stone and Groves (1968). Performance on Weston's Landolt ring task was evaluated over a large range of glare indices. The main performance differences were due to subjects and to practice. This supports the view that glare discomfort is not retinal in origin since impairment of retinal functions should reduce visual acuity and contrast sensitivity. Fry and King (1971) have suggested that the source of discomfort is related to stimulation of pain nerve endings in the iris due to the complex pupillary response to the non-uniform luminance conditions.

Preferred luminance ratios

Although discomfort glare has no direct effect on performance, the long-term effects may be to distract attention from the task. A distracting effect of a bright source within the field of view was found by Hopkinson and Longmore (1959). This has a relevance for designing an ideal range of luminances in the environment in relation to task luminance. Attention remains on the task more effectively if it has a brighter luminance than the general surroundings. Studies of observer preferences indicate that the luminance of the immediate task surround should not be less than about one-third of the task luminance (Bodmann, 1967). The American National Standards Institute (1973) recommend that the luminance ratios of task to surround to more remote surfaces should be approximately 10:3:1, or where the task has a low luminance such as a VDT screen, 1:3:10.

Visual fatigue

In many occupations involving prolonged visual work complaints of visual fatigue and eyestrain are common (Weston, 1962). In recent years this has become particularly apparent amongst users of VDTs (Dainoff, 1979; Grandjean and Vigliani, 1980). Unfortunately, little systematic research has been carried out on the effects that lighting parameters have on visual fatigue that has a general application to visually demanding tasks, although it is usually taken for granted that poor lighting causes visual fatigue. This is because subjective reports of visual fatigue often refer to lighting conditions as a cause (for example, Dainoff, Happ, and Crane, 1981).

Any discussion on visual fatigue is made difficult by the absence of an agreed definition. This is partly because it is often not possible to differentiate the symptoms of visual fatigue from those associated with physical and mental fatigue. For example, changes in a person's posture while performing a task can be caused by fatigue in muscles responsible for maintaining a particular posture and by the mental load imposed by the task, as well as from the operator avoiding the effects of glare sources in the visual field of view. Nevertheless there are a group of symptoms which are traditionally associated with visual fatigue and they include itching or inflamed eyes; burning, throbbing or aching sensations in the eyes; blurred vision; double vision;

difficulty focusing; giddiness; headache; irritability, and difficulty in maintaining attention (Weston, 1962).

Attempts to provide objective measures of fatigue have tended to be inconclusive. Such measures include decrements in performance, increased blink rate, increased recognition times, lowering of CFF, and changes in eye movement parameters, fixation times, pupil diameter, dark adaptation time, and brightness discrimination (for example, Brozek, 1949; Brozek, Simonson, and Key, 1950; Kovalenko, 1970; Geacintov and Peavler, 1974; Ostberg, Gunnarsson, and Calissendorf, 1976; Stone, Clarke, and Slater, 1980).

Weston (1962) identifies eyestrain as involving undue action of the intrinsic and extrinsic eye muscles resulting in fatigue. The extrinsic muscles control eye movements and convergence while the intrinsic muscles are concerned with pupil size and accommodation. Temporary changes in certain eye movement parameters have been induced by Bahill and Stark (1975), but these were not due to the introduction of adverse lighting conditions. On the other hand there is some controversial evidence (Aboimova, 1974) that permanent damage to the accommodation system can result from close visual work performed over a period of several years. Recently, there has been some encouraging work on the measurement of temporary changes in the accommodation response of the eye induced by fatiguing conditions (Ostberg, 1980). Visual work at a VDT which subjects reported was fatiguing produced a temporary myopia (over-accommodation) for distance vision and a hyperopia (under-accommodation) for near vision.

Some of the effects of poor lighting on vision can be inferred from what has already been said in this chapter. Discomfort glare is likely to fatigue the pupil control system. Potential glare sources will be avoided at a cost of observers adopting fatiguing postures. The angle of vision accompanying these unsatisfactory postures may lead to fatigue of the extrinsic eye muscles. In cases where poor lighting causes a reduction in task contrast or contrast sensitivity, such as low illuminance, disability glare, and veiling reflections, the eye may futilely attempt to clarify the retinal image through changes in accommodation or the observer may bring the task closer to the eyes (Lyons, 1970b). Both these may lead to fatigue of the accommodation and convergence mechanisms.

One would expect that under poor lighting conditions performance over long periods of work should show a greater decrement than under more favourable conditions. Surprisingly enough, there is very little evidence that this is the case. One of the few studies to demonstrate this result was made by Brozek, Simonson, and Key (1959). Subjects performed over 2-hour periods on a task requiring them to identify very small moving letters at illuminances ranging from 22 lx to 3230 lx. Performance generally improved with illuminances up to 540 lx and then levelled off. Under all conditions there was a decrement in performance over time, but this was greatest for the 22 lx condition. One reason for the paucity of evidence of this kind in practical tasks is given by Boyce (1971) who suggested that performance decrements arising from fatigue can be overcome by supplying an increase in effort. Using a series of Landolt ring cancellation tasks similar to Weston's, Boyce found that as illuminances were reduced subjects reported an increase in subjective ratings of effort. These results suggest that an alternative way of looking into the effects of lighting conditions might be to consider them in the context of models of how effort or processing capacity is allocated to tasks (Kahneman, 1973).

SUMMARY

From what has been said in this chapter, the reader can be excused for concluding that lighting plays a minor role in influencing performance and productivity. Certainly, adequate lighting can only compensate to a limited extent for the low levels of performance that result from poorly developed task features such as low contrast and small size of detail. On the other hand, the standards of current lighting practice are inadequate and this is reflected in the frequent complaints that refer to lighting as a cause of discomfort and annoyance. What is more, as Boyce (1981) emphasizes, there is plenty of evidence to suggest that in most environments the levels of illumination are excessive. This results in a waste of scarce resources and in unnecessary costs. What is needed is more consideration to be given to the quality of illumination and to the requirements of individuals.

REFERENCES

Aboimova, V. M. (1974). The development of myopia in persons working with computer equipment. *Voenno-Meditsinskii Zhurnal*, 67–68. (In Russian.)

American National Standards Institute. (1973). *American National Standard Practice for Industrial Lighting* (New York: Illuminating Engineering Society).

Bahill, A. T., and Stark, L. (1975). Overlapping saccades and glissades are produced by fatigue in the saccadic eye movement system. *Experimental Neurology*, 48, 95–106.

Bellchambers, H. E., and Godby, A. C. (1972). Illumination, colour rendering and visual clarity. *Lighting Research and Technology*, 4, 104–106.

Beuttell, A. W. (1934). An analytical basis for a lighting code. *Illuminating Engineer*, 27, 5–11.

Blackwell, H. R. (1959). Specification of interior illumination levels. *Illuminating Engineer*, 54, 317–353.

Blackwell, H. R. (1970). Developments of procedures and instruments for visual task evaluation. *Illuminating Engineer*, 65, 267–291.

Bodmann, H. W. (1967). Quality of interior lighting based on luminance. *Transactions of the Illuminating Engineering Society* (London), 27, 71–87.

Boyce, P. R. (1971). *The measurement of effort in performance of a visual task* (Capenhurst, Cheshire: Electricity Council Research Centre Memorandum M370).

Boyce, P. R. (1976). Illuminance, lamp type and performance in a colour discrimination task. *Lighting Research and Technology*, 4, 104–106.

Boyce, P. R. (1979). *Veiling reflections: an experimental study on their effects on office work* (Capenhurst, Cheshire: Electricity Council Research Centre Memorandum 1230).

Boyce, P. R. (1981). *Human Factors in Lighting* (London: Applied Science Publishers).

Boyce, P. R., and Simons, R. H. (1977). Hue discrimination and light sources. *Lighting Research and Technology*, **9**, 125–136.

British Standards Institution (1968). *Test Charts for Determining Distance Visual Acuity*. BS4274.

Brown, W. R. J. (1951). The influence of luminance level on visual sensitivity to colour. *Journal of the Optical Society of America*, **41**, 684–688.

Brown, W. R. J. (1952). The effect of field size and chromatic surrounding on colour discrimination. *Journal of the Optical Society of America*, **42**, 837–844.

Brozek, J. (1949). Qualitative criteria of oculomotor performance and fatigue. *Journal of Applied Physiology*, **2**, 247–260.

Brozek, J., Simonson, E., and Key, A. (1950). Changes in performance and ocular functions resulting from strenuous visual inspection. *American Journal of Psychology*, **63**, 51–66.

Campbell, F. W., and Maffei, L. (1974). Contrast and spatial frequency. *Scientific American*, **231**, 106–114.

Cochram, A. H., Collins, J. B., and Langdon, F. J. (1970). A study of user preferences for fluorescent lamp colours for daytime and night-time lighting. *Lighting Research and Technology*, **2**, 249–256.

Cole, B. L. (1978). Some observations on disability glare. *IES Lighting Review*, **40**, 82–85.

Commission Internationale de l'Éclairage. (1972). *A Unified Framework of Methods for Evaluating Visual Performance Aspects of Lighting* (Paris: CIE Publication 19) (TC-3.1).

Commission Internationale de l'Éclairage. (1975). *Guide on Interior Lighting* (Paris: CIE Publication 29) (TC-4.1).

Commission Internationale de l'Éclairage. (1980). *An Analytical Model for Describing the Influence of Lighting Parameters upon Visual Performance* (Paris: Draft CIE Publication 19/2) (TC-3.1).

Cornu, L., and Harlay, F. (1969). Modifications de la discrimination chromatique en fonction de l'éclairement. *Vision Research*, **9**, 1273–1287. (In French.)

Crouch, C. L., and Cornell, H. (1977). Research basis for IES illumination levels. *Lighting Design and Application*, **7**, 32–36.

Cushman, W. H. (1980). Selection of filters for dark adaptation goggles in the photographic industry. *Applied Ergonomics*, **11**, 93–99.

Dainoff, M. J. (1979). *Occupational Stress Factors in Secretarial/Clerical Workers* (Cincinnati, Ohio: National Institute of Occupational Safety and Health).

Dainoff, M. J., Happ, A., and Crane, P. (1981). Visual fatigue and occupational stress in VDT operators. *Human Factors*, **23**, 421–438.

De Boer, J. B. (1977). Performance and comfort in the presence of veiling reflections. *Lighting Research and Technology*, **9**, 169–176.

Dekoker, N., and Frier, J. P. (1969). Visibility of specular and semi-specular tasks in sheet metal surfaces. *Illuminating Engineering*, **64**, 167–175.

Dickens, D. G., Evans, J., Perry, C., and Tidman, G. G. (1967). *Lighting for Inspection, Part IV*. The British Glass Industry Research Association Technical Report No. 106.

Ditchburn, R. W. (1973). *Eye Movements and Visual Perception* (London: Oxford University Press).

Eastman, A. A. (1971). Compatible visibility measurements. *Illuminating Engineering*, **66**, 99–106.

Farnsworth, D. (1943). The Farnsworth–Munsell 100-hue and dichotomous tests for colour vision. *Journal of the Optical Society of America*, **33**, 568–578.

Faulkner, T. W., and Murphy, T. J. (1973). Lighting for difficult visual tasks. *Human Factors*, **15**, 149–162.

Feinstein, J. (1970). 'Human Factors in the Woollen Industry'. Unpublished doctoral thesis, Loughborough University of Technology.

Fry, G. A., and King, V. M. (1971). The role of the pupil in discomfort glare. *Proceedings of the CIE 17th Session*, Barcelona.

Geacintov, T., and Peavler, W. S. (1974). Pupilography in industrial fatigue assessment. *Journal of Applied Psychology*, **59**, 213–216.

Gillies, G. J. (1975). Glass inspection. In Drury, G. C., and Fox, J. G. (eds.) *Human Reliability and Quality Control* (London: Taylor & Francis).

Grandjean, E., and Vigliani, E. (eds.) (1980). *Ergonomic Aspects of Visual Display Terminals* (London: Taylor & Francis).

Hecht, S. (1931). *The Retinal Processes Concerned with Visual Acuity and Colour Vision*. Bulletin No. 4 of the Howe Laboratory of Ophthalmology (Cambridge, Massachusetts: Harvard Medical School).

Hecht, S., and Smith, E. L. (1936). Intermittent stimulation by light. VI. Area and the relation between critical fusion frequency and intensity. *Journal of General Physiology*, **19**, 979–991.

Hecht, S., Haig, C., and Chase, A. M. (1937). The influence of light adaptation on subsequent dark adaptation of the eye. *Journal of General Physiology*, **20**, 831–850.

Holladay, L. L. (1926). The fundamentals of glare and visibility. *Journal of the Optical Society of America*, **12**, 271–319.

Hopkinson, R. G., and Collins, J. B. (1970). *The Ergonomics of Lighting* (London: Macdonald Technical and Scientific).

Hopkinson, R. G., and Longmore, J. (1959). Attention and distraction in the lighting of workplaces. *Ergonomics*, **2**, 321–333.

Hunter, R. S. (1975). *The Measurement of Appearance* (New York: John Wiley).

Illuminating Engineering Society (1967). *Evaluation of Discomfort Glare: The IES Glare Index System for Artificial Lighting Installations*. IES Technical Report No. 10 (London: IES).

Illuminating Engineering Society (1977). *IES Code for Interior Lighting* (London: IES).

Johnson, C. S., Keltner, J. L., and Balestrery, F. (1978). Effects of target size and eccentricity on visual detection and resolution. *Vision Research*, **18**, 1217–1222.

Kahneman, D. (1973). *Attention and Effort* (New Jersey: Prentice-Hall).

Kerr, J. L. (1971). Visual resolution in the periphery. *Perception and Psychophysics*, **9**, 375–378.

Kovalenko, I. G. (1970). Hygienic requirements in working with microfilms. *Hygiene and Sanitation*, **35**, 344–348.

Lyons, S. (1970a). Practical colour matching in industry. *Light and Lighting*, **63**, 264–268.

Lyons, S. (1970b). Lighting for close work. *Light and Lighting*, **63**, 36–38.

Megaw, E. D. (1979). Factors affecting visual inspection accuracy. *Applied Ergonomics*, **10**, 17–25.

Muntz, W. R. A., Baddeley, A. D., and Lythgoe, J. N. (1974). Visual resolution under water. *Aerospace Medicine*, **45**, 61–66.

Ostberg, O. (1980). Accommodation and visual fatigue in display work. In Grandjean, E., and Vigliani, E. (eds.) *Ergonomic Aspects of Visual Display Terminals* (London: Taylor & Francis).

Ostberg, O., Gunnarsson, E., and Calissendorf, B. (1976). *Literature review and pilot study on visual fatigue and intense microimage reading*. Arbetarskyddsstyrelsens Undersoknings-rapporter, AMF 108/76. (In Swedish.)

Petherbridge, P., and Hopkinson, R. G. (1950). Discomfort glare and the lighting of buildings. *Transactions of the Illuminating Engineering Society* (London), **15**, 39–79.

Petherbridge, P., and Hopkinson, R. G. (1955). A preliminary study of reflected glare. *Transactions of the Illuminating Engineering Society* (London), **20**, 255–257.

Pirenne, M. H. (1967). *Vision and the Eye* (London: Chapman & Hall).

Poulton, E. C., Kendall, P. G., and Thomas, R. J. (1966). Reading efficiency in flickering light. *Nature*, **209**, 1267–1268.

Ronchi, L., and Neri, M. (1974). Speed of reading versus target contrast. *Atti della Fondazione Giorgio Ronchi*, **29**, 957–963.

Ross, J. (1979). Human perception of visual display units. In McPhee, D. and Howie, A. (eds.), *Proceedings of a Conference in Ergonomics and Visual Display Units*, Australia.

Rowlands, E., Loe, D. L., Waters, I. M., and Hopkinson, R. G. (1973). Visual performance in illuminance of different spectral quality. *Proceedings of the CIE 17th Session*, Barcelona.

Saito, M., and Tanaka, T. (1977). Visual bottle inspection performance in highly paced belt-conveyor systems. *Journal of Ergology*, **6**, 127–137.

Sinclair, M. A. (1979). The use of performance measures on individual examiners in inspection schemes. *Applied Ergonomics*, **10**, 17–25.

Smith, S. W., and Rea, M. S. (1978). Proofreading under different levels of illumination. *Journal of the Illuminating Engineering Society*, **88**, 47–52.

Smith, S. W., and Rea, M. S. (1979). Relationships between office task performance and ratings of feelings and task evaluations under different light sources and levels. *Proceedings of the CIE 19th Session*, Kyoto.

Spencer, H., Reynolds, L., and Coe, B. (1977). *The Effects of Image/Background Contrast on the Legibility of Printed Materials* (London: Royal College of Art) Readability of Print Research Unit.

Stevens, W. R., and Foxell, C. A. P. (1955). Visual acuity. *Light and Lighting*, **48**, 419–424.

Stiles, W. S., and Crawford, B. H. (1933). The luminous efficiency of rays entering the eye pupil at different points. *Proceedings of the Royal Society*, **B112**, 428–450.

Stone, P. T., Clarke, A. M., and Slater, I. (1980). The effect of task contrast on visual performance and visual fatigue at a constant illuminance. *Lighting Research and Technology*, **12**, 144–159.

Stone, P. T., and Groves, S. D. P. (1968). Discomfort glare and visual performance. *Transactions of the Illuminating Engineering Society* (London), **33**, 9–15.

Tinker, M. A. (1939). The effect of illumination intensities upon speed of perception and upon fatigue in reading. *Journal of Educational Psychology*, **30**, 561–571.

Troscianko, T. S. (1977). Effect of subtense and surround luminance on the perception of a coloured field. *Colour Research and Application*, **2**, 153–159.

Voke, J. (1979). Colour bars of an occupational kind. *Occupational Safety and Health*, **99**, 10–12.

Weale, R. A. (1961). Retinal illumination and age. *Transactions of the Illuminating Society* (London), **26**, 95–100.

Weale, R. A. (1963). *The Ageing Eye* (London: H. K. Lewis).

Weitzman, D. O., and Kinney, J. A. S. (1969). Effect of stimulus size, duration, and retinal location upon the appearance of colour. *Journal of the Optical Society of America*, **59**, 640–643.

Weston, H. C. (1935). *The Relation Between Illumination and Visual Performance; I: The Effect of Size of Work*. Joint Report of the Industrial Health Research Board and the Illumination Research Committee (reprinted 1953) (London: HMSO).

Weston, H. C. (1945). *The Relation Between Illumination and Visual Performance; II: The Effect of Brightness and Contrast*. Industrial Health Research Board Report No. 87 (reprinted 1953) (London: HMSO).

Weston, H. C. (1962). *Sight, Light and Work* (London: H. K. Lewis).

Wyatt, S., and Langdon, J. N. (1932). *Inspection Processes in Industry*. MRC Industrial Health Research Board, Report No. 63 (London: HMSO).

The Physical Environment at Work
Edited by D. J. Oborne and M. M. Gruneberg
©1983 John Wiley & Sons Ltd.

Vibration at Work

D. J. OBORNE
Department of Psychology,
University College of Swansea,
Singleton Park, Swansea, UK

Of all of the aspects of a worker's physical environment, vibration is possibly one of the most fundamental. It underlies the production and perception of noise and sounds in the environment and, depending on the theory to which one ascribes, the production and perception of light stimuli. Understanding the basis of vibration, therefore, allows some understanding of the properties of other environmental stimuli.

As individuals we perceive vibration from before birth to death. For example a foetus receives vibration that is transmitted through the mother's body from her heart and from outside, whilst the developing and developed individual is exposed to tactile vibration from machinery, from transport, and from any aspect of the environment which moves. It must be accepted from the outset, however, that much of this vibration is unlikely to affect the individual much—if at all. Most is absorbed within the body structure, perhaps because of the individual's own behaviour such as changes in posture, thus causing few detrimental effects on health, performance, or comfort. Nevertheless there are still many situations in which vibration can affect an operator detrimentally, for example reading displays and operating controls, and it is the purpose of this chapter to consider the circumstances surrounding these effects.

It is perhaps appropriate at this stage to define vibration and its parameters. In its most basic form a body is said to vibrate if it oscillates about a fixed point in space. A weight on the end of a spring, for example, will vibrate if the spring is extended and then released, and in this case the 'fixed point' is the position of the weight before it was moved. With vibration defined in this way it follows that a body can vibrate in a number of different directions, although the International Standards Organization (1974) suggests that any movement

143

should be defined and measured in terms of three orthogonal components: x—front to back; y—side to side; and z—up/down. Using these components a person jumping up and down, for example, would be vibrating in the z direction. If the same person were rotating about an axis from shoulder to shoulder (for example tumbling face-forwards from a roof) then the body would be vibrating in the x and z axes at the same time. Finally, a weightless astronaut in space may rotate uncontrollably in a spherical fashion and would be vibrating in all three axes together. For most experimental purposes, however, the effects of vibration are normally considered in one axis only since only one vibration axis normally predominates in any given situation (although on vehicles such as ships or aeroplanes the structure could be vibrating in many directions at once).

Once the direction of the motion has been determined the *extent* to which the object vibrates is defined in terms of two parameters: its 'speed' and 'intensity'.

The 'speed' of a vibrating body is expresed in terms of its frequency of movement—simply the number of times the body, the weight on the end of the spring for example, completes one cycle of movement (i.e. from its fixed, reference point to its highest point, to its lowest point, and finally back to its reference point) within a specific time period (usually 1 second). The faster the body vibrates, therefore, the more cycles that occur per second. The normal unit of frequency is the Hertz (Hz), where 1 Hz = 1 cycle per second.

The vibration intensity is normally expressed in terms of the amount by which the body departs from the fixed point—usually its distance or amplitude (in cm or in mm). More recently, however, the units of acceleration have been used to define vibration intensity. These are conventionally expressed in g units (1 g being the amount of acceleration needed to lift a body off the earth's surface); although the convention has been changed slightly in recent years to use the metric units of ms^{-2} (1 g = 9.81 ms^{-2}).

Although the types of vibration stimuli discussed so far are relatively simple in nature, everyone who has experienced vibration from machines will know that in the majority of cases a vibrating body does not behave in this simple, harmonic way. Often the vibration experienced at work is complex in nature, varying in both frequency and intensity. Luckily, however, using a statistical process known as Fourier analysis (which is too complex to be described here) it is possible to take any complex or random vibration and reduce it to its component simple harmonic motions of the sort described earlier. This allows initial laboratory experiments to be performed using simple vibration stimuli to determine how specific aspects of the vibration affect operator behaviour, and then studies of more complex, combined stimuli can be carried out at a later stage. Eventually, therefore, it should be possible to predict operator behaviour when confronted with 'real-life' stimuli.

THE BASES OF VIBRATION EFFECTS

The purpose of this chapter is to consider how vibration can affect a person's performance and, to some extent, health. These performance effects occur in both vision and in motor control so causing problems in perceiving displays and operating equipment. Whatever aspects of vibration are considered, however, and irrespective of whether the vibration is local or is perceived over the whole body, the detrimental effects are due to one problem—the operator's inability to control the movement of the affected body part. Because of this vibration can cause damage to health by buffeting body organs and other structures, by decrements to motor control making it difficult to control limb movements, and by reductions in visual performance because of uncontrollable eye movements. Understanding how vibration makes it difficult to control body parts, therefore, might explain how vibration can cause performance difficulties and perhaps allow the problem to be prevented or reduced in some way.

Any simple structure: this book, a table, a door, a building, can be excited at a particular frequency which is known as its natural or resonant frequency. If vibration is applied to the structure at or near this frequency then it will vibrate at an intensity which is higher than that applied to it. This amplification is known as resonance. (Indeed this effect can also occur if the original vibration input is situated close to, but not actually touching, the structure—this is how sopranos can sometimes shatter glass.) At other frequencies the opposite of resonance can occur, so that the body structure absorbs and so reduces the input intensity. This process is known as dampening or attenuation.

When discussing the human body it is necessary to consider an extremely complex structure which is composed of different organs, bones, joints and muscles. Each of these parts, both individually and together, can be affected in the ways described above so that at some frequencies they might vibrate at higher intensities than the vibrations applied to them whereas at others they could absorb and attenuate the inputs. It is for this reason that body movements can sometimes become difficult for the operator to control.

The resonant frequency of a particular system, for example the hand–arm complex; the head–neck complex; or the whole body itself, can be determined by comparing the vibration intensity of the system both at the point of stimulation and at the point of 'exit' for different frequencies. For example, to consider the resonance characteristics of the whole body, vibration measuring devices (accelerometers) could be placed at the feet (entry) and the top of the head (exit) of a standing person. The resonant frequencies, then, are those at which the 'exit' intensities exceed the 'input' intensities, i.e. when the exit:input intensity ratio is greater than 1. If the 'transmissibility' ratio is less than unity the system is absorbing, and is thus said to be dampening, the vibration. Naturally, if this occurs with significant levels of vibration input, the energy in the absorbed vibration could cause structural damage. Producing these ratios over a wide range of frequencies enables a 'map' to be drawn which illustrates the transmissibility of the system over these frequencies. In turn this allows some understanding of the types of vibration stimuli that are likely to affect the system's control (visual or motor) detrimentally, and should also provide information regarding the vibration frequencies likely to cause structural damage at high enough intensities.

A number of investigators have considered the biodynamic response of the whole body and there is general agreement that, for vertical vibration, the body has a whole-body resonance around 5 Hz (for example, Dieckmann, 1958; Guignard and Irving, 1960; Coermann, 1962; Lovesey, 1975). This is illustrated in Figure 1 which indicates the average (foot–head) transmissibility obtained by the author from 95 subjects standing in an upright but non-rigid posture. Quite clearly the body absorbs (and so dampens) vibration extremely efficiently above about 15 Hz. Between about 4 and 8 Hz, however, the amplification of incoming vibration intensity can be quite considerable.

Figure 1 also illustrates an interesting anomaly in the curve between about 12 and 15 Hz, since some resonance appears also to occur in this region. Although the anomaly also appears in many of the curves produced by other investigators (for example, Coermann, 1962; Lovesey, 1975), little explanation has been forthcoming to suggest reasons for its occurrence.

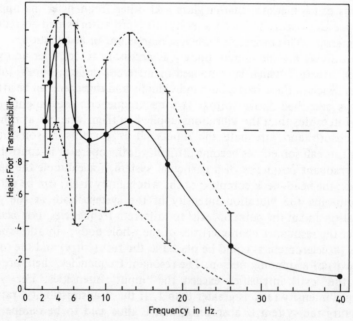

Figure 1. Head–foot transmissibility obtained from 100 standing subjects (mean ± 1 SD)

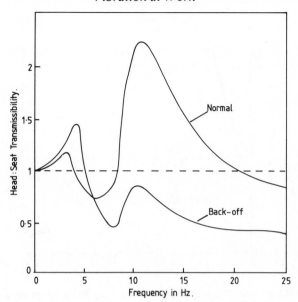

Figure 2. Head–seat transmissibility for subjects sitting either normally or without using the backrest. (From Rowlands, 1977.) Crown copyright reserved

The seated operator may be exposed to different vibration inputs compared with a standing person, particularly if the seat has a backrest. This, itself, helps to transmit vibration to the operator, as was demonstrated well by Rowlands (1977). The upper trace of Figure 2 illustrates the seat–head transmissibility of a subject sitting normally in the seat but pressed against the seat back. In the lower trace, however, the posture was such that the subject's back was away from the seat back. The reduction in transmissibility at 10 Hz is quite marked, and the implications of such findings for a seated operator's ability to perform control tasks should be obvious.

Seat–shoulder transmissibility

In addition to considering whole-body transmissibility, Rowlands (1977) also placed accelerometers at the subjects' shoulders (held by two loops of elastic passed under the armpits and over the shoulder). His results for one typical subject are shown in Figure 3, again for the 'normal' and 'back-off' seated postures. Similar curves were also obtained by Guignard and Irving (1960) for a seat without backrests. Comparing the curves in Figures 2 and 3, whereas the 5 Hz peak transmissibility is again apparent in Figure 3 the second peak at 10–12 Hz is not so. Furthermore the significant reduction in transmissibility in the 'back-off' condition seen previously in the whole-body curves is not

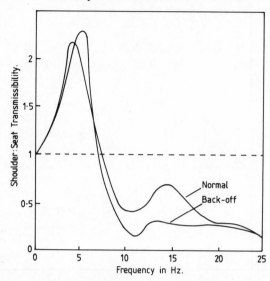

Figure 3. Shoulder–seat transmissibility for subjects sitting either normally or without using the backrest. (From Rowlands, 1977.) Crown copyright reserved

apparent. Since transmissibility between seat and shoulder excludes potential visual problems but includes shoulder control problems the results suggest, at this stage of analysis at least, that manual control in tasks using the arms may not be so severely degraded by the backrest in a normal seated position as would be the control of functions requiring the head (for example vision).

Hand–arm transmissibility

The biodynamic response of the hand–arm system is important for two reasons. First most control tasks involve this system and second there is a growing awareness of the possibility of damage to the hand from using high-speed vibrating tools. Until relatively recently, however, little work had been carried out to investigate the dynamic response of the hand–arm system.

Abrahams and Suggs (1969) analysed the vibration characteristics of a cadaver hand and arm by mounting accelerometers on to the bones. Their results showed that as the vibration frequency introduced into the hand increased, less vibration was transmitted up the arm. Similar conclusions were reached by Reynolds and Soedel (1972) and by Reynolds and Angevine (1977). Reynolds and Angevine (1977) placed accelerometers at seven points between the fingers and shoulders of five subjects, who were asked to grip a vibrating handle. Their results are shown in Figure 4 (the graph co-ordinates are arranged logarithmically to cover the ranges measured), from which it is clear that less vibration is transmitted the further up the arm the test site is situated.

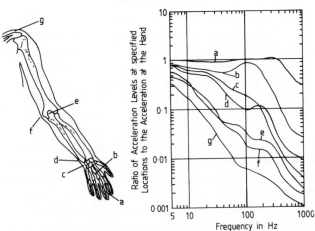

Figure 4. Hand–arm transmissibility obtained by Reynolds and Angevine (1977) at different test sites along the arm. Reproduced with permission. Copyright: Academic Press Inc. (London) Ltd

Indeed vibration frequencies above about 100 to 150 Hz are almost totally absorbed in the hand itself. Reynolds and Soedel (1972) also demonstrated that changes in the position and stiffness of the arm had no significant effect on the vibration response of the hand–arm system. Not unexpectedly, however, grip tightness had a significant influence.

In response to the need to control the extent of vibration experienced by workers in industry, the British Standards Institution (1975) and the International Organization for Standardization (1979) have recently produced draft guides for exposure limits to hand vibration. As with most such standards, however, the guides provide no information relating to the experimental evidence upon which the respective committees made their assessments (this will be discussed later).

Head–eye transmissibility

Just as the dynamics of the hand–arm–shoulder systems have implications for understanding manual control difficulties under vibration, the behaviour of the eyes in their sockets can affect the operator's visual ability. In this case two aspects are apparent: first the movement of the head and eyes together, and second the resonant characteristics of the eyes themselves.

The eyes are clearly not fixed inside the skull but are able to move by the action of muscles that attach them to the orbit in the skull. When the head changes position, feedback from the vestibular apparatus in the ear produces a reflex action of these eye muscles so that the eye moves in an opposite direction to that of the head. For example flexing the neck back so that the face points upwards causes the eyes to rotate down; the eyeballs then 'gravitate' to the *status quo*. Such a statokinetic reflex (Alpern, 1972) enables the observer to perceive the presence of vibration, and also to track an apparently moving object. Indeed Benson and Barnes (1978) and Barnes, Benson and Prior (1978) have suggested the presence of two reflex systems. First, a retinal reflex (which operates at frequencies below about 2 Hz) uses information gained from the moving image on the retina to maintain a stable image by moving the eye. The second system (which operates up to about 7 to 10 Hz) uses information gained from the vestibular apparatus to infer head position and again maintain a stationary retinal image by inducing compensatory eye movements. This is the statokinetic oculomotor system.

Because of these feedback systems, the ways in which the eyes move during whole-body vibration are not necessarily the same as the head movements.

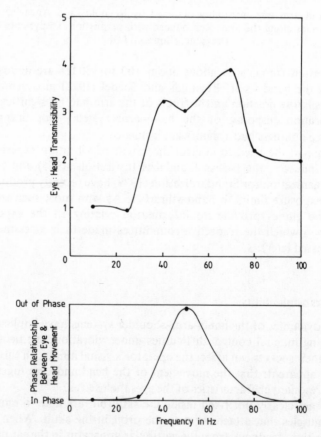

Figure 5. Eye–head transmissibility and phase. (From Stott, 1980.)

Indeed both Lee and King (1971) and Wells and Storey (1980) have demonstrated considerable dampening effects in head–eye transmissibility. Although the authors appear to differ slightly in their assessment of the extent to which this dampening occurs, both agree that the minimum dampening occurs above 20 Hz.

At higher frequencies the eyeballs themselves are in danger of resonating— irrespective of the head movement. Stott (1980) was able to map the course of these resonance effects for five subjects by measuring the movement of a spot of light shone on to the cornea of the eye. His results (shown in Figure 5) demonstrate the beginnings of eyeball resonance after about 30 Hz, with a maximum (vibrating approximately 4 times as much as the head alone) at 70 Hz. (The transmissibility increase that can be seen above about 20 Hz can possibly be ascribed to the head–eye movements discussed above). Interestingly, too, Figure 5 also indicates the phasic relationships between the eye and head at each frequency. This is important since even if the two structures were vibrating at the same level (i.e. with a transmissibility ratio of 1), if they are out of phase then the resultant retinal image is likely to be blurred. As can be seen in Figure 5, very wide variations in phase occur between about 30 and 100 Hz.

HEALTH PROBLEMS DUE TO VIBRATION

Although the relationship between vibration and productivity at work must be concerned mainly with the effects of vibration on operator performance, for two reasons its effects on health cannot be dismissed. First an operator whose health is being degraded is likely to perform at a less efficient level than one who is not so affected. An obvious example is the effects of noise on hearing. A worker who is becoming deaf due to industrial noise is less likely to be able to perform well in tasks requiring, for example, the comprehension of verbal instructions or perception of auditory displays. The second implication of health damage to the level of overall productivity lies in the cost to the organization caused by a worker who suffers industrial damage. These costs may include at the least time off work for visits to medical services or for recovery and, possibly, legal compensation.

The health effects of vibration lie basically in two areas. First damage caused to body organs as a result of their being buffeted by high vibration levels at relatively low frequencies. These effects are basically intensity dependent. Second the breakdown of body tissues due either to continued resonance or to their absorption of high-energy vibration. These effects are primarily frequency dependent.

For the majority of working environments the potential damage to large body organs or to the musculoskeletal system by high-intensity buffeting is unlikely to be a problem. In vehicles which ride over rough terrain, however, the levels of vibration experienced for very short periods may, over time, cause structural damage. How vibration can cause these effects in vehicles such as tractors, earth movers, heavy lorries, and military vehicles is described by Guignard (1965):

Such vehicles are poorly sprung in comparison with most passenger carriers and may even be practically devoid of springing. Particularly when operating over rough ground, their occupants are subjected to severe shaking at frequencies lying mainly within the band from 1 to 10 Hz (Radke, 1958). The vertical forces applied may exceed 1 g from time to time, with the result that the rider is jerked from his seat, returning to it with a spine-jarring impact. Similar accelerations can be experienced in motor patrol boats driven at high speed through choppy seas.

Rosseger and Rosseger (1960) carried out a comprehensive survey of the health complaints of 371 tractor drivers (who frequently have to drive over rough, ploughed terrain) and recorded two forms of damage resulting from long periods of tractor operation: stomach complaints and disorders of the spine (particularly in the lumbar and thoracic regions). Both the number and severity of such cases increased proportionately with the length of service as a tractor driver. Traces of blood in the urine have also been found in the drivers of these vehicles, which is probably due to kidney damage (although this breakdown could be caused as much by resonating the kidneys as by damage due to high-intensity vibration *per se*).

Injuries which are caused by the frequency aspects of vibration normally occur after prolonged exposure to the vibrating stimulus, and this mainly in the higher frequency ranges. In contemporary working environments the problem arises particularly from the use of powered hand-held machinery such as road drills, stone breakers and chain saws.

Intense vibration from hand tools can be transmitted to the fingers, hands, and arms of the operator from the machines themselves and from objects which are held by the hand and vibrated by the appliance. When this happens, structural damage to the peripheral blood and nervous systems in the fingers can occur which, over time, produces 'intermittent numbness and clumsiness of the fingers, intermittent blanching of either all or part of the extremities, and a temporary loss of muscular control of the exposed parts of the body' (Agate, 1949). Such conditions could clearly affect many forms of motor performance. Because of the appearance of the affected limbs, the condition is often referred to as 'white finger' although since the symptoms are similar to a disease first described by Raynaud in 1862 it is sometimes referred to as 'Raynaud's disease of occupational origin' (Taylor, 1974). In 1970, however, the Industrial Injuries Advisory Council rejected the various names in favour of the descriptive term 'vibration induced white finger' (VWF), and described the complex of symptoms associated with vibrating tools as 'the vibrating syndrome'. These additional effects may include any or all of neuritis, damage to bones, joints or muscles (Taylor, 1974).

The mechanisms by which vibration causes these effects are still far from understood. Whether they are due to the long-term resonance of parts of the fingers or to the growth of callouses on the fingers affected by pressure which interferes with the peripheral blood flow (Stewart and Goda, 1970), the fact remains that higher proportions of workers using vibratory tools over long periods develop VWF than would be expected from a non-vibrating tool user population (for example, Grounds, 1964; Taylor, Pelmear, and Pearson, 1974).

As with the cause of this affliction, the precise levels and frequencies of vibration to be avoided are also little understood. A draft International Standard and British Standard for hand–arm vibration has been produced which, with other potential standards, has been discussed in detail by Keighley (1974). However, because of the length of time needed to induce the disease and its damaging potential, little laboratory work appears to have been performed in this area.

The work which is available has been carried out at two levels. First, by determining the transmissibility characteristics of the hand–arm system it should be possible at least to predict the vibration frequencies which are causing the damage. To this end the data produced by Reynolds and Angevine (1977), discussed earlier, should prove useful. Their results suggested that frequencies above about 100–150 Hz tended to be absorbed in the hand itself, and these are likely to be causing the damage.

The second line of attack has been to consider vibration or touch thresholds of the hand or finger. Thus Taylor, Pelmear, and Pearson (1974) discuss work by Thomson and Kell in 1969 who demonstrated that a sample of chain saw users had significantly higher vibrotactile thresholds than non-users. Pelmear, Taylor, and Pearson (1974) demonstrated gradual reductions in touch sensitivity with increasing severity of the disease. By extending investigations such as these, relationships between vibration type and the probability of VWF may be obtained in the future. Furthermore to maintain the output of tasks involving any aspect of manual dexterity, data such as these demonstrate well the need for the organization to ensure that the operator's health is not damaged as a result of vibration.

In summary, therefore, it is clear that vibration can, over long periods, cause health problems for workers. Whether these problems result in a financial or a performance loss to the organization will depend on the duration and type of vibration experienced.

PERFORMANCE EFFECTS OF VIBRATION

Because body parts tend to vibrate in sympathy with vibrating machinery either nearby or on which they may rest, the effects of vibration on performance are mainly to degrade motor control. This might be the control of a limb (causing, for example, reduced hand or arm steadiness) or of the head or eyeballs (causing fixation difficulties and blurring), and attempts to compensate for any of these control difficulties are likely to lead to muscular fatigue. As will be discussed later, there is little evidence available to suggest that vibration can affect central, intellectual processes.

A. Visual performance effects of vibration

A clearly formed image of an object will only be perceived in the visual cortex of the brain if a stable image falls on the retina. A moving figure stimulates different sets of receptors in the retina, so producing a signal of overlapping and confused images. This is clearly likely to make it difficult to detect much of the object's detail, particularly if the retinal image oscillates with a relatively large amplitude.

Although a fair amount of work has been carried out to investigate visual vibration effects, it is difficult to draw too many conclusions about the types and levels of vibration that affect visual performance. This is because different investigators have used different tasks to measure visual performance—for example, acuity using the Landolt C or vernier separation, recognition of dial settings or numbers, the time taken to read passages, etc. (O'Briant and Ohlbaum, 1970). Because these different tasks require subjects to perform different activities, it would be difficult to relate them to each other or to any standard performance criteria.

Three arrangements by which the observer and the object are vibrated can exist to produce a situation in which a moving image is perceived. Firstly if the object alone is vibrated; secondly when only the observer is vibrated; and thirdly when both the observer and the object are vibrated. In this third case the degree of blurring will depend not only on the nature of the vibration experienced but on the phase relationship between the two moving bodies. The effects of these three aspects will be considered separately.

Vibrating the object alone

The detrimental effects of vibrating the object alone appear to be a function mainly of the vibration frequency and, to some extent, of its intensity.

If the object is vibrating at a low enough frequency (below about 1 Hz), the optical system is able to track it and so maintain a stable image on the retina. However it should be remembered that by doing so the optic muscles need to work hard, so that muscular fatigue may occur quite quickly. Since the tracking task (known as pursuit eye movements) is performed in the nature of a closed-loop control system, it is likely that the eye movement will initially lag behind that of the object movement but will then soon 'catch up'. The latency of the initial delay has been estimated by Robinson (1965) to be 125 ms but the efficiency of the system to catch up with the moving stimulus depends on both the stimulus frequency and its predictability. An object moving sinusoidally, for example, produces a highly predictable retinal image and soon enables the observer to predict the position of the object at any one time. If the object is moving randomly, however, this prediction is not possible and the tracking performance needs to be carried out more efficiently to ensure the same level of success. This aspect of a tracking task in 'keeping up with' the object movement is described in terms of the phase relationship between the object and the eye movement. Thus if the eye maintains a perfect track (i.e. as the object moves 'up' so does the eye) then the eye and the object are said to be *in phase*. If the object is moving in an upward direction but the eye is in its downward part of the oscillation, however, the system is said to be *out of phase*. Clearly, then, different tracking abilities can be defined in terms of different phases.

In addition to phase, a further measure of pursuit eye movement efficiency is the extent to which the amplitude of the eye movement relates to that of the object. (The 'eye amplitude' to 'object amplitude' ratio is known as the system 'gain'.) At very low frequencies the eye is able to pursue the object movement perfectly in almost a 1:1 relationship, i.e. with a gain of 1. As the object frequency increases, however, the eye amplitude tends to reduce so that it tracks only the central portion of the object's movement.

A number of investigators have considered the relationships of these two measures of pursuit eye movement efficiency to the frequency of the object vibration, and some of their results are collated in Figure 6. A similar figure was also produced by Huddleston (1969) for predictable (sine wave) motions only. As can be seen from Figure 6, at frequencies below 1 Hz the optical system is able to track the predictable object and so maintain a stable image. Thus the gain remains fairly stable at around unity and the phase difference between the two is insignificant. Above 1 Hz, however, the system effectiveness decreases considerably until by about 2–4 Hz and above the tracking ability is almost non-existent. Interestingly, Figure 6 also demonstrates that at very low frequencies the tracking performance for unpredictable motions is almost as good as for predictable stimuli. With increasing frequency, however, this ability soon disappears, but at around 2–4 Hz and above (when pursuit eye movements are no longer effective) the system's inability to track unpredictable stimuli appears to be no worse than its inability to track predictable stimuli.

At higher object frequencies, when pursuit eye movements cannot usefully track a vibrating object, any performance reduction will be related directly to the degree of blurring on the retina. The quality of the image, then, will be inversely proportional to the number of extra retinal cells stimulated (i.e. the vibration amplitude), although at the same time it will be proportional to the length of time for which any one cell is stimulated. Since the time taken for an object to move through one cycle is inversely proportional to the frequency, it

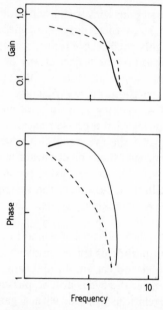

Figure 6. Gain and phase relationships for the optic system (——, sinusoidal stimuli; – – – –, unpredictable stimuli). (After Carpenter, 1977.)

follows that the performance efficiency will be related to both the frequency and the amplitude of the vibrating image. Indeed O'Hanlon and Griffin (1971) have suggested that at frequencies above about 5 Hz an observer's error rate in perceiving fine detail in a moving object is proportional to the product of the frequency and the square root of the amplitude of the vibrating image. This relation appears to fit the data produced by O'Hanlon and Griffin, and Meddick and Griffin (1976) state that the model was later confirmed by Alexander (1972).

In an attempt to map the relationships between vibration frequency and visual performance, Huddleston (1970) measured the proportion of time that subjects were able to maintain a stable image of an object vibrating at one of two different amplitudes. His results, shown in Figure 7, illustrate well the observer's problems involved in coping with vibrating material. Thus, for the smaller amplitude, the eye is able to track the moving object quite well at low frequencies. As the frequency is increased, this ability is reduced in the manner described in Figure 6. The attempt to track the object continues, although with decreasing efficiency, until at about 5 Hz the subject relinquishes the attempt and stabilizes on the object. At this point, then, the decrement is related more to the degree of image blurring. For the higher amplitude vibration, however, the relinquishing of pursuit tracking occurs at a lower frequency, with the result that the upturn in performance occurs earlier.

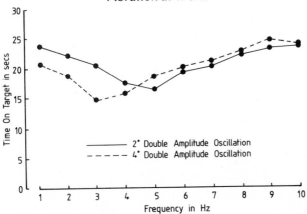

Figure 7. Tracking performance under vibration, showing how the main frequency effect is modified by an amplitude effect. (From Huddleston, 1970.) Copyright (1970) by the American Psychological Association. Adapted by permission of the author

With regard to the effect of the amplitude of the moving object, studies by Drazin (1962) and by Huddleston (1970) demonstrate that at frequencies below about 4 Hz (in which pursuit eye movements are possible), visual performance is reduced with increasing vibration amplitude. At higher frequencies, however, these deficiencies are not sustained. Indeed, Huddleston's data shown in Figure 7 suggest that at 5 Hz the higher amplitude was beneficial, and Drazin's results suggest that at 6 and 8 Hz the larger amplitudes produced lower error scores than did the smaller amplitudes. Griffin and Lewis (1978), however, argue that these results should not lead to a general conclusion that reading becomes easier with increased displacement. They suggest that the larger amplitudes were large enough to reduce the amount of confusion in the blurred image; more confusion is likely to result from smaller amplitudes and, when this occurs, the O'Hanlon and Griffin model of $E \propto f \sqrt{a}$ still holds true. No evidence is yet available to support or to refute this hypothesis. It must be remembered, however, that their model was proposed for performance reductions in a visual acuity task (perceiving the gap in a Landolt C). Griffin himself questions (1976a) whether it also holds true for other types of perceptual tasks. Indeed data from Meddick and Griffin (1976), who used digits of the form recommended in British Standard 3693A, suggest that the error rate for this type of material is *not* proportional to $f \sqrt{a}$.

Finally, in an attempt to produce some simplified model of the effects of object vibration—at least above 5 Hz—Griffin (1975) argues that data relating to the threshold of visual blur could be used to predict the minimum levels of object vibration needed to affect visual acuity. This level, he suggests, is equal to a displacement of 1 minute of arc at the eye. However, since this

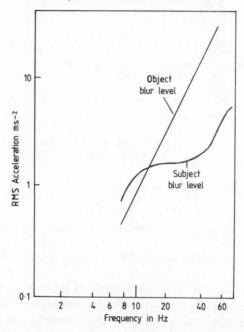

Figure 8. The average levels of vertical vibration needed to produce blur, compared with object blur levels. (Reproduced with permission from Griffin, 1976.) Copyright: Academic Press Inc. (London) Ltd

would probably be over-restrictive in all but the most critical conditions, he later suggested (1976a) that displacements of greater than ± 2 minutes of arc may, depending on the difficulty of the task, start to affect reading ability. Figure 8 illustrates this boundary.

Vibrating the observer alone

Precisely the same problems are apparent when the observer is vibrated as when the object is vibrated—namely those concerning the tracking ability of the optical system and the degree of blur experienced. These problems, however, are confounded by the dynamic characteristics of the body in which the eyes reside. These may be such as to produce head and eye motions that have different intensities to the input motion and, because the body is a flexible structure, the resultant eye motions may not even occur in the same axis as the input motion. (Indeed Griffin, 1976b, has demonstrated that vertical vibration is likely to cause some angular motions of the eyes when applied to seated subjects.)

Because of these confounding problems, and because so much variability exists between individuals in their whole-body transmissibility (see, for example, Figure 2), the only reasonable procedure for determining the effects of whole-body vibration on vision is to measure the level of vibration experienced at the head. Only if the subject's seat or feet to head transmissibility at each frequency is known would it be sensible to use seat or feet (input) intensity data. Unfortunately, however, many experiments in this area have ignored the observer (and sometimes even the seat) transmissibilities.

During their study of seat to shoulder and head transmissibility, Guignard and Irving (1960) also asked subjects to scan blocks of typescript letters 'c' and to count randomly placed letters 'o'. The seated subject received vibration at five frequencies between 2.4 and 9.5 Hz, each at 0.25 g, measured at the seat/subject interface. Using the average time taken to complete the task as their measure of reading performance, Guignard and Irving demonstrated very close similarity between the shape of the performance curve as a function of frequency and that of the velocity of the head motion. Unfortunately, however, only four subjects were tested which, given the levels of individual variability known to exist for these types of reading task (for example, Griffin, 1976b) is likely to limit the value of the results.

Considering the frequency of the vibration alone, the problems which occur when a vibrating observer views a stationary display are similar to those which occur when only the display is vibrated; i.e. they operate in two frequency bands. First low frequencies in which the moving observer's problem is to stabilize the eyes to maintain a stationary image and second, at higher frequencies, in which eyeball resonance is involved.

Because the low-frequency task is essentially one involving stabilizing the eyes on a stationary display (rather than moving the eyes to keep up with a moving display), it is often referred to as compensatory (rather than pursuit) tracking. The difference between the two terms, however, is more than simply semantic. For example Guignard and Irving suggest that the upper frequency limit for compensatory eye movements is higher than that for pursuit movements. Furthermore Benson (1972) and Benson and Barnes (1978) suggest that compensatory eye movements occur as a result of the vestibulo-ocular reflexes discussed earlier rather than from a voluntary control mechanism.

In an experiment designed to investigate these various aspects, Benson (1972) used two sets of subjects, each undergoing two trials. In the first trial the subject was vibrated whilst the object remained stationary (the subject's head was clamped to the vibrator, thus alleviating seat to head transmissibility problems). In the second trial the object alone was vibrated. The first group comprised eight seated subjects who viewed numbers whilst exposed to vertical rotational (yaw) vibration between 0.5 and 10 Hz. (A person is in 'yaw' when vibrating in both the lateral and fore–aft directions simultaneously; for example, if standing on an oscillating turntable.) The second group comprised only one subject who performed the same tasks under the same conditions. Due to injury, however, this subject had no semicircular canal function

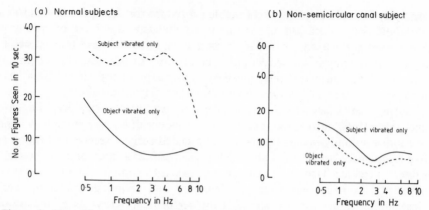

Figure 9. The effect of object and subject vibration on visual performance. (From Benson, 1972.)

and thus was unable to take advantage of any vestibulo-ocular reflexes.

Benson's results are shown in Figure 9 in terms of reading efficiency (the number of digits seen in 10 s), for both the normal and the non-semicircular canal subjects. Clear differences can be seen between the performances under the two conditions. Thus when the target alone was vibrated, the two groups performed similarly: performance was maintained below 1 Hz using pursuit eye movements, although after about 1–2 Hz this form of tracking was relinquished. When the 'normal' observers were vibrated, however, compensatory eye reflexes enabled the performance to be maintained for longer so that efficiency did not begin to decline until after 4 Hz. For the subject without the semicircular canal function, however, compensatory eye movement was not apparent and the performance in both the observer and the object vibrating conditions was very similar. Comparing the results from the two groups then, demonstrates well that compensatory eye movements are at least facilitated by the vestibulo-ocular reflex system.

At frequencies higher than those which allow compensatory tracking, the problem of eyeball resonance must clearly be taken into account. As discussed earlier Stott (1980) demonstrated the beginnings of resonance in the eye–orbit complex at about 30 Hz, with a maximum at 70 Hz.

With regard to the intensity aspects of the vibrating observer, the obvious problem relates to visual blur. In an experiment to map the frequency course of blurring when the observer alone is vibrated, Griffin (1975) exposed 12 subjects to vertical vibration at frequencies between 7 and 75 Hz. At each frequency the subjects were required to adopt postures that resulted in the 'maximum sensation' at the head. They were then asked to adjust the vibration level to the minimum at which they observed any definite blurring of points of light. (Because subjects always adjusted down the intensity range, it is likely that this technique will produce 'conservative' estimates of the blur level.)

Griffin's average 'minimum blur level' over the frequency range is also illustrated in Figure 8, along with the levels of vertical object vibration needed to produce blur. The divergence of these two curves at higher frequencies illustrates, once again, the effect of eye movement relative to head movement. From these curves, however, it is not possible to determine by how much the eyeball resonance affects visual performance. Furthermore, any interpretation of these curves must take account of Griffin's own cautions regarding the high level of inter- and intra-subject variability which were obtained.

In an attempt to produce equal performance decrement contours, Lewis and Griffin (1980a,b) considered the effects of vibration frequency (2.8 Hz to 63 Hz) on a number reading task. In addition, employing a model which supposed a linear relationship between error rate and vibration intensity experienced at the head at each frequency, the authors predicted performance contours outside the range of intensities which they investigated. Their results are shown in Figure 10.

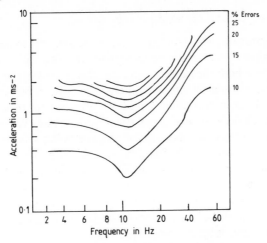

Figure 10. Levels of vibration needed to produce equal error rates for a reading task. (Reproduced with permission from Lewis and Griffin, 1980a.) Copyright: Academic Press Inc. (London) Ltd

With regard to the effect of task factors on visual performance, the most obvious factor to consider is that of object size. Clearly larger objects are easier to see and this is likely also to be true under vibrating conditions. This was illustrated by Lewis and Griffin (1979a) who used four character heights (ranging from 1 to 2 mm) whilst seated subjects were exposed to one of two vibration frequencies (4 and 11.2 Hz) at one of six vibration levels (no vibration and vibration between 0.04 and 0.2 g). Their results demonstrate significant increases in percentage reading errors, both with increases in vibration intensity and reductions in character size.

Finally the question whether it is 'better' or 'worse' to vibrate the object rather than the observer might appear at this stage to have practical consequences. However it is one which is difficult to answer, primarily because of the effects of the frequency of stimulation. Certainly Benson's (1972, 1978) results suggest that, for rotational vibration at least, compensatory tracking at low frequencies (caused by vibrating the observer) is more efficient than pursuit eye movements (resulting from object vibration). These conclusions can be supported by data from Dennis (1965) who performed a similar experiment to Benson's using vertical axis vibration. His results indicated that below 6 Hz vibrating the display produced higher visual impairment than when the subject alone was vibrated. Above 14 Hz, however, the converse was the case. The final answer to this question whether to vibrate the object or the subject, however, cannot be provided until any motor aspects of the task are accounted for. These will be discussed in the next section.

Vibrating the object and the observer together

Although the previous two conditions have illustrated the many problems of viewing an object in a dynamic environment, they are quite simple compared with that in which both the observer and the object are vibrating. Unfortunately, however, this is a situation which is likely to prevail in real-life environments whenever the observer and objects are both attached to, or are inside, a piece of vibrating machinery, such as a passenger or driver in a vehicle.

When both the observer and the object are being vibrated, a number of conditions may occur—each of which is likely to affect the resultant visual performance in an individual manner. For example the two may be vibrating at different frequencies or intensities, they may be moving in phase or out of phase, and they could even be moving in different axes. Because of these problems, very few well-controlled studies have been carried out to investigate combined object and subject vibration effects.

One specific situation which has been investigated however, is that in which the display is in some way attached to an observer's helmet. These helmet-mounted displays allow information to be presented continuously to an operator such as a pilot—regardless of the head position.

Barnes, Benson, and Prior (1978) investigated this form of the observer-object relationship for angular motion of the head (using both the 'yaw' and 'pitch' motions). Their results demonstrated a marked decrease in the ability to read the displayed digits with frequencies above about 1 Hz. Furthermore the rate of this decrease was faster for the smaller digit size. A slight difference in the performance in each axis was apparent, however, in so far as the overall number of digits read correctly was lower, and the reduction in reading efficiency higher, in the pitch than in the yaw axis.

A similar type of experiment was reported by Furness and Lewis (1978)

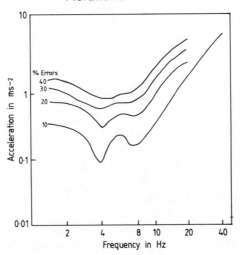

Figure 11. Average contours of vibration levels required to produce equal percentage reading errors on a helmet-mounted display. (From Furness and Lewis, 1978.)

although their subjects were vibrated in the vertical axis only (1.4 to 45 Hz). As with the Lewis and Griffin (1980a,b) studies, from the performance measures Furness and Lewis produced equal performance decrement contours over the frequency range studied. These are illustrated in Figure 11. Comparing these contours with those shown in Figure 10 it would appear that performance begins to degrade at lower frequencies in the helmet-mounted display condition than when only the observer is vibrated. Using the evidence of, for example, Benson and Barnes (1978), therefore, it is not unrealistic to hypothesize that when the object and observer are vibrated together at the same level and frequency, the resultant reduction in visual performance (at least at low frequencies) appears to be display-based. Thus a driver's performance in viewing displays in a moving vehicle, for example, will be affected more in the fashion of the curves shown by Huddleston (1970) in Figure 7 than by Lewis and Griffin's (1980b) subject-based vibration performance curves in Figure 10.

In summary it is clear that the effects of vibration on visual performance are extremely complex. They depend on whether the observer or the object is vibrating, on the frequency and intensity of the vibration, and on the size (and thus the distance from the observer) of the object. In general it would appear that the extent of performance reduction is determined largely by the vibration frequency. At low frequencies it is a function of the optical system's ability to track an object to maintain a stable retinal image. At higher frequencies it is a function simply of the degree of blur. The cut-off frequency of these two bands, however, is determined by whether it is the observer or the object which is being vibrated. Because of the existence of vestibulo-ocular reflexes, vibrating observers are able to track a stationary object at higher frequencies than a stationary observer is able to track a vibrating object.

B. Motor performance effects of vibration

Two types of task are normally used by experimenters to investigate the effects of vibration on motor performance, and both require the operator to use the arms or legs to operate controls in order to maintain a particular course. They are generally known as tracking tasks and take the form either of pursuit tracking or of compensatory tracking.

In pursuit tracking, the operator's function is to move the controls so that the object (usually a spot on an oscilloscope) follows a predetermined course (possibly following another moving spot). A 'real-life' example, in this case, could be a car driver's task of moving a steering wheel to keep the car on a winding road. The operator corrects errors then, by comparing the movement of the 'spot' (the car) with that of a standard (the road).

In the compensatory tracking task the operator 'sees' only errors. The task is to maintain an otherwise moving 'spot' in a particular position—to use the controls to compensate for the machine's movement. The spot only moves when the task is not performed correctly. The car driver's attempt to maintain a steady speed (i.e. to keep the speedometer needle in a particular place) is an example of such a task. Variations in the vehicle dynamics, the road incline, the weather, or other environmental conditions may all act to influence the car speed and so make the driver have to compensate for these influences by controlling the accelerator and other pedals.

As Poulton (1974) argues, compensatory tracking is clearly more difficult to perform than pursuit tracking. An operator tracking in a compensatory manner cannot see what is being done, nor predict what is meant to be done; the operator can only compensate when an error has occurred. Tracking in a pursuit manner, however, the operator can see the movements produced by the track programme, in addition to seeing the effects of the control movements.

Although the two forms of tracking task differ in their difficulty, it would appear that they are not differentially affected by vibration. Thus Lewis (1980) asked subjects to perform, separately, both types of tracking task whilst being subjected to different vibration stimuli. His results suggest that, irrespective of the measures used to record the subject's performance, and although different frequency stimuli affected the performance to different degrees, the performance curves for the two types of task were very similar in shape.

Whatever measure of motor performance is used, there appears to be general agreement that at low frequencies (less than about 15 Hz) performance reductions are related to the amount of vibration experienced at the controlling limb. In this case, therefore, the important variable to be considered is again the individual's seat or foot to arm (shoulder) transmissibility. Thus Levison (1976) demonstrated that performance decrements in a vertical tracking task were linearly correlated with shoulder acceleration in the range 2–10 Hz. Furthermore Buckhout (1964) demonstrated tracking error to follow very closely a linear relationship with the intensity of vertical vibration measured at the sternum (at 6, 8, and 10 Hz).

Since the effects of vibration on motor performance appear to be determined largely by the amount of vibration transmitted through the body it would be reasonable to expect the frequency dependence of performance (i.e. the shape of a performance accuracy versus frequency graph) to follow that of body transmissibility. Unfortunately no study has related individual subjects' transmissibility data with their performance scores, but some support for the hypothesis may be seen by comparing tracking scores over frequency with typical transmissibility data. Figure 12 illustrates very crude bands of tracking decrement produced by Shurmer (1967). He surveyed 15 experiments prior to 1967 and, on the basis of the reports, tentatively divided the data into bands of 'no', 'slight', 'moderate', and 'severe' decrements. As can be seen, the maximum tracking error appears to occur at between 3 and 5 Hz, a similar frequency range to that of peak seat–shoulder transmissibility shown in Figure 3. It must be emphasized, however, that the bands illustrated in Figure 12 are very rough approximations, drawing together results from different studies having different tasks, subjects, aims, and techniques. They should, therefore, be interpreted with extreme care.

With regard to the intensity domain, the results from a number of studies are extremely consistent and suggest that tracking performance decreases as the vibration intensity transmitted to the limb increases (for example, Catterson, Hoover, and Asche, 1962; Lewis and Griffin, 1979b). This is also illustrated in Figure 12.

The lowest level of vibration required to affect performance appears to be very variable. Reviewing the field, for example, Lewis and Griffin (1978) point out that the levels of vibration at which some experimenters had failed to obtain an effect were higher than those at which other experimenters had obtained significant reductions in performance. They conclude, therefore, that

It seems reasonable to draw the general conclusion that increases in vibration level, above some threshold effect, will result in progressive degradation of performance. However, because of the great number of task variables which may affect the performance of specific systems during vibration . . . it is not reasonable to expect to be able to discover an absolute threshold of effect, above which performance is affected by vibration and below which it is not.

Finally, Fraser, Hoover, and Asche (1961) investigated the combined effects of vibration frequency and intensity on a tracking task. On the basis of their results they argued that the subjects' average tracking error (the number of

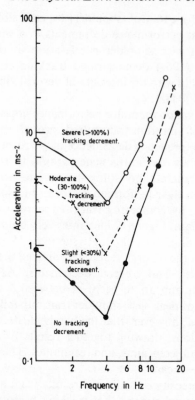

Figure 12. Equal tracking performance contours derived by Shurmer (1967)

subjects used was not reported) was proportional to the product of the vibration amplitude and the square root of the frequency (over the frequency range 2–12 Hz) (i.e. $E \propto a \sqrt{f}$). This is interesting, particularly when the expression is compared with that reported earlier by O'Hanlon and Griffin in terms of visual acuity errors ($E \propto f \sqrt{a}$). The two expressions clearly imply that visual performance degradation is mainly a function of the vibration frequency, whereas manual performance degradation is primarily intensity-dependent.

With regard to the direction of the motion being applied to the operator, all of the studies conducted so far agree that the primary detrimental effect to tracking ability occurs in the axis in which the operator is being vibrated. For example Fraser, Hoover, and Asche (1961) demonstrated that horizontal tracking performance was affected more by y-axis vibration than by z-axis vibration of the same intensity. Vertical tracking was affected more by z-axis vibration than by y-axis vibration. Front–back (x) axis vibration had no effect on either horizontal or vertical tracking. Similar conclusions were reached by

Shoenberger (1970) who argues, not unreasonably, that the results suggest the primary mechanism responsible for decrements on tasks of this nature to be the interference with perceptual processes and hand control caused by the short-duration whole-body vibration.

The studies by Fraser, and co-workers, and by Shoenberger were carried out using separate axes in different trials. Lovesey (1974), however, describes an experiment to investigate the effects of combined y- and z-axis vibration on a compensatory tracking task. He presented subjects with vibration at $0.2\,g$ in the z axis (2, 5, and 7 Hz) and $0.1\,g$ vibrations of the same frequency in the y axis. In addition these frequencies and levels were used in combination at $2z + 5y$, $2z + 7y$, $5z + 7y$, $7z + 2y$, and $7z + 5y$. His results are interesting since, in addition to illustrating decrements in tracking performance with all single-axis vibrations, when the axes were combined tracking performance tended to be degraded by an amount equal to the product of the tracking decrements produced by each single axis alone, i.e.

$$\text{combined error} = z\,\text{error} \times y\,\text{error}.$$

Lovesey does add, however, that this equation only holds true for cases when the task difficulty was great enough to be affected adversely by the single-axis vibrations. It does not hold if either the z or y error was zero or if the vibration actually helped to improve performance. (More will be said later regarding the possibility of performance increases under vibrating conditions.)

In addition to the vibration itself as a variable that could affect performance, the task to be performed by the operator must also be considered. In this respect its duration and the physical equipment provided could play important roles.

The variable of exposure duration (or 'time dependency') is one which is presently receiving much debate since it forms an important part in the levels set by the International Standards Organization (1974) for exposure to whole-body vibration. Unfortunately, as will be discussed later, there is little evidence to support the contention that performance decreases the longer that the individual is exposed to the vibration stimulus (for example, Lewis and Griffin, 1979a,b; Guignard, Landrum, and Reardon, 1976; Maslen, 1972; Hornick, 1962; Hornick and Lefritz, 1966). This is best exemplified by a very long-duration study carried out by Gray *et al.* (1976). They exposed their subjects for 3 hours to 5 Hz vertical vibration at $0.12\,g$ but, although tracking performance was worse under the vibration as opposed to the static conditions, the authors were unable to demonstrate any reduction in performance over the 3-hour period. Indeed, if anything, a slight improvement in performance was observed.

With regard to the quality of the equipment provided for the operator, an obvious variable to consider is the type and degree of body restraint afforded during the task. Without such support the action of the vibration will be to destabilize the body and make the manual control task more difficult to accomplish effectively. In this respect two restraint systems can be considered— harnesses and arm rests.

Although at first sight it would appear sensible to argue that a restraining harness is likely to increase stability and thus improve performance, the effects of the harness on the amount of vibration transmitted through the body must be considered. Thus, as noted earlier, Rowlands (1977) demonstrated significant increases in vibration transmitted to the shoulder when the back was against the backrest. Given the very strong relationship between the amount of vibration reaching the shoulder and performance decrement then, it could well be hypothesized that a restraining harness would have a detrimental effect on motor control. This was illustrated by Lovesey (1971) for tracking in both the y and z axes.

As far as armrests are concerned, Torle (1965) tested three subjects on a tracking task using a 'small', a 'large', or no armrest (unfortunately dimensions were not provided). His results demonstrated some improvement in tracking ability using the armrest, although he observed no difference between the types of armrest used. The armrest improvement increased with increasing vibration intensity. Whether the improvement was due to increased total body stability created by the armrests, or simply to fore-arm or elbow stability is not, unfortunately, able to be deduced from the experimental report.

In summary, therefore, whole-body vibration clearly degrades motor control, particularly when the task demands movement in the same plane as the vibration. Furthermore the degree of degradation is primarily intensity-dependent and is thus a strong function of the manner in which vibration is transmitted through the body.

C. The effects of vibration on the speed of reaction and information processing

For a number of years, particularly during the late 1950s and 1960s during the 'space race' era, a number of studies were carried out to investigate whether vibration is likely to affect an operator's response (reaction) time.

Fast reactions demand both central and peripheral abilities: a stimulus (for example a light) is perceived; the information is transmitted to the brain where a decision is made; and a motor action (for example pressing a button) is taken. Any, or all, of these processes could be affected by vibration even though the task places minimal demands on the sensory and motor functions.

Much of the research which has been carried out in this area has demonstrated that reaction time is relatively unaffected by vibration (for example Weisz, Goddard, and Allen, 1967; Holland, 1965). For example Hornick (1962) asked subjects to press a foot pedal each time a particular sequence of coloured lights appeared. He tested frequencies from 0.9 to 6.5 Hz at accelerations of 0.15, 0.25 and 0.35 g in each of the three axes. Under no condition was reaction time increased although, interestingly, he reported an increase in reaction time during a post-vibration test after vibration in the y and z axes. In the light of information on similar responses after the cessation of other stressors (for example Wohlwill *et al.*, 1976), it could be argued that the vibration is acting in this case as a general stressor which causes the operator to have to work harder to maintain the same level of performance. When the stressor ends, however, a 'let-down' effect occurs which shows itself as reduced performance.

Despite experiments such as this showing no effect of vibration, Shoenberger (1970) did demonstrate significant performance reductions using vibration, separately, in the x, y, and z axes. The main effect was in the y (side–side) axis with highly significant decrements occurring at 1 Hz and 3 Hz. Very little reduction in reaction time occurred at either 11 Hz in the y axis or in the other two axes at any frequency. It may be suggested, however, that Shoenberger's results simply reflect his apparatus arrangements: the stimulus lights and response buttons were arranged in a row (i.e. along the y axis) in front of the subject. Interference in the motor component of the reaction time task could, therefore, have caused the increased reaction time—an hypothesis supported by the fact that the increased reaction time occurred mainly during the low-frequency vibration in which transmissibility is high. Indeed Shoenberger himself had earlier advanced this possibility when he concluded (1967) that 'direct mechanical interference with the motor aspects of the task may be the most significant factor contributing to performance decrements during relatively low intensity short duration vibration'.

An interesting validation of the hypothesis of peripheral, rather than central, interference, was produced by Shoenberger (1974). He used a memory reaction time task in which subjects were required first to memorize letters of the alphabet and then to react (verbally) to the presence or absence of letters presented on a screen. The motor component of the reaction time task, therefore, was reduced to one of controlling the diaphragm for speech. Using an analysis technique developed by Sternberg (1966), Shoenberger was able to determine whether any reaction time increase was due to the central processing time or to the input/output process. Thus Sternberg had demonstrated that reaction time increases linearly with the task difficulty (number of items to remember) such that

reaction time $= A + B \times M$,

where:

$\quad A$ = the time required for input and output processes,
$\quad B$ = the central processing time required to determine whether or not the displayed item is a member of the memory set:
$\quad M$ = the number of items to be remembered.

Using this analysis with different task difficulties (*M*), Shoenberger (1974) demonstrated that reaction time performance on this type of task at least is susceptible to mechanical interference with the peripheral processes (i.e. the perception of the test letter and the verbalization of the response), but is essentially immune to any central processing effects of the vibration.

In terms of intellectual (cognitive) tasks, Shoenberger's conclusions of no vibration effects have been supported by some experimenters but not by others. For example Schohan, Rawson, and Soliday (1965) showed no appreciable effects of vibration on a navigation task, whilst Simons and Schmitz (1958) found no effects on mental arithmetic using 2.5 and 3.5 Hz vibrations at up to 0.31 *g*. On the other hand Huddleston (1964), using a 'rolling arithmetic' task (which combined mental addition and recent memory) demonstrated that performance was significantly slower at 4.8, 6.7, 9.5, and 16 Hz at 0.5 *g* than during the static control condition. The wide frequency range demonstrates that the performance reductions were not frequency-dependent, as are both visual and motor control decrements. In a subsequent experiment Huddleston (1965) used the same intensity at 4.8 and 6.7 Hz and confirmed these results.

The results of the effects of vibration on cognitive tasks, therefore, appear to be inconclusive. However it must be remembered that with such tasks a number of possible variables can interfere to cause unpredictable results unless they are controlled. The individual's level of arousal, for example, is known to have effects (both facilitative and detrimental) on subsequent performance (see, for example Fox's chapter in this volume). In this vein Poulton (1978) argues that vibration at 5 Hz can act as an alerting mechanism to increase performance. Furthermore, the level of arousal is known to be related to the

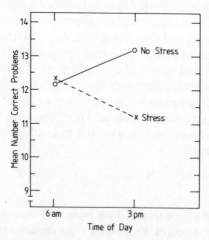

Figure 13. The effect of stress (vibration and noise) and time of day on a mental arithmetic task (after Sommer and Harris, 1970)

time of day as a result of the human body's cyclical (circadian) activities. Thus Sommer and Harris (1970) have demonstrated time of day effects on the relationship between a combined vibration and noise stressor and mental performance. Subjects were tested on a mental subtraction task at either 6 a.m. or 3 p.m. whilst exposed to either a 5 Hz, 0.25 g vibration and 110 dB noise stressor or to no stress. As can be seen in Figure 13, whereas the stress condition produced poorer performance at 3 p.m., at 6 a.m. no difference in performance was observed. Thus, the significant reduction in performance at 6 a.m. under the 'no stress' condition further supports the hypothesis that the degree of 'arousal' or 'alertness' plays a significant role in whether or not the stressor will affect performance.

A VIBRATION STANDARD

Since 1964 attempts have been made to combine all of the preceding types of data on the effects of vibration on health and performance (and also comfort), to compose an accepted standard for human exposure to whole-body vibration. Such a standard was finally produced in 1974—ISO 2631; *Guide for the Evaluation of Human Exposure to Whole-body vibration* (see Cowley, 1976).

The guide lays down limits of exposure to both vertical and lateral vibration

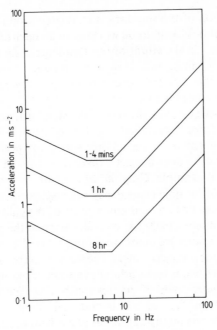

Figure 14. ISO Fatigue-decreased proficiency boundaries for vertical vibration

under three criteria: the preservation of health (exposure limit), working efficiency (fatigue-decreased proficiency boundary, FDP), and comfort (reduced comfort boundary, RCB). As an innovation the levels for each criterion, within the frequency range 1–80 Hz, are defined in terms of the maximum time for which an operator should be exposed to the vibration — from 1 minute to 8 hours. For any exposure time, exposure limit = 2 × FDP, and RCB = FDP/3.15. Figure 14 illustrates some of the levels produced for vertical vibration.

Before commenting on the Standard, it should be remembered that the limits are not the result of an experimental investigation specifically designed to produce a standard. They have been produced by a Technical Committee set up by the International Standards Organization (TC 108) to review previous work. This leads to a number of confusions, not the least being which experimental data were used to produce the standard and how much weight was put on the evidence of any one investigation. As Oborne (1976) comments on the final draft (ISO/DIS 2631):

It is not clear from which sources the ISO Working Party drew their information. The reference list at the end of the document covers most of the experimental and review papers published prior to 1972 and does not distinguish between those of general interest and those used in producing the standard.

The major innovation of the standard is to relate vibration to exposure time. Thus an operator who is likely to be working in an environment for 8 hours in which, for example, 20 Hz vibration predominates, should only receive an average of 0.8 ms^{-2} vibration before performance deteriorates. The same person experiencing the same frequency vibration, however, but for a short, 16-minute, period would be able to accept about 5.3 ms^{-2}.

Unfortunately, however, like the rest of the standard, experimental evidence for this time dependency is sadly lacking. Indeed Allen (1975) points to recent evidence that indicates that for casual exposures, any performance decrement which is due to vibration does not get worse with time — at least for exposures up to 3 hours (for example Gray *et al.*, 1976). A useful review of the experimental evidence for time dependency has been produced by Clarke (1979).

How much trust can be laid on many aspects of the guide, therefore, is open to debate. Indeed, Oborne (1983) has critically assessed the evidence upon which the ISO recommendations are made, and found their bases to be deficient. As a guide, however, the ISO document provides a useful starting point from which designers may begin to decide appropriate vibration levels, but these decisions will be more valid if its restrictions are understood. Thus the document refers, primarily, to whole-body vibration applied to seated or standing 'man'. It provisionally applies to recumbent or reclining man but not to local (for example, hand–arm) vibration. Further it covers only people in 'normal health', and most of the evidence for the limits appears to be based on averaged laboratory data obtained from fit young men. (Jones and Saunders, 1972, for example, have demonstrated some significant differences between men's and women's reactions to higher frequency (greater than 30 Hz) vibration stimuli). Finally, and this restriction applies to all composite curves, different individuals react differently to vibration, and curves such as the ISO standards which depict average reactions may mask these differences (see, for example, Oborne and Humphreys, 1976).

SUMMARY

When exposed to vibration of any significant amount, this chapter has demonstrated that considerable health and performance effects can occur with possible resultant losses in system efficiency and productivity. These effects can be related to the frequency and intensity of the vibration experienced, and to the task performed.

REFERENCES

Abrahams, C. F. Jr., and Suggs, C. W. (1969). *Chain saw vibration: isolation and transmission through the human arm.* Paper presented to Annual Meeting of the American Society of Agricultural Engineers, Indiana, June.

Agate, J. N. (1949). An outbreak of cases of Raynaud's phenomenon of occupational origin. *British Journal of Industrial Medicine*, **6**, 144–163.

Alexander, C. (1972). *Performance Changes due to the Single and Dual Frequency Vibration of Reading Material.* Ph.D. thesis, University of Southampton.

Allen, G. R. (1975). *Ride quality and International Standard 2631.* Paper presented to Ride Quality Symposium, Williamsburg, August. NASA TM X-3295.

Alpern, M. (1972). Effector mechanisms in vision. In Kling, J. W., and Riggs, L. A., (eds.) *Experimental Psychology* (New York: Methuen).

Barnes, G. R., Benson, A. J., and Prior, A. R. J. (1978). Visual–vestibular interaction in the control of eye-movement. *Aviation, Space and Environmental Medicine*, **49**, 557–564.

Benson, A. J. (1972). *Effect of angular oscillation in yaw on vision.* Paper presented to Human Response to Vibration Meeting, Sheffield.

Benson, A. J., and Barnes, G. R. (1978). Vision during angular oscillation. The dynamic interaction of visual and vestibular mechanisms. *Aviation, Space and Environmental Medicine*, **49**, 340–345.

British Standards Institution (1975). *Guide to the Evaluation of Exposure of the Human Hand-Arm System to Vibration.* BSI DD 43.

Buckhout, R. (1964). Effect of whole body vibration on human performance. *Human Factors*, **6**, 157–163.

Carpenter, R. H. S. (1977). *Movements of the Eyes* (London: Pion Ltd.).

Catterson, A. D., Hoover, G. N., and Asche, W. F. (1962). Human psychomotor performance during prolonged vertical vibration. *Aerospace Medicine*, **33**, 598–602.

Clarke, M. J. (1979). A study of the available evidence on duration effects on comfort and task proficiency under vibration. *Journal of Sound and Vibration*, **65**, 107–123.

Coermann, R. R. (1962). The mechanical impedance of the human body in sitting and standing position at low frequencies. *Human Factors*, **4**, 227–253.

Cowley, D. M. (1976). International standards in the vibration field. In Tempest, W. (ed.) *Infrasound and Low Frequency Vibration* (London: Academic Press).

Dennis, J. P. (1965). Some effects of vibration upon visual performance. *Journal of Applied Psychology*, **49**, 245–252.

Dieckmann, D. (1958). A study of the influence of vibration on man. *Ergonomics*, **1**, 347–355.

Drazin, D. H. (1962). Factors affecting vision during vibration. *Research*, **15**, 275–280.

Fraser, T. M., Hoover, G. N., and Asche, W. F. (1961). Tracking performance during low frequency vibration. *Aerospace Medicine*, **31**, 829–835.

Furness, T. H., and Lewis, C. H. (1978). *Helmet mounted display reading performance under whole-body vibration*. Paper presented to Human Response to Vibration Meeting, Silsoe, Beds.

Gray, R., Wilkinson, R. T., Maslen, K. R., and Rowlands, G. F. (1976). *The effects of 3 hrs of vertical vibration at 5 Hz on the performance of some tasks*. Royal Aircraft Establishment Technical Report 76011.

Griffin, M. J. (1975). Levels of whole-body vibration affecting human vision. *Aviation, Space and Environmental Medicine*, **46**, 1033–1040.

Griffin, M. J. (1976a). Vibration and visual activity. In Tempest, W. (ed.) *Infrasound and Low Frequency Vibration* (London: Academic Press).

Griffin, M. J. (1976b). Eye motion during whole-body vibration. *Human Factors*, **18**, 601–606.

Griffin, M. J., and Lewis, C. H. (1978). A review of the effects of vibration on visual acuity and continuous manual control. Part I: Visual acuity. *Journal of Sound and Vibration*, **56**, 383–413.

Grounds, M. D. (1964). Raynaud's phenomenon in users of chain saws. *Medical Journal of Australia*, **1**, 270–272.

Guignard, J. C. (1965). Vibration. In Gillies, J. A. (ed.) *A Textbook of Aviation Physiology* (Oxford: Pergamon).

Guignard, J. C., and Irving, A. (1960). Effects of low frequency vibration on man. *Engineering*, 9 September, 364–367.

Guignard, J. C., Landrum, C. J., and Reardon, R. E. (1976). *Experimental Evaluation of International Standard (ISO 2631) for Whole-body Vibration Exposures*. University of Dayton Research Institute. UDRI-TR-76-79.

Holland, C. L. (1965). Performance effects of long term random vertical vibration. *Human Factors*, **9**, 93–104.

Hornick, R. J. (1962). The effects of whole-body vibration in three directions upon human performance. *Journal of Engineering Psychology*, **1**, 93–101.

Hornick, R. J., and Lefritz, N. M. (1966). A study and review of human reaction to prolonged random vibration. *Human Factors*, **8**, 481–491.

Huddleston, J. H. F. (1964). *Human Performance and Behaviour in Vertical Sinusoidal Vibration*. Institute of Aviation Medicine Report 303.

Huddleston, J. H. F. (1965). *Effects of 4.8 and 6.7 c.p.s. Vertical Vibration on Handwriting and a Complex Mental Task, With and Without Abdominal Restraint*. Institute of Aviation Medicine Memo 60.

Huddleston, J. H. F. (1969). Oculomotor pursuit of vertical sinusoidal targets. *Nature*, **222**, 572.

Huddleston, J. H. F. (1970). Tracking performance on a visual display apparently vibrating at 1–10 Hz. *Journal of Applied Psychology*, **54**, 401–408.

Industrial Injuries Advisory Council (1970). *Interim Report on the Vibration Syndrome National Insurance (Industrial Injuries) Act, 1965*. Cmd 4430 (London: HMSO).

International Organization for Standardization (1974). *Guide for the Evaluation of Human Exposure to Whole-body Vibration*. ISO 2631 — 1974.

International Organization for Standardization (1979). *Draft International Standard— Principles for the Measurement and the Evaluation of Human Exposure to Vibration Transmitted to the Hand.* ISO/DIS 5349.

Jones, A. J., and Saunders, D. J. (1972). Effects of postural and methodological changes on equal comfort contours for whole body, vertical, sinusoidal vibration. *Applied Acoustics,* **5**, 279–299.

Keighley, G. D. (1974). Safe working limits of vibration level for continuous and interrupted exposure. In Taylor, W. (ed.) *The Vibration Syndrome* (London: Academic Press).

Lee, R. A., and King, A. I. (1971). Visual vibration response. *Journal of Applied Physiology,* **30**, 281–286.

Levison, W. H. (1976). *Biomechanical response and manual tracking performance in sinusoidal, sum of sines and random vibration environments.* Army Medical Research Laboratories Report. AMRL-TR-75-94.

Lewis, C. H. (1980). *The interaction of control dynamics and display type with the effect of vibration frequency on manual tracking performance.* Paper presented to Human Response to Vibration meeting, Swansea.

Lewis, C. H., and Griffin, M. J. (1978). A review of the effects of vibration on visual acuity and manual control. Part II: Continuous manual control. *Journal of Sound and Vibration,* **56**, 415–457.

Lewis, C. H., and Griffin, M. J. (1979a). The effect of character size on the legibility of numeric displays during vertical whole-body vibration. *Journal of Sound and Vibration,* **67**, 562–565.

Lewis, C. H., and Griffin, M. J. (1979b). Mechanisms of the effects of vibration frequency, level and duration on continuous manual control performance. *Ergonomics,* **22**, 855–889.

Lewis, C. H., and Griffin, M. J. (1980a). Predicting the effects of vertical vibration frequency, combinations of frequencies and visual distance on the reading of numeric displays. *Journal of Sound and Vibration,* **70**, 355–377.

Lewis, C. H., and Griffin, M. J. (1980b). Predicting the effects of vibration frequency and axis, and seating conditions on the reading of numeric displays. *Ergonomics,* **23**, 485–501.

Lovesey, E. J. (1971). *An investigation into the effects of dual axis vibration, restraining harness, visual feedback and control force on a manual positioning task.* Royal Aircraft Establishment Technical Report 71213.

Lovesey, E. J. (1974). The occurrence and effects upon performance of low frequency vibration. In Tempest, W. (ed.) *Infrasound and Low Frequency Vibration* (London: Academic Press).

Lovesey, E. J. (1975). The helicopter—some ergonomic factors. *Applied Ergonomics,* **6**, 139–146.

Maslen, K. R. (1972). *Efficiency under prolonged vibration and the ISO 'Guide'.* Royal Aircraft Establishment Technical Memo EP 512.

Meddick, R. D. L., and Griffin, M. J. (1976). The effect of two-axis vibration on the legibility of reading material. *Ergonomics,* **19**, 21–33.

Oborne, D. J. (1976). A critical assessment of studies relating whole-body vibration to passenger comfort. *Ergonomics,* **19**, 751–774.

Oborne, D. J. (1983). Whole-body vibration and ISO 2631: A critique. *Human Factors,* **25**, 55–70.

Oborne, D. J., and Humphries, D. A. (1976). Individual variability in human response to whole-body vibration. *Ergonomics,* **19**, 719–726.

O'Briant, C. R., and Ohlbaum, M. K. (1970). Visual acuity decrements associated with whole-body Gz vibration stress. *Aerospace Medicine,* **41**, 79–82.

O'Hanlon, J. G., and Griffin, M. J. (1971). *Some effects of the vibration of reading material upon visual performance.* ISVR Technical Report 49 (University of Southampton).

Pelmear, P. L., Taylor, W., and Pearson, J. (1974). Raynaud's phenomenon in pedestal grinders. In Taylor, W., (ed.) *The Vibration Syndrome* (London: Academic Press).

Poulton, E. C. (1974). *Tracking Skills and Manual Control* (New York: Academic Press).

Poulton, E. C. (1978). Increased vigilance with vertical vibration at 5 Hz: an alerting mechanism. *Applied Ergonomics,* **9**, 73–76.

Radke, A. O. (1958). Vehicle vibration. *Mechanical Engineering,* **80**, July, 38–41.

Reynolds, D. D., and Angevine, E. N. (1977). Hand–arm vibration. Part II: Vibration transmission characteristics of the hand and arm. *Journal of Sound and Vibration,* **51**, 255–265.

Reynolds, D. D., and Soedel, W. S. (1972). Dynamic response of the hand–arm system to sinusoidal input. *Journal of Sound and Vibration,* **21**, 339–353.

Robinson, D. A. (1965). The mechanics of human smooth pursuit eye movement. *Journal of Physiology,* **180**, 569–591.

Rosegger, R., and Rosegger, S. (1960). Health effects of tractor driving. *Journal of Agricultural Engineering Research,* **5**, 241–275.

Rowlands, G. F. (1977). *The transmission of vertical vibration to the heads and shoulders of seated men.* Royal Aircraft Establishment Technical Report TR77068.

Schohan, B., Rawson, H. E., and Soliday, S. M. (1965). Pilot and observer performance in simulated low altitude high speed flight. *Human Factors,* **7**, 257–265.

Shoenberger, R. W. (1967). Effects of vibration on complex psychomotor performance. *Aerospace Medicine,* **38**, 1264–1269.

Shoenberger, R. W. (1970). *Human performance as a function of direction and frequency of whole-body vibration.* Army Medical Research Laboratories Report AMRL-TR-70-7.

Shoenberger, R. W. (1974). An investigation of human information processing during whole-body vibration. *Aerospace Medicine,* **45**, 145–153.

Shurmer, C. R. (1967). *A review of the effects of low frequency vibration on man and his tracking performance.* BAC (Bristol) Guided Weapons Div. Report R 41A/20/RES/415.

Simons, A. K., and Schmitz, M. A. (1958). *The effect of low frequency, high amplitude whole-body vibration on human performance.* (Washington DC: Office of the Surgeon General, Research and Development Div.).

Sommer, H. C., and Harris, C. S. (1970). *Combined effects of noise and vibration on mental performance as a function of time of day.* Army Medical Research Laboratories Report AMRL-TR-70-36.

Sternberg, S. (1966). High-speed scanning in human memory. *Science* **153**, 652–654.

Stewart, A. M., and Goda, D. F. (1970). Vibration syndrome. *British Journal of Industrial Medicine,* **27**, 19–27.

Stott, J. R. R. (1980). *Mechanical resonance of the eyeball.* Paper presented to Human Response to Vibration Meeting, Swansea.

Taylor, W. (1974). The vibration syndrome: Introduction. In Taylor, W. (ed.) *The Vibration Syndrome* (London: Academic Press).

Taylor, W., Pelmear, P. L., and Pearson, J. (1974). Reynaud's phenomenon in forestry chain saw operators. In Taylor, W. (ed.) *The Vibration Syndrome* (London: Academic Press).

Torle, G. (1965). Tracking performance under random acceleration: effects of control dynamics. *Ergonomics,* **8**, 481–486.

Weisz, A. Z., Goddard, C., and Allen, R. W. (1965). *Human Performance under Random and Sinusoidal Vibration.* Aerospace Medical Research Laboratories, Ohio, Report AMRL-TR-65-209.

Wells, M. J., and Storey, N. (1980). *Investigations of vibration-induced eye movements under whole-body vibration.* Paper presented to Human Response to Vibration meeting, Swansea.

Wohlwill, J. F., Nasar, J. L., Dejoy, D. M., and Foruzani, H. H. (1976). Behavioral effects of a noisy environment: task involvement versus passive exposure. *Journal of Applied Psychology*, **61**, 67–74.

The Physical Environment at Work
Edited by D. J. Oborne and M. M. Gruneberg
©1983 John Wiley & Sons Ltd.

Industrial Noise and Man

PAUL L. MICHAEL AND GORDON R. BIENVENUE
*Environmental Acoustics Laboratory,
Pennsylvania State University,
University Park, PA 16802, USA*

Industrial noise problems have increased substantially during the past 30 years due to the increased number and types of machines used in industry, and this trend may be expected to continue. The most critical effect of noise on the industrial worker is the temporary and/or permanent damage to hearing that may result from exposure to high-level noise. Noise that interferes with the hearing of speech and warning signals may also be a significant safety hazard in some workplaces. The interference of noise with speech communication and work performance is of concern to production specialists in industry. Away from work, noise may disturb relaxation and sleep. Less is known about the effects of stress resulting from noise exposures but recent studies have indicated that noise-induced stress may, in some situations, combine with other stresses to contribute to stress-related diseases.

This chapter concentrates primarily on the effects of noise, with a particular emphasis on stress effects, and on the measurements necessary to provide the most useful descriptors of noise.

NOISE-INDUCED HEARING IMPAIRMENT

Background

Noise-induced hearing impairment has been recognized as a significant problem at and away from work environments for more than 100 years. Even so, estimates have been made that there are still between 5 and 15 million workers in the United States exposed to potentially hazardous noise levels (Glorig, 1958; EPA, 1977; OSHA, 1981). An accurate estimate of the number of people having significant noise-induced hearing impairment caused by workplace noise exposure is not available because many industrial workers are also exposed to very high noise levels away from work. Furthermore, the characteristics of hearing losses resulting from such factors as ageing, childhood diseases, drugs, and other stresses are similar to those from noise exposure so that the aetiologies of individual impairments are often uncertain (Lawrence, Gonzalez, and Hawkins, 1967; Rosen, 1967; Kryter, 1970).

A considerable amount of research on noise-induced hearing impairment has been completed during the past 30 years leading to a general agreement that high-level noise exposure can cause degeneration of receptor cells in the organ of Corti, a sensorineural hearing impairment (Kryter, 1963; Baughn, 1966, 1973; Ward, 1968, 1976).

Regulations have been developed that limit noise exposures in work environments but these regulations have been based on studies that have shown wide variations in the effects of noise on hearing (OSHA, 1970, 1981; NIOSH, 1972; ISO, 1975, 1980; BSI, 1976). There is still much to be learned about the effects of intermittent and impulsive noise exposures on hearing thresholds, and about the effects of noise on other aspects of hearing. The many different combinations of level, frequency, and temporal characteristics of noise, along with the wide differences among individuals in their susceptibility to noise-induced hearing impairment, complicate the task of establishing meaningful damage-risk criteria. Evidence of the difficulty of this task is shown by the fact that the American National Standards Institute (ANSI) has not been able to develop a standard on hearing conservation criteria after more than 30 years of work. Unpublished draft proposals have been issued, however, by ANSI and by the International Organization for Standardization.

The conflicting results found between some studies, and the slow progress made towards the development of a widely accepted standard for damage risk, may be due, in part, to the fact that most research has been based on only one measure of hearing, the threshold of hearing for pure tones. Unfortunately, hearing threshold levels do not necessarily reflect the ability of an ear to perform other functions, for example, to distinguish differences in loudness or to detect a particular sound in the presence of a masking noise. Also, noise-induced hearing impairment may be found in the ability of an ear to discriminate loudness differences, and/or to distinguish certain sounds in the presence of masking noise, as well as in the impairment of hearing thresholds (Michael and Bienvenue, 1976; Bienvenue and Michael, 1977, 1979, 1980; Bienvenue et al., 1977; Michael et al., 1978).

A test battery approach to detecting hearing changes

Research carried out by the Environmental Acoustics Laboratory (EAL) at The Pennsylvania State University during the past 5 years on loudness discrimination and level of initial masking, along with conventional threshold measurement procedures, has shown that these three test results are non-redundant (Bienvenue and Michael, 1977; Michael *et al.*, 1978). The use of all three tests as a test battery which will be discussed later, provides more complete information on hearing changes than that provided by threshold measurements alone. The test battery has also been shown to be a significantly more sensitive indicator of noise-induced hearing changes than conventional threshold measurements used alone.

A loudness discrimination test

Paradoxically, a sensorineurally impaired ear shows recruitment in that it can identify small changes in the level of a test tone with greater sensitivity and accuracy than a normal ear. The testing procedure proposed by Michael and Bienvenue (1976) was designed to determine an individual's ability to detect specific increments of loudness above a continuous presentation of a pure tone. Thus, if an individual demonstrates a shift in his/her capability for detecting increments of loudness from one measurement to the next, the individual may be in the process of developing sensorineural hearing changes.

Temporary threshold shifts (TTS) that are statistically significant, but small enough not to cause permanent threshold shifts (PTS), generally recover rapidly and will become insignificant within about ½ hour (Ward, 1973, 1975). The TTS recovery rate is so rapid that specific time periods of about 2 minutes (TTS_2) after exposure must be used to get reasonably reliable test-retest results. Obviously, this short time period is difficult, or impossible, to use in field tests because a quiet test room is generally located at a significant distance from the work areas. Loudness discrimination (LD) shifts, however, have been shown to persist for significantly longer periods of time than TTS effects so that LD shifts are much better suited for field use (Bennett *et al.*, 1977).

The concept of loudness discrimination index (LDI), introduced in 1977 by Bienvenue and his colleagues, enhances the sensitivity of the loudness discrimination test procedures by assigning a single number score for each subject (also Bennett *et al.*, 1977). The LDI was developed to be responsive to the largest shift for each individual regardless of the increment magnitude at which it occurs, thereby avoiding individual differences in baseline LD ability and greatly enhancing the sensitivity of the LD measurements.

A level of initial masking test

A masking test, called the level of initial masking (LIM) utilizes a tone-on-tone masking task (Bienvenue and Michael, 1977). A high-frequency test tone (4000 Hz) is presented to a subject simultaneously with each of six different masking tones. Starting at the lowest masker frequency, each masker tone is increased in level until the subject indicates that the test tone is inaudible.

The masker level producing this initial masking of the 4000 Hz test tone is recorded for each masker frequency as the level of initial masking (LIM).

The evaluation and practical usefulness of the test battery

Laboratory studies using the test battery, comprising the TTS, LDI, and LIM test, were concerned with the temporary effects on hearing caused by noise exposures (Bennett *et al.*, 1977; Bienvenue and Michael, 1977; Bienvenue, Bennett, and Michael, 1977; Michael *et al.*, 1978). In these studies, significant shifts in hearing were found in 60–70 per cent of the noise-exposed subjects with each of the three component tests (TTS, LDI, LIM). Further, the subjects having significant shifts were not necessarily the same for each test so that about 90 per cent of the subjects showed a significant shift for at least one test procedure. The use of the test battery was thereby demonstrated to be a more effective means of identifying hearing shifts than the use of any single test alone.

In one of these studies a group of 60 normal-hearing untrained listeners were given various noise exposures and tested with the three-component test battery (Michael *et al.*, 1978). Results of test battery measurements were essentially the same for untrained listeners as for trained laboratory subjects. Thus, the test battery should provide viable results using untrained listeners in industrial settings. In addition, correlations among the three test components were low and were not statistically significant. This independence of data from the three tests justifies the use of all three tests wherever detailed information on a variety of hearing parameters is required.

The practical feasibility of the the test battery for use with untrained subjects in actual workplace locations was tested in a pilot study by Schrock (1979). Small, lightweight, portable instrumentation was developed for administering the testing battery. The study was conducted in a local industry where the test battery could be used in an existing test booth. Test battery measurements were made on ten employees before normal work shifts on 10 work days over a 14-day period. To determine test-retest reliability, each individual's mean test scores obtained before work for the first week (5 days) were compared with his or her mean scores obtained under the same conditions from a second week (5 days). All measurements were made on the day shift so that measurement times were carefully controlled. In all cases, these test–retest results showed no statistically significant differences between the data from the first and second weeks of study. There was also no significant difference between the abilities of the subjects used in these field studies and those used in laboratory studies in regard to their performance of the test battery tasks. Obviously, the number of subjects used in this field study does not provide enough information to establish meaningful normative data for persons in various age groups and with different noise exposure histories, but these normative data are not necessary if the test battery is to be used for comparison tests on the same subject at different times. Normative data will be required before the test battery results can be used effectively for assessing susceptibility to noise-induced hearing impairment, for monitoring levels in hearing conservation programmes, and for other purposes requiring absolute data levels.

Another practical consideration, the test time, averaged about 15 minutes for a complete test battery throughout these pilot study measurements. This test time is comparable to conventional threshold tests, and so these studies have shown that reliable and sensitive test results can be provided with the EAL test battery in real-life work environments in a practical period of time.

NOISE INTERFERENCE WITH SPEECH AND WARNING SIGNALS

A. Speech interference

Speech interference from noise is usually considered as one aspect of the overall phenomenon of subjective masking. Speech is so redundant, and the typical listener is so familiar with the language, that a considerable amount of information can be missed from this complicated sequence of sounds and the speech will still be understood.

Variables related to speech interference

Variables that influence the extent to which noise will interfere with speech include the characteristics of the speaker and listener, the characteristics of the message, and the characteristics of the masking noise.

Noise tends to interfere with speech reception to a greater extent if the speaker has poor articulation, or if the listener and speaker use different dialects. Also lack of extensive knowledge of, and experience with, the language will render communication more difficult in noise. Decrements in hearing acuity due to the ageing process (presbycusis) also necessitate lower background noise levels for adequate speech communication (Kryter, 1970).

Research has demonstrated that communications containing simple and predictable information are less subject to interference from noise (Klumpp and Webster, 1963; Webster, 1969, 1970).

As a general rule, the higher the noise level the greater will be its interference with speech. The frequency spectrum of the noise is also very important in that the extent to which a given noise will interfere with speech depends, to a large extent, on the sound pressure levels of the noise at the speech frequencies (Kryter, 1970).

The effect of intermittent or impulse noise on speech intelligibility is difficult to assess. As the frequency and duration of noise bursts increase, the level of speech intelligibility is reduced.

Measures of speech interference

Various procedures have been developed to characterize noise with respect to its speech-masking abilities. The three best known are the articulation index (AI) (ANSI, 1969) the speech interference level (SIL) or the preferred speech interference level (PSIL) (Webster, 1969, 1970) and the A-weighted overall sound level (Kryter, 1970).

The AI is the most complicated of the three measures, with the SIL or PSIL next in complexity, and the single-number A-weighted measurement procedure being by far the simplest. In most cases having complex masking noise characteristics, the levels of accuracy of these three measurement procedures are directly related to the degree of complexity. For the simpler noise characteristics in some cases the SIL or A-weighted measurements are satisfactory.

The level of complexity of these tests is caused, for the most part, by the amount of resolution provided by the measurement procedure. The AI procedure uses 20 frequency bands over a frequency range of 200 to 6100 Hz, while the SIL, or PSIL procedures use three or four frequency bands over a range of about 300 to 4800 Hz. The overall, single-number A-weighted measurement gives emphasis to those sounds having frequencies between 1000 and 5000 Hz with decreasing emphasis given to lower frequencies (-50 dB at 20 Hz) and to higher frequencies (-9 dB at 20,000 Hz).

Implications of speech interference

Research on community noise indicates that speech interference is a primary source of noise-related annoyance. In certain situations noise may mask signals that, if not heard, could lead to property damage or personal injury. Although people can adapt to even relatively high levels of background noise, there is evidence that they develop non-communicating lifestyles degrading their quality of life (Hockey, 1970a,b; Gulian, 1973; EPA, 1974).

B. Warning signal interference

Warning signals have many different level, frequency, and temporal characteristics so that general guidelines beyond those given above for speech interference are not justified (Michael, Saperstein, and Prout, 1972, 1973; Wilkins and Martin, 1981). Obviously, measurement and detection of these warning sounds must be considered separately for each situation. Unfortunately, only limited information is available on this subject.

NOISE EFFECTS ON COGNITIVE TASK PERFORMANCE

Comprehensive studies of the effects of noise on task performance have failed to yield a consistent pattern of effects (Broadbent, 1957; Cohen, 1966; Kryter, 1970). Overall, it is probably safe to conclude from these studies that the effects of noise on short-term task performance are not severe in most cases, and that the detection of these decrements can be made only on noise-sensitive tasks using detailed performance assessment techniques.

Characteristics of the noise

In a literature review compiled by the EPA in 1974, the following conclusions were reached pertaining to task performance in noise:

(1) continuous noise without special meaning does not generally impair performance unless the sound exposure level exceeds 90 dB(A);
(2) intermittent and impulsive noises are more disruptive than steady-state noises of the same level;
(3) high-frequency components of noise (above approximately 2000 Hz) usually produce more interference with performance than low-frequency components of noise;
(4) noise is more likely to increase error rates and variability as opposed to rate of work.

Characteristics of the task

Most performance decrements caused by noise have been found in tasks that require (1) continuous performance, (2) prolonged vigilance, or (3) the performance of two tasks simultaneously. Tasks that require simple, repetitive operations are unaffected and sometimes enhanced by noise. Obviously, tasks that require the operator to attend to auditory cues for successful performance are most susceptible to impairment from noise.

Noise-related impairments are often found in overloading or demanding task situations because the individual has a limited capacity information processing system and, where noise is present, less spare capacity exists for task information relative to quiet conditions (Hockey, 1970ab; Kahneman, 1973). Performance on simple or boring tasks might be improved in the presence of an arousal-increasing stimulus such as noise because the arousal level may be increased toward an optimal level (Hebb, 1956).

Characteristics of the individual

There appears to be a great amount of variation in the way different individuals respond to noise and, although this is a common observation, very little is known about the nature of these differences. There has, however, been an attempt to apply the inverted-U theory of arousal to the problem of individual differences (Welford, 1965, 1968). The basic supposition of this approach is that individuals differ in their chronic levels of arousal. If one individual is chronically more aroused than another, additional arousal afforded by the presence of noise would be more likely to lead to a condition of over-arousal for this individual than for a less chronically aroused individual. Tentative findings also suggest that introverts perform better than extroverts in boring and monotonous task situations, and that introverts appear to be more adversely affected by noise than extroverts.

Cumulative and post-noise exposure effects

Research indicates that the adverse effects of noise tend to appear towards the end of task performance sessions (Broadbent, 1971), particularly if the noise exposure duration is lengthy (Hartley, 1973).

Recent studies have shown that although noise may not affect performance during the actual exposure, it may produce impairments which occur after the noise has been terminated (Glass and Singer, 1972; Wohlwill *et al.*, 1976). More severe after-effects were found with irregular–intermittent and intense (108 dB(A)) noises. In addition when subjects were provided with the means to terminate the noise, the magnitude of the post-noise effect was reduced even when this control was not exercised (Glass and Singer, 1972; Wohlwill *et al.*, 1976).

Field studies of task performance

Actual work situations often present obstacles to controlled experimentation, so that many field studies show methodological deficiencies (Kryter, 1970). Recent work involving a 5-year study of medical, attendance, and accident files for 1000 factory workers shows that workers in high noise settings (> 95 dB(A)) had more job-related accidents, sickness, and absenteeism than their counterparts in more quiet settings (< 80 dB(A)) (Cohen, 1973). It is usually difficult to separate the effects attributable to noise from those related to other physical stressors such as heat and air pollution, or to considerations of accident threat and job security. Evaluation of the positive effects of noise reduction efforts are often confounded by positive morale and motivation changes that also accompany the intervention in the work environment.

Implications of task performance effects

Assessment of the effects of noise on task performance requires consideration of the particular noise involved, the type of task in question, and the individuals performing the task. In general, the overall rate of work is not affected, but variability in the rate of work is often increased. Demanding tasks or tasks that must be performed for relatively long periods of time are more subject to disruption by noise. Although in some situations performance during noise is unaffected, subsequent performance or behaviour sometimes suffers as a result of previous noise exposure.

NOISE EFFECTS ON ANNOYANCE, RELAXATION AND SLEEP

A. Annoyance

Annoyance reactions, perhaps the most widespread response to noise, are good examples of noise effects having the potential for significant psychological and physiological implications. Annoyance has been studied from two general perspectives: annoyance reactions of the individual and annoyance reactions to the community.

Individual reactions

Individual annoyance reactions to noise have been investigated in most cases in the laboratory (Broadbent, 1957; Galloway, 1970; Wohlwill *et al.*, 1976). Comparisons are usually made between pairs of sounds to determine the degree of unpleasantness of, or other subjective responses to, a particular set of sounds. Generally, annoyance increases with sound level, and high-frequency sounds (above 1000 Hz) are found more annoying than sounds having predominantly low-frequency characteristics. Temporal patterns of exposure and personal attitudes towards the noise sources are also important factors.

Community reactions

Community annoyance reactions to noise are usually investigated through social surveys (Galloway, 1970; Fidell, Horonjeff, and Green, 1981; Tracor, 1971; Alexandre, 1973). Most have been made on populations exposed to either aircraft or surface transportation noises because a large number of people have been adversely affected by these noises. The results of this research have shown that a number of personal, social, and situational factors can influence any particular individual's response to noise. It is possible, however, to predict with reasonable accuracy the percentage of individuals who will express annoyance to a given noise exposure in a particular community. Inclusion of certain personal and social factors, such as those listed below, has been shown to improve the accuracy of prediction (Galloway, 1970; Tracor, 1971). Generally, listeners are more readily annoyed when:

(1) they are indoors rather than outdoors;
(2) the exposure is at night rather than during the day;
(3) they live in suburban rather than urban areas;
(4) they perceive the noise level, or the source, to be unnecessary;
(5) they perceive the noise exposure to be a threat to their personal health or safety;
(6) they perceive the noise or the source to be a threat to an economic investment (property value);
(7) they are dissatisfied with other aspects of their environment;
(8) they believe the noise, or the source, is not within their control;
(9) they believe they were treated unfairly or ignored by the authorities.

The socioeconomic status of the community, and the community's past experience with noise exposures, are also related to the degree of annoyance expressed but the effect is very complicated.

Noise attitude surveys

The terms survey, interview, and questionnaire are often used interchangeably. However, these terms are not synonymous and should be distinguished from each other. The term survey refers to the general act of acquiring information. It does *not* refer to an actual method or instrument used for such purpose. Interviews and questionnaires, on the other hand, are two popular ways to collect information; thus, they are two survey instruments. Attitudes then may be surveyed through the use of interviews or questionnaires.

There are certain advantages in employing interviews rather than questionnaires. In an interview, questions can be explained, unexpected responses can be interpreted, and more in-depth questions can be included. On the other hand, questionnaires are usually less expensive; however, people tend not to fill out or return questionnaires.

The design of social noise surveys

A widely employed framework for the design of social noise surveys includes the following four factors for consideration (Cohen, 1966; Borsky, 1970; Tracor, 1971; Gulian, 1973):

(1) perception of awareness of noise,
(2) activities affected or interrupted by noise,
(3) annoyance or hostility resulting from interruption by noise,
(4) complaints resulting from interruption by noise.

The first factor pertains to the large individual differences that exist in terms of perception and awareness of noise. Some people are extremely sensitive to noise, while others are quite insensitive to it. Thus, people who are exposed to the same noise will not all react to it in a similar manner.

The second factor considered in this framework stems from the observation that the adverse effects of noise are closely related to the variety of activities intruded upon by noise, and the extent or magnitude of this intrusion.

The third factor, the extent to which people feel annoyed or irritated by different types of noise, is highly dependent upon social, psychological, and situational variables.

The fourth factor pertains to complaint activity. A survey of complaint activity should include both the extent to which people desire to complain, and the extent to which they actually do register such complaints. Such information is typically included in noise surveys because there is often administrative interest in predicting complaint activity. Research has shown, however, that complaint rate represents a serious underestimation of annoyance level (Schieber, 1968; Thiessen, 1969; Lukas, 1972).

Each of these factors suggests a general category of questions that should be included in a community noise questionnaire or interview protocol.

Survey content

A complete survey should contain items pertaining to the following four content areas: (1) description and assessment of the noise environment, (2) activity disruption and interference from noise, (3) psychosocial situational variables, and (4) personal–demographic background. Each of these areas is discussed in detail.

Description of the noise environment

Questions should be directed at assessing the respondents' perceptions of the noise environment in which they live. The first question might simply inquire about sources of dissatisfaction in the person's environment so as to assess how noise compares with other problems in the environment. Note that no prompting of the respondent regarding noise has taken place.

Next, an overall 'neighbourhood' noise level rating should be obtained. Similar overall ratings might be solicited for noise levels inside the home, and for the city or town in general.

After the overall noise exposure information has been obtained, the contribution of various noise sources such as aircraft, trucks, industry, barking dogs etc., should be assessed. Ranking procedures should be used to assess the magnitude of the contribution of each of the sources. Information pertaining to the times at which these noises are most obvious should also be obtained.

Respondents might also be asked if they have ever complained to the authorities about noise, or if they have ever thought of registering a complaint.

Activity interference from noise

It has been found that the extent to which noise is annoying depends in part on the extent to which it disrupts ongoing activities (Hebb, 1956; Hockey, 1970a,b; Lukas, 1972, 1977). Questions should be included that ask the respondent about the types of activities that are disrupted by noise, and the degree of the disruption. A list of such activities might include: TV/radio listening, conversation, telephone use, relaxing inside/outside, listening to music, sleeping, reading, eating, etc. Questions should also be asked about direct annoyance and some questions should be included that determine the extent to which the respondent has altered daily activities to cope with the noise. The individual may not feel that noise interferes with his sleep or TV watching, but almost without awareness of the relationship of the noise to his behaviour, may report that he sleeps with the air conditioner on all through the year or that he always keeps the front windows closed. These are effects of noise that often go unnoticed.

Psychosocial and situational variables

Previous survey research has shown that there are a number of intervening personal, social, and situational factors that appear to affect responses to noise (Schieber, 1968; Thiessen, 1969; Tracor, 1971; Lukas, 1972). For example, reactions to environmental noise have been found to be more adverse if the noise is perceived as being unnecessary, unpredictable, or uncontrollable, or if the noise is thought to represent a threat to personal health and safety. Also, individuals who rate themselves as being sensitive to noise tend to be more adversely affected by it (Schieber, 1968; Thiessen, 1969; Hockey, 1970a,b; Lukas, 1972).

Personal–demographic backgrounds

Socioeconomic background information typically collected in the course of any type of interview, fulfils several functions. Information is provided concerning the socioeconomic makeup of the sample, and the extent to which the sample is representative of the general population. Also, patterns of response to items in other parts of the interview may depend on socioeconomic variables such as age, income, sex, national origin, occupation, or educational level. Information on the person's previous occupational and non-occupational noise exposures should also be recorded.

Special survey techniques should be used that allow solicitation of personal information while respecting the privacy of the respondent. For example, sometimes broad categories of response are used to obtain information on items such as income level. This information should not be omitted from the community noise survey solely on the grounds that it is sometimes difficult to obtain.

B. Relaxation and sleep disturbance

Two important considerations in the study of relaxation and sleep disturbance are: (1) arousal or waking due to noise, and (2) changes within the sleeping individual who does not awaken with the noise (Schieber, 1968; Thiessen, 1969; Lukas, 1972, 1977; Williams, 1973).

Sleep disturbance variables

Important variables related to response to noise during sleep are age, sex, sleep stage, and noise level (Lukas, 1972; Williams, 1973).

(1) *Age*: Middle-aged and older subjects are more affected than children and young persons at all stages of sleep.
(2) *Sex*: Women are typically more sensitive to noise during sleep than men. Middle-aged women are especially sensitive to subsonic jet aircraft fly-overs and simulated sonic booms (Nixon, 1971).
(3) *Stages of sleep*: People tend to be most responsive to noise exposures during lighter sleep stages. Often, noise during the deeper sleep stages does not produce behavioural awakening, but does result in shifts in sleep stage. Usually, the shift is from a deep to a light sleep. It has been observed that more meaningful stimuli elicit greater response. In general, behavioural awakening is more likely to occur the longer someone has been sleeping.
(4) *Noise level*: As a general rule, the higher the noise level, the greater the probability of sleep interference (Thiessen, 1969).

Implications of sleep disturbance effects

Sleeping in noisy environments appears to produce adverse effects either in the form of wakening the sleeper, or in the form of shifts in the stages of sleep. Existing data arise mostly from laboratory studies employing relatively few participants. Community noise surveys, however, have also shown sleep disturbance to be a major source of annoyance (Lukas, 1977).

Very little is known about the long-term effects of sleep disturbance although it is probable that significant sleep disturbance could lead to adverse health effects.

STRESS AND ITS RELATION TO NOISE EXPOSURE

General physiological responses to noise

The extra-auditory effects of noise both in humans and animals have been reviewed by several authors (Kryter, 1970, 1972, 1976; Welch and Welch, 1970; Miller, 1971, 1974). Initial physiological responses to noise include reflexive contractions of the tensor tympani and stapedius muscles of the middle ear (Davis, 1950), startle responses such as eye blink, facial grimace, muscle flexion, and tension, head and posture adjustments (Hoffman and Fleshler, 1963) and orienting and defensive reflexes (Sokolov, 1963). These reflexive mechanisms are transient responses which tend to arouse, alert, and protect the individual at the onset of acoustic stimulation. In addition to these phenomena researchers have noted that the central nervous system becomes more excitable during noise exposure (Busnel, Busnel, and Lehman, 1973), that alterations are observable in patterns of electroencephalographic recordings (Bell, 1966) and that there are alterations in the ribonucleic acid levels observable in both neural and glial cells of the central nervous system (Anthony, 1973).

The circulatory effects observed in conjunction with noise exposure indicate that noise affects several parameters of the circulatory system including blood pressure, heart rate, and pulse rate (Bell, 1966; Jansen, 1969; Cuesdean, 1977; Johnson, 1977). There is evidence that workers in high-level noise environments demonstrate a greater incidence of circulatory disorders than workers in low-noise environments (Jansen, 1961). However, it is extremely difficult to attribute these effects to noise *per se* since other stress-producing agents are present in the work environments tested.

Variations in respiration rate have also been noted subsequent to or concomitant with noise exposure (Bell, 1966; Jansen, 1969; Sokolik, 1977). Variations in the digestive tract have been observed in conjunction with noise exposure as well as variations in galvanic skin resistance (Davis, 1932; Davis, Buchwald, and Frankman, 1955).

In addition, it has been observed that noise affects eye pupil dilation (Jansen, 1970). The magnitude of the pupillary dilation tends to increase with the level of the noise, reaching a maximum at approximately 110 dB sound pressure level. Also, in some instances, considerably lower noise levels than these may result in disturbances in the balance mechanism, especially if the stimulation is unequal at the two ears (Nixon, 1971). The immediate vestibular symptoms of the high-level noise exposure include vertical nystagmus, disorientation, nausea, and vomiting (McCabe and Lawrence, 1958; Glorig, 1969). Long-term vestibular effects have not been observed.

The stress response to noise

One of the most notable of the non-auditory physiological effects of high-level noise on human beings is what is termed the N-response (Davis, Buchwald, and Frankman, 1955; Kryter, 1970). The N-response is characterized by the vasoconstriction of peripheral blood vessels as well as by the minor changes in blood pressure and heart rate noted above. In addition, it includes slow and deep breathing, changes in electrodermal sensitivity, and a brief change in skeletal-muscle tension.

A large variety of noxious agents or stressors are capable of producing a general stress reaction in the organism (Selye, 1956, 1974). The organism's response to a stressor is generally referred to as the general adaptation syndrome (GAS). The GAS has three stages: the alarm stage, in which a system prepares to fend off a stressor; the resistance stage, in which the body fights off the stressor; and the exhaustion stage that occurs if the body can no longer withstand the stressor (Selye, 1956, 1974). Prolongation of the resistance stage of the GAS may result in lowered resistance to infection and the development of so-called diseases of adaptation, such as gastro-intestinal ulcers, elevated blood pressure, arthritis, etc. (Selye, 1974).

Noise of an extremely high level has been shown to act as a stressor that can, at least in some cases, lead to some of the reactions associated with the GAS (Ettema, 1980). In evaluating the effects of noise as a stressful agent consideration must be given to the interaction of various stressors, individual differences in susceptibility to stress, and the apparent adaptability of the human organism to stressful environments. In the next sections the phenomenon of noise as a stress-inducing agent will be considered in some detail.

Hormonal secretions due to noise

Existing research has shown that noise can serve to activate the hypothalamic–pituitary–adrenal axis resulting in specific hormone secretions (Anthony, 1973; Anthony, Ackerman, and Lloyd, 1959). Specifically, noise has been shown to cause an increase of hypothalamic corticotrophin releasing factor (CRF) in the rat brain (Hiroshige *et al.*, 1969), increased secretions of adrenocorticotrophic hormone (ACTH) (Geber, Anderson, and Van Dyne, 1966), and a greater production of adrenal cortical steroids, particularly corticosterone (Sackler *et al.*, 1959). In one particular study destruction of the auditory receptors prevented this increase in corticosterone in a group of comparison animals (Henkin and Knigge, 1963), a finding which suggests that the noise stress phenomenon acts primarily through the auditory system.

While the fact that noise acts as a neurogenic stressor, potentially operating through various central nervous system and endocrine pathways, has been reasonably well documented in animals, studies involving human subjects have been somewhat contradictory (Arguelles *et al.*, 1962, 1970; Atherly, Gibbons, and Powell, 1970; Brandenberger, Follenius, and Termolières, 1977; Favino, 1978), however, sufficient evidence has been developed to conclude that noise exposure will, under certain conditions, precipitate a stress response in humans.

One significant factor to consider in evaluating research on various adrenal–cortical secretions subsequent to and concomitant with noise exposures is that there are many inherent problems in the design of such experiments. The studies referenced in this section may generally be viewed to suffer from at least one of the following difficulties: either (a) a lack of identical control runs with which to compare the noise conditions; (b) unaccounted-for circadian effects (that is daily variations in adrenal–cortical hormone secretion levels); (c) an extremely small number of subjects for meaningful statistical analysis; (d) poor control and/or definition of acoustical parameters of the noise; and (e) a failure to run intra- and inter-assay controls. It is especially important to keep in mind the necessity of determining quiet baseline levels of adrenal–cortical hormone secretions. Temporal fluctuations in cortisol have been recognized since it was noted by Pincus in 1943 and it has been demonstrated more recently that this daily circadian pattern can contribute significantly to fluctuations and variations seen in experimental results (Tyler *et al.*, 1954).

A hormonal mediation model for auditory and non-auditory noise effects

The particular significance of the hormonal phenomena that have been noted have to do with the relationship between the non-auditory (or extra-auditory) and the auditory responses to noise exposure. The circulatory alterations are of particular interest in this case. This constriction of peripheral blood vessels (Dega, 1977) leads to impaired circulation to the surface tissues (Cuesdean, 1977) while concentrating blood supply away from the skin and into the deep muscles of the skeletal muscular system (Williams, 1975).

The link between stress response, circulatory changes, and auditory changes resulting from noise exposure really only becomes apparent with a consideration of auditory embryology. The inner ear structure of the human being, and in fact of all mammalians, develops from the ectodermal germ layer of the embryo (Northern and Downs, 1974). As these structures have evolved embryologically from ectodermal tissue, their blood supply is essentially an ectodermal type of blood supply. Thus, when the individual is experiencing stress, the inner ear along with other surface tissues will experience notably reduced blood supply.

Evidence for hormonal mediation of noise effects

If the hormonal mediation model outlined above is to be considered viable, one must expect to find in the literature indications that noise stress results in reduced blood supply to the cochlear end organ for hearing, and that there is some indication that this reduced blood supply is a mediating mechanism to the phenomenon of noise-induced hearing shift. Evidence for this particular phenomenon does exist.

The cochlear potentials have been demonstrated to be dependent upon a normal blood supply (Weaver *et al.*, 1949; Knoshi, Butler, and Fernandez, 1961). Specifically, it has been demonstrated that the blood supply to the cochlea is reduced under high-level noise exposure (Bekesy, 1951; Tonndorf, Hyde, and Brogan, 1955; Gulick, 1958).

In addition researchers have noted that either hypoxia or high-level sound stimulation will result in significantly reduced oxygen tension in the cochlear tissues (Misrahy, Shinabarger, and Arnold, 1958; Misrahy *et al.*, 1961; Koide *et al.*, 1960; Schneider, 1974). Generally, therefore, the presence of high-level sound appears to cause some physiological alteration that results in significant reductions of oxygen supplies to the organ of Corti structures. Finally it has been noted that, following exposure to high-level sound, blood vessels in the stria vascularis region and in the spiral vessel region of basilar membrane, demonstrate a notable lack of red cells (Lawrence, Gonzalez, and Hawkins, 1967). In addition these vessels tend to demonstrate occlusion phenomena under conditions of high-level noise (Lawrence, 1971; Spoendlin, 1971). Thus, evidence from electrophysiological, biochemical, and morphological areas tends to support the notion that the cochlea suffers a reduced blood supply during high-level noise exposure.

One further area with relevance to the question being examined has to do with individuals who demonstrate disorders in the hormonal response mechanism. Research with subjects demonstrating adrenal–cortical insufficiency indicated that pure tone detection thresholds were significantly more sensitive in these individuals than in normal individuals (Henkin *et al.*, 1967). In the same studies, subjects with anterior pituitary insufficiency (i.e., panhypo-pituitarism) also demonstrated this hypersensitivity for low-level auditory signals. Subsequent research in this same area has indicated that individuals with these deficiencies in hormonal responses to environmental stressors, while demonstrating heightened auditory capacity, do demonstrate poorer-than-normal speech discrimination, poorer-than-normal performance for pure tone sounds in masking noise, and impaired auditory localization ability (Henkin and Daly, 1968). Thus, the impaired hormonal response to environmental stressors gives heightened sensitivity on some parameters at the expense of losing capability in other aspects of audition. Research in this area included the treatment of individuals with both adrenocortical insufficiency and panhypopituitarism with prednisolone and adrenocorticotropic hormone. In both treatment conditions, the introduction of a carbohydrate-active steroid to the abnormal patient population resulted in a return of their auditory threshold capability to a condition equivalent to normal auditory threshold, while at the same time leading to enhanced capacity in the areas of speech discrimination, pure tone threshold in noise, and auditory localization ability (Henkin and Daly, 1968). Research has also been completed with subjects who demonstrate excessive endogenous levels of carbohydrate-active steroids, a condition referred to as Cushing's syndrome (Henkin, 1975a,b). These patients, when tested auditorily, show increased pure tone thresholds compared to normal subjects, and decreased auditory integration ability as well as decreases in frequency range and increased auditory pain threshold. Thus, patients with untreated Cushing's syndrome display hearing impairments that are the reciprocal or the opposite of the auditory capability in untreated individuals who show adrenocortical insufficiency (Henkin, 1975a,b). Treatment of the excessive endogenous glucorticoid secretions in these individuals results in a return of hearing abilities to normal levels of operation. Generally, then, this research indicates that abnormal levels of adrenocortical hormones can lead to specific abnormalities of hearing and, therefore, the trend of this research is certainly congruent with a hypothesis that noise-induced hearing changes may be hormonally mediated.

A summary of stress and its relation to noise exposure

A variety of non-auditory stress effects of exposure to high-level noise has been reviewed and the possible relationships between non-auditory and auditory noise exposure effects have been examined. Noise may give rise to several physiological phenomena including reflexive muscular responses, increased excitability of the central nervous system, and a variety of circulatory effects. Additional noise exposure effects include: variations in respiration parameters, heightened skeletal muscle tonus, variations in the activities of the gastro-intestinal system, pupillary dilation, and a variety of effects related to the vestibular system.

The non-auditory effects noted above are all known to be phenomena related to the whole-body pattern of response when the body is immersed in a stressful environment. Current research indicates that noise can act as an environmental stressor. It has been noted that noise exposure will trigger the secretion of certain hormones as a part of the overall stress response. Of particular interest in this area are the adrenocortical hormones which are secreted in the presence of a high-level noise stressor. A major physiological change induced by the stress response of the individual is a reduced blood supply to surface tissues with a concomitant increase in the concentration of blood to the deep, skeletal muscles. The proposed hormonal mediation model suggests that the auditory changes observed concomitant with high-level noise exposure are in part the by-product of the reduction in blood supply to the cochlea that is the body's normal reaction to environmental stressors. The immersion in high-level noise is of long duration in many sectors of our society (notably, the industrial settings). This long duration of noise exposure is a chronic immersion in an environmental stressor which may lead to maladaptive responses in the individual.

The hormonal mediation model for noise-induced hearing change is supported by the fact that noise exposure results in reduced blood supply to the cochlea. In addition persons with abnormal hormonal response to environmental stressors demonstrate a variety of auditory abnormalities as compared with their hormonally normal counterparts. Treatment with carbohydrate-active steroids has been shown to result in a return to normal hearing in these individuals. Thus, current evidence on the nature of the hearing mechanism and its interaction with the endocrine system would suggest that the model proposed in this section is a viable scheme for characterizing mechanisms of noise-induced hearing impairment.

NOISE MEASUREMENT

General

All objectives of a noise survey must be carefully considered before sound pressure level measurements are made. The necessity for a comprehensive definition of purpose and scope of a noise survey cannot be over-emphasized. The choice of instruments, measurement techniques, and data recording procedures will be determined from the survey design. There are four general types of noise surveys for the purposes of:

(1) monitoring work area noise levels for hearing conservation,
(2) determining speech or warning signal interferences,
(3) determining psychological disturbance (annoyance) levels, and
(4) providing information for noise control purposes.

Monitoring noise exposures for hearing conservation purposes usually requires measurements at the listener's location using A-weighted frequency characteristics (ANSI, 1966, 1967, 1971a,b,c; AIHA, 1975; Michael, 1978). Measurements of noise to determine its interference with speech and warning signals may use octave band and/or overall A-weighted frequency characteristics, and these measurements are also usually made at the listener's location. Data sampling and recording techniques may differ somewhat between survey types 1 and 2. The third survey type is also based on an A-weighted measurement in most cases but more detailed information, in the form of narrow-band measurements, is often required to pinpoint offending sources in areas where there are several different noise sources (Webster, 1970; Yerges and Bollinger, 1973; EPA, 1974). The fourth survey type generally requires octave or narrower band measurements in order to pinpoint major offending sources of noise (ANSI, 1971b). The following discussions of specific survey types will rely heavily upon readily available references on common noise measurement procedures. More space will be given to newer noise descriptors and measurement procedures.

Surveys of work areas

Most of the early studies of noise-induced hearing impairment, prior to 1969, used octave band measures of noise (Intersociety Committee, 1967). Octave band measurements require a relatively high level of skill by the operator, expensive equipment, and the time required for measurement and analysis of the data is also relatively high. Rules, regulations, and guidelines concerned with noise-induced hearing impairment enacted during the last 12 years have caused many persons who have had very little training and/or experience to become involved with noise measurement and analysis. Also, measurements must be made under difficult conditions with severe time restraints. Most of these noise regulations, therefore, have been based on single A-weighted sound pressure measurements that are considerably simpler and less expensive to obtain than octave, or narrower, band analyses. Although somewhat less information is provided with A-weighted measurements than with band analyses, the A-weighted levels have proved to be satisfactory in many cases.

Most specifications concerned with limiting noise exposures also specify the time of exposure (OSHA, 1970, 1981; NIOSH, 1972; ISO, 1975, 1980; BSI, 1976). The times of exposure to various A-weighted sound pressure levels, therefore, must be recorded manually when using conventional sound level meters (Environmental Acoustics Laboratory, 1980). This can be a very difficult task when sound levels change rapidly, and various sampling techniques may be required to afford the desired accuracy of measurement.

Dosimeters, first introduced more than twenty-five years ago, have been used by many hearing conservationists in recent years particularly for measurements of rapidly changing noises (OSHA, 1981; Michael, 1978; ANSI, 1967, 1978). These instruments are generally worn mounted on the collar or shoulder of a worker throughout a normal work shift in a noisy area. At the end of the work shift, the dosimeter is attached to a readout instrument which, in turn, provides a dose reading having noise exposure level, frequency, and time characteristics. In most cases the dose reading is based on a specified noise exposure limit and the readout is given as a percentage of the allowed daily dose. The use of a dosimeter requires less skill and individual, or area, exposures can be sampled by a relatively inexpensive procedure. A disadvantage of using a dosimeter is that some inaccuracies may result, particularly at high frequencies, from using the microphone mounted close to the body.

Data recording methods and time intervals between measurements will vary depending upon the time-level exposure patterns. For simple time-level patterns direct readings from a sound level meter and manual recording procedures are generally adequate. A more sophisticated sampling technique, or the use of a dosimeter, may be necessary for more complicated time-level patterns. Measurements need not be repeated in most cases until changes are made which could influence exposure levels; for example, changes in the noise source, or sources, or in job locations. Unexpected shifts in monitored hearing thresholds would, of course, be another indication for noise exposure to be measured again.

Determining speech or warning signal interference

Speech interference level surveys have been made with narrow-band, octave-band, overall A-weighted frequency, and with other overall frequency-weighted levels. Warning signal interference measurements generally require narrow-band or octave-band measurements depending upon the signal and background noise characteristics. The purpose of these surveys, and the physical characteristics of the signals and the background noise, will in most cases determine the degree of detail needed, and hence the means of measuring the noise.

Determining annoyance levels

A considerable amount of flexibility is required in measurement procedures directed towards the estimation of annoyance levels. Psychological, physiological, and physical parameters are involved in very complicated ways so that responses may show a wide range of reactions (Yerges and Bollinger, 1973).

When common broad-band noises are involved, measurements using A- or other frequency weightings are just as effective as narrow-band analyses for estimating annoyance levels. If a particular noise exposure has a high percentage of energy in narrow frequency bands, a narrow-band analysis will in most cases provide better correlation with annoyance responses than measurements using wider frequency bands. Narrow frequency bands may also be required to measure or pinpoint a single source's contribution when there are multiple sources contributing to the overall nosie level.

A single overall frequency weighting is much easier to record and to analyse than bands of noise, particularly when levels are changing rapidly over a significant period of time. Most noise ordinances have been based on this relatively simple single-frequency weighting because enforcement activities must be carried out by persons with limited experience and with very basic instrumentation (Yerges and Bollinger, 1973).

Statistical distribution of noise levels (L_N)

Statistical distribution of noise levels makes use of sound pressure level measurements taken at predetermined time intervals over some specified observation period (Yerges and Bollinger, 1973; EPA, 1974). From these data the percentage of time that any specified sound level is exceeded can be determined. Alternatively, the sound level that is exceeded a specified percentage of the observation time such as 10 per cent (L_{10}), 50 per cent (L_{50}), and 90 per cent (L_{90}), can be determined. The A-weighted sound level exceeded 10 per cent of the time, L_{10}, is commonly used to describe community noise levels while the level exceeded 90 per cent of the time, L_{90}, is used as the ambient or background level. The level exceeded 50 per cent of the time, L_{50}, is the mean level for a normal distribution of levels.

The length of the observation period must be adequate to describe the variation in sound level. A rule of thumb for determining the required period of observation is that the time period should be long enough to accumulate at least a number of samples equal to 10 times the total sound level fluctuation. For example, if the sound levels fluctuate over a range of 14 dB (± 7 dB), the total number of samples should be in excess of 140. From previous studies (Safeer, Wesler, and Rickley, 1972; Yerges and Bollinger, 1973) it has been determined that a sampling rate of once every 10 seconds will result in an L_{10} value that is within 3 dB of the correct value. For the example given above, the total observation time necessary to take 140 samples will be about 23 minutes.

Equipment: The basic equipment required for manual sampling is a sound level meter (SLM), a timing device, and a data sheet (see Figure 1). A small tape recorder also may be desirable by some operators to describe source and measurement conditions (not for recording the sound being measured). Care should be taken to prevent verbal communications between the operator and the recorder from being picked up by the SLM microphone during measurements.

Procedure: The procedure for determining the statistical distribution and the corresponding L_{10} and L_{90} values is as follows:

(1) Check the functioning, calibration, and operation of the sound level meter (SLM) and associated equipment.
(2) Locate the SLM microphone at the point of interest.
(3) Set the SLM weighting switch to the 'A' position and the meter response switch to the 'FAST' position.
(4) Turn on the SLM and observe the range of the meter fluctuations. Multiply this range by 10 to compute the total number of samples required. (If this range increases during the course of taking data, the number of samples required will also increase; however, the number of samples required is not changed if the fluctuation range decreases.)

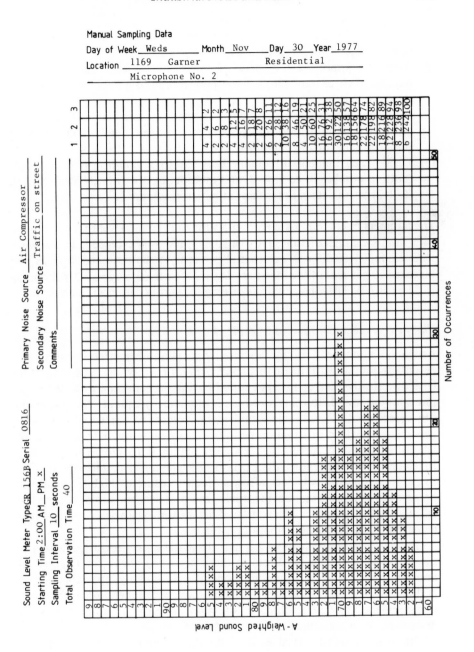

Figure 1. Data sheet example

(5) Every 10 seconds read the instantaneous A-weighted sound level and record this level as an occurrence by making a check in the appropriate row of the data sheet (see Figure 1).

(6) After the appropriate number of samples have been taken, add the number of check marks in each row and record this number in column 1 of the data sheet.

(7) Add the row totals in column 1 beginning with the highest sound pressure level total (top figures) and record these numbers in column 2 (i.e., from the top of column 2:4 = 4,4 + 2 = 6,4 + 2 + 2 = 8, etc.).

(8) Divide each number in column 2 by the total number of occurrences (bottom number in column 2) and multiply by 100 (i.e., $(4/242) \times 100$, $(6/242) \times 100$, etc.). Enter these numbers in column 3.

The numbers in column 3 are percentiles for each sound level that correspond with the percentage of time that the sound level was exceeded. In the work sheet example, 80 dB was exceeded 7 per cent of the time and 78.5 dB was exceeded 10 per cent of the time (i.e., L_{10} = 78.5 dB(A), L_{50} = 70.0 dB(A), L_{90} = 54.8 dB(A)). These percentile determinations are accurate within ± 3 dB.

Energy equivalent continuous level (L_{eq})

An energy equivalent continuous level, L_{eq}, is another effective means for describing sounds with fluctuating levels (EPA, 1974). By definition, L_{eq} is the level of a steady-state continuous sound having the same energy as the actual time varying sound. In other words, it is numerically equal to the continuous dB(A) level that has the same sound energy content as the actual fluctuating sound (over a given observation period). L_{eq} accounts for both duration and level of all sounds occurring during a given observation time period. Since L_{eq} is related to energy (rather than pressure) averaging it emphasizes the high sound levels, and thus it does afford a good measure of high-level intrusive noises such as those from moving trucks, motorcycles, and aircraft. Details of calculating the L_{eq} will not be addressed herein as they are described elsewhere (Environmental Acoustics Laboratory, 1980).

Obviously, measurements of L_{eq} must have the same general guidelines for the length of measurement times as those described above for L_{10} and L_{50}. Short cuts can be taken if the source operates with highly repeatable periodic cycles, as with trash compactors or domestic air conditioners. Also, short-term measurements may be justified in situations where it is only necessary to determine that a prescribed L_{eq} level has been exceeded.

The most straightforward method for determining L_{eq} is, of course, to measure it directly. Unfortunately, instruments for this purpose are expensive and they are not widely used at this time.

Determining day–night level (L$_{dn}$)

The L_{dn} descriptor is similar to the energy-based L_{eq} except that it provides greater weight to night-time noises. Normally it is equivalent to the 24-hour L_{eq} level with a 10 dB night-time penalty added to the noise levels between 10 p.m. and 7 a.m. Thus, this measure takes into consideration the greater intrusiveness of night-time noises.

Tape recorders

For special cases it may be convenient to record a sound so that an analysis may be made at a later date. A tape recording is particularly helpful when a series of analyses are required or when the sound source is on for only a short period of time. Extreme care must be taken, however, in the use of tape recorders. Tape recorders are difficult to calibrate and to use, so this work should be left to highly qualified professionals whenever possible.

Obviously, when a tape recorder is used, the manufacturer's instructions must be followed closely. Also, the specifications of the tape recorder should be studied closely to determine if it will provide the required frequency range and overall accuracy. It is strongly recommended that 'instrumentation-type' recorders be used (rather than the less expensive 'audio-type') because of their tight tolerances, their long-term stability, and the convenience of calibration and use. A discussion of tape recording is provided in the Society of Automotive Engineers recommended practice SAEW J184(13).

SUMMARY

Noise will continue to be a significant environmental problem for many industrial employers and their employees. These employers must be aware of their responsibilities to employees in the prevention of noise-related health and safety problems. Efforts must be made to reduce the noise levels in the work areas by controlling the sources and, if these efforts are not successful, personal protective devices must be chosen to provide the best possible combination of protection and communication. The effective control of noise exposures and communication in work areas should also improve work effectiveness and production efficiency in many cases. Education programmes must make employees aware of noise problems away from work as well as in their work areas.

Employers must also take the responsibility of controlling noise that may be generated into surrounding communities. They should take the initiative in working with surrounding communities to maintain a high standard for the community environment.

REFERENCES

Alexandre, A. (1973). Decision criteria based on spatio-temporal comparisons of surveys on aircraft noise. In Ward, W. D. (ed.) *Proceedings of the International Congress on Noise as a Public Health Problem.* U.S. EPA No. 550/9-73-008.

American Industrial Hygiene Association (1975). *Industrial Noise Manual.* 3rd edn. (1975) (Ohio: AIHA).

American National Standards Institute (1966). *American Standard Specifications for Octave, Half-Octave, and Third-Octave Filter Sets.* SI.11-1966 (New York: ANSI).

American National Standards Institute (1967). *American National Standard for Preferred Frequencies and Band Numbers for Acoustical Measurements.* SI. 6-1967 (New York: ANSI).

American National Standards Institute (1969). *American National Standard for the Calculation of the Articulation Index.* S3.5-1969 (New York: ANSI).

American National Standards Institute (1971a). *American National Standard Specification for Sound Level Meters.* SI.4-1971 (R1976) (New York: ANSI).

American National Standards Institute (1971b). *American National Standard Specification for Sound Level Meters.* SI.4-1971 (New York: ANSI).

American National Standards Institute (1971c). *American National Standard Methods for the Measurement of Sound Pressure Levels.* S1.3-1971 (R1976) (New York: (ANSI).

American National Standards Institute (1978). *American National Standard Specification for Personal Noise Dosimeters.* SI.25-1978 (ASA 25-1978) (New York: ANSI).

Anthony, A. (1973). Azure B-RNA changes in the adrenal and cerebral cortex of rats exposed to intense noise. *Federation of the American Societies of Experimental Biology Proceedings,* **32,** 2093–2097.

Anthony, A., Ackerman, E., and Lloyd, J. (1959). Noise stress in laboratory rodents. I. Behavioral and endocrine response of mice, rats, and guinea pigs. *Journal of the Acoustical Society of America,* **31,** 1430–1437.

Arguelles, A. E., Ibeas, D., Ottone, J. P., and Chekherdemian, M. (1962). Pituitary-adrenal stimulation by sound of different frequencies. *Clinical Endocrinology and Metabolism,* **22,** 846–852.

Arguelles, A. E., Martinez, M. A., Pucciarelli, E., and Disito, M. V. (1970). Endocrine and metabolic effects of noise in normal, hypertensive, and psychotic subjects. In Welch, B. L. and Welch, A. S. (eds) *Physiological Effects of Noise* (New York: Plenum Press).

Atherly, G., Gibbons, S., and Powell, J. (1970). Moderate acoustic stimuli: the inter-relation of subjective importance and certain physiological changes. *Ergonomics,* **13,** 536–545.

Baughn, W. L. (1966). Noise control: percent of population protected. *International Audiology,* **5,** 331–338.

Baughn, W. L. (1973). *Relation between daily exposure and hearing loss based on the evaluation of 6835 industrial noise exposure cases.* AMRL-TR-73-53. Aerospace Medical Research Laboratory, Wright Patterson Aerospace Force Base, Ohio.

Bekesy, G. V. (1951). D. C. potentials and energy balance of the cochlear partition. *Journal of the Acoustical Society of America,* **23,** 576–582.

Bell, A. (1966). *Noise. An occupational health hazard and public nuisance.* Public Health Papers, No. 30 (Geneva: World Health Organization).

Bennett, T., Bienvenue, G. R., Michael, P. L., and Anthony, A. (1977). 'Physiologic and audiometric indices of noise susceptibility.' 94th meeting, Acoustical Society of America, 9 June.

Bienvenue, G. R., and Michael, P. L. (1977). 'Test battery approach to the early detection of noise induced hearing impairment.' 94th meeting, Acoustical Society of America, 9 June.

Bienvenue, G. R., and Michael, P. L. (1979). Digital processing techniques in speech discrimination testing. In Yanick, P. Jr. (ed.) *Rehabilitation Strategies for Sensorineural Hearing Loss* (New York: Grune & Stratton).

Bienvenue, G. R., and Michael, P. L. (1980). Permanent effects of noise exposure on results of a battery of hearing tests. *American Industrial Hygiene Association Journal*, **41**, August.

Bienvenue, G. R., Bennett, T., Anthony, A., and Michael, P. (1977). 'Effects of asymptotic noise exposure on a battery of tests.' American Audiology Society Meeting, December 12.

Borsky, P. N. (1970). The use of social surveys for measuring community response to noise environments. In Chalupnik, J. D. (ed.) *Transportation Noises: A Symposium on Acceptability Criteria* (Seattle: University of Washington Press).

Brandenberger, G., Follenius, M., and Termolières, C. (1977). Failure of noise exposure to modify temporal patterns of plasma cortisol in man. *European Journal of Applied Physiology*, **36**, 237–246.

British Standards Institution (1976). *Method of Estimating the Risk of Hearing Handicap Due to Noise Exposure*. BS 5330.

Broadbent, D. E. (1957). Effects of noise on behaviour. In Harris, C. M. (ed.) *Handbook of Noise Control* (New York: McGraw-Hill).

Broadbent, D. E. (1971). *Decision and Stress* (London: Academic Press).

Busnel, R. G., Busnel, M. C., and Lehman, A. G. (1973). Synergic effects of noise and stress on general behavior. *Life Science*, **16**, 131–137.

Cohen, A. (1966). 'Effects of noise on performance.' Proceedings of the International Congress on Occupational Health. Vienna, Austria, A IV.

Cohen, A. (1973). Industrial noise and medical absence and accident record data on exposed workers. In Ward, W. D. (ed.) *Proceedings of the International Congress on Noise as a Public Health Problem*. EPA NO. 550/9-73-008.

Cuesdean, I. (1977). Study of cardiovascular and auditory pathophysiological implications in a group of operatives working in noisy industrial surroundings. *Physiologica*, **14**, 53–61.

Davis, H. (1950). Temporary deafness following exposure to loud tones and noise. *Acta Otolaryngologica*, **88**, 1–57.

Davis, R. C. (1932). Electrical skin resistance before, during, and after a period of noise stimulation. *Journal of Experimental Psychology*, **15**, 108–117.

Davis, R. C., Buchwald, A. M., and Frankman, R. W. (1955). Autonomic and muscular responses and their relation to simple stimuli. *Psychological Monographs*, **69**, 405.

Dega, K. (1977). The effects of noise on some indexes of the circulatory system efficiency of shipyard grinders. *Bulletin of the Institute of Maritime and Tropical Medicine Odynia*, **28**, 143–150.

Environmental Acoustics Laboratory (1980). *Community Noise Fundamentals*. The Pennsylvania State University. Developed under Contract 68-01-5853, U.S. Environmental Protection Agency.

Environmental Protection Agency (U.S.) (1974). *Information on Levels of Environmental Noise Requisite to Protect Public Health and Welfare with an Adequate Margin of Safety*. EPA, March.

Environmental Protection Agency (U.S.) (1977). *Toward a National Strategy for Noise Control*. EPA, ONAC, Washington, DC, 20460, April.

Ettema, J. H. (Chairman) (1980). Team III Report: Nonauditory physiological effects induced by noise. In *Noise as a Public Health Problem; Proceedings of the*

Third International Congress, ASHA Reports No. 10, American Speech–Language–Hearing Association, April.

Favino, A. (1978). Concentrations of certain hormones in the blood of human males subjected to steady-state noise. In Assenmacher, I., and Franer, D. S. (eds.) *Environmental Endocrinology* (New York: Springer-Verlag).

Fidell, S., Horonjeff, R., and Green, D. M. (1981). Statistical analysis of urban noise. *Noise Control Engineering,* **16,** 75–80 (March–April).

Galloway, W. J. (1970). Predicting community response to noise from laboratory data. In Chalupnik, J. D. (ed.) *Transportation Noises: A Symposium on Acceptability Data* (Seattle: University of Washington Press).

Geber, W., Anderson, T., and Van Dyne, B. (1966). Physiologic responses of the albino rat to chronic noise stress. *Archives of Environmental Health,* **12,** 751–754.

Glass, D. C., and Singer, J. E. (1972). *Urban Stress: Experiments on Noise and Social Stressors* (New York: Academic Press).

Glorig, A. (1958). *Noise and Your Ear* (New York: Grune & Stratton).

Glorig, A. (1969). Non-auditory health effects. In Ward, W. D. (ed.) *Sixth Congress of Environmental Health* (Chicago: American Medical Association).

Gulian, E. (1973). Psychological consequences of exposure to noise: facts and explanations. In Ward, W. D. (ed.) *Proceedings of the International Congress on Noise as a Public Health Problem.* U.S. EPA No. 550/9-73-008.

Gulick, W. L. (1958). The effects of hypoxemia upon the electrical response of the cochlea. *Annals of Otology, Rhinology and Laryngology,* **67,** 148–169.

Hartley, L. R. (1973). Effects of prior noise or prior performance on serial reaction. *Journal of Experimental Psychology,* **101,** 255–261.

Hebb, D. O. (1956). Drives and the C.N.S. *Psychological Review,* **62,** 243–254.

Henkin, R. I. (1975a). Effects of ACTH, adrenocorticosteroids and thyroid hormone on sensory function. In Stumpf, W., and Grant, L. (eds.) *Anatomical Neuro-endocrinology* (Basel: Karger).

Henken, R. I. (1975b). The role of adrenal corticosteroids in sensory processes. In Blaschko, H., Sayers, G., and Smith, D. (eds.) *Handbook of Physiology, Endocrinology* (Washington, DC: American Physiological Society).

Henkin, R. I., and Daly, R. L. (1968). Auditory detection and perception in normal man and in patients with adrenal cortical insufficiency: effect of adrenal cortical steroids. *Journal of Clinical Investigations,* **47,** 1269–1280.

Henkin, R. I., and Knigge, K. M. (1963). Effect of sound on the hypothalamic–pituitary–adrenal axis. *American Journal of Physiology,* **204,** 710–714.

Henkin, R. I., McGlone, R., Daly, R. L., and Bartter, F. C. (1967). Studies on auditory thresholds in normal man and in patients with adrenal cortical insufficiency: the role of adrenal cortical steroids. *Journal of Clinical Investigations,* **46,** 429–435.

Hiroshige, T., Sato, T., Ohta, R., and Itoh, S. (1969). Increase in corticotrophin-releasing activity in the rat hypothalamus following noxious stimuli. *Japanese Journal of Physiology,* **19,** 866–875.

Hockey, G. R. J. (1970a). Effect of loud noise on attentional selectivity. *Quarterly Journal of Experimental Psychology,* **22,** 28–36.

Hockey, G. R. J. (1970b). Signal probability and spatial location as possible basis for increased selectivity in noise. *Quarterly Journal of Experimental Psychology,* **22,** 37–42.

Hoffman, H. S., and Fleshler, M. (1963). Startle reaction: modification by background acoustic stimulation. *Science,* **141,** 928–930.

International Organization for Standardization (1975). *Acoustics: Assessment of Occupational Noise Exposure for Hearing Conservation Purposes.* ISO Standard 1999 (Geneva: ISO).

International Organization for Standardization (1980). *First Draft Proposal ISO/DP/ 1991/1. For Acoustic Assessment of Occupational Noise Exposure with Respect to Hearing Impairment* (Geneva: ISO).

Intersociety Committee (1967). Guidelines for noise exposure control. *American Industrial Hygiene Association Journal*, **28**, 418.

Jansen, G. (1961). Adverse effects of noise on iron and steel workers. *Stahl und Eisen*, **81**, 217–220.

Jansen, G. (1969). Effects of noise on physiological state. In Ward, W., and Fricke, J. (eds.) *Noise as a Public Health Hazard*. ASHA Reports No. 4 (Washington D.C.: American Speech Hearing Association).

Jansen, G. (1970). Relation between temporary threshold shift and peripheral auditory effects of sound. In Welch, B. L. and Welch, T. L. (eds.) *Physiological Effects of Noise* (New York: Plenum Press).

Johnson, A. (1977). Prolonged exposure to a stressful stimulus (noise) as a cause of raised blood pressure in man. *Lancet*, **1** (8002), 86–88.

Kahneman, D. (1973). *Attention and Effort* (Englewood Cliffs, NJ: Prentice-Hall).

Klumpp, R. G., and Webster, J. C. (1963). Physical measurements of equally speech-interfering Navy noises. *Journal of the Acoustical Society of America*, **35**, 1328–1338.

Knoshi, R., Butler, R. A., and Fernandez, C. (1961). Effect of anoxia on cochlear potentials. *Journal of the Acoustical Society of America*, **33**, 349–356.

Koide, Y., Yoshida, M., Konno, M., Nakano, Y., Yoshikawa, Y., and Nogaba, M. (1960). Some aspects of acoustic trauma. *Annals of Otology, Rhinology and Laryngology*, **69**, 661–697.

Kryter, K. D. (1963). Exposure to steady-state noise and impairment of hearing. *Journal of the Acoustical Society of America*, **35**, 1515.

Kryter, K. D. (1970). *The Effects of Noise on Man* (New York: Academic Press).

Kryter, K. D. (1972). Non-auditory effects of environmental noise. *American Journal of Public Health*, **3**, 389–398.

Kryter, K. D. (1976). Extra-auditory effects of noise. In Henderson, D. *et al.* (eds.) *Effects of Noise on Hearing* (New York: Raven Press).

Lawrence, M. (1971). The function of the spiral capillaries. *Laryngoscope*, **81**, 1314–1322.

Lawrence, M., Gonzalez, G., and Hawkins, J. E. Jr. (1967). Some physiological factors in noise-induced hearing loss. *American Industrial Hygiene Association Journal*, **26**, 425–431.

Lukas, J. S. (1972). Awakening effects of simulated sonic booms and aircraft noise on men and women. *Journal of Sound and Vibration*, **20**, 457–466.

Lukas, J. S. (1977). *Measures of noise level: their relative accuracy in predicting objective and subjective responses to noise during sleep*. U.S. EPA No. 660/1-77-010.

McCabe, B. F., and Lawrence, M. (1958). The effects of intensive sound on the non-auditory labyrinth. *Acta Otolaryngologica*, **49**, 147–157.

Michael, P. L. (1978). Industrial noise and conservation of hearing. In Clayton, G. D., and Clayton, F. E. (eds.) *Patty's Industrial Hygiene and Toxicology*, 3rd edn, Vol. I (New York: John Wiley & Sons).

Michael, P., and Bienvenue, G. (1976). A procedure for the early detection of noise-susceptible individuals. *American Industrial Hygiene Association Journal*, **36**, 52–55.

Michael, P., Bienvenue, G., Kerlin, R., and Prout, J. (1978). *Early detection of noise-induced hearing impairment*. Final Report for Contract No. 68-01-4498. U.S. Environmental Protection Agency.

Michael, P. L., Saperstein, L. W., and Prout, J. H. (1972). *Aspects of noise generation and hearing protection in underground coal mines*. U.S. Bureau of Mines Final Report Grant No. G0122004.

Michael, P. L., Saperstein, L. W., and Prout, J. H. (1973). *A study of roof warning signals and the use of personal hearing protection in underground coal mines*. U.S. Bureau of Mines Final Report Grant No. G0133026.

Miller, J. D. (1971). *Effects of noise on people*. EPA Report, NTID 300.7:1-153.

Miller, J. D. (1974). Effects of noise on people. *Journal of the Acoustical Society of America*, **56**, 729–764.

Misrahy, G. A., Shinabarger, E. W., and Arnold, J. E. (1958). Changes in cochlear endolymphatic oxygen availability, action potential, and microphonics following asphyxia, hypoxia and exposure to loud sounds. *Journal of the Acoustical Society of America*, **30**, 701–704.

Misrahy, G. A., Spradley, J. F., Dzinovic, S., and Brooks, C. J. (1961). Effects of sound, hypoxia and kanamycin on the permeability of cochlear partitions. *Annals of Otology, Rhinology and Laryngology*, **70**, 572–581.

National Institute of Occupational Safety and Health (1972). *Criteria for a Recommended Standard. Occupational Exposure to Noise*, HSM 73, 11001, NIOSH, U.S. Dept. of Health, Education and Welfare.

Nixon, C. W. (1971). *Some effects of noise on man*. AMRL-TR-71-53, Aerospace Medical Research Laboratory, Wright-Patterson AFB, Ohio.

Northern, J. L. and Downs, M. P. (1974). *Hearing in Children* (Baltimore: Williams & Wilkins).

Occupational Safety and Health Act of 1970 (1970). *Public Law 91-596*, 29 December.

Occupational Safety and Health Administration (1981). *Regulation on Occupational Noise Exposure: Hearing Conservation Amendment*, U.S. Department of Labor, Federal Register, 46 FR 4161, 16 January.

Pincus, G. (1943). A diurnal rhythm in the excretion of urinary ketosteroids by young men. *Journal of Clinical Endocrinology and Metabolism*, **3**, 195–199.

Rosen, S. (1967). Hearing studies in selected urban and rural populations. *Transactions of the New York Academy of Sciences*, **29**, 9–21.

Sackler, A., Weltman, A., Bradshaw, M., and Jursthuk, P. (1959). Endocrine changes due to auditory stress. *Acta Endocrinologica*, **31**, 405–418.

Safeer, H. B., Wesler, J. E., and Rickley, E. J. (1972). Errors due to sampling in community noise level distribution. *Journal of Sound and Vibration*, **24**, 365–376.

Schieber, J. P. (1968). 'Étude analytique en laboratoire de l'influence du bruit sur le sommeil.' Centre d'Études Bioclimatiques du CNPS, Strasbourg, France, April.

Schneider, E. A.(1974). A contribution to the physiology of the perilymph. Part III: On the origin of noise-induced hearing loss. *Annals of Otology, Rhinology and Laryngology*, **83**, 406–412.

Schrock, R. R. (1979). *A manual test battery for measuring noise exposure effects on three parameters of hearing*. Master of Science paper for Audiology, The Pennsylvania State University.

Selye, H. (1956). *Stress of Life* (New York: McGraw-Hill).

Selye, H. (1974). *Stress Without Distress* (Philadelphia: J. B. Lippincott).

Sokolik, I. I. (1977). Pneumoconiosis associated with a disease caused by vibration and noise in miners. *Vrach Delo*, **9**, 127–131.

Sokolov, Y. N. (1963). Higher nervous functions: the orienting reflex. *Physiological Review*, **25**, 545–580.

Spoendlin, H. H. (1971). Primary structural changes in the organ of Corti after acoustic stimulation. *Acta Otolaryngologica*, **71**, 166–176.

Thiessen, G. J. (1969). *Effects of noise from passing trucks on sleep*. Report Q1 presented at 77th meeting of Acoustical Society of America, Philadelphia, April.

Tonndorf, J., Hyde, R. W., and Brogan, F. A. (1955). Combined effect of sound and oxygen deprivation upon cochlear microphonics in guinea pigs. *Annals of Otology, Rhinology and Laryngology*, **64**, 392–406.

Tracor, J. (1971). *Community response to airport noise*. NASA Report CR-1961.

Tyler, F. H., Migeon, D., Florentin, A. A., and Samuels, L. T. (1954). Twenty-four hour cycle of cortisol secretion. *Journal of Clinical Endocrinology*, **14**, 774–779.

Ward, W. D. (ed.) (1968). *Proposed Damage Risk Criteria for Impulse Noise 'Gunfire'*. Report of working group 57, NAS-NRC Committee on Hearing Bioacoustics and Biomechanics.

Ward, W. D. (1973). Adaptation and fatigue. In Jerger, J. (ed.) *Modern Developments in Audiology* (New York: Academic Press).

Ward, W. D. (1975). Studies of asymptotic TTS. *Aerospace Medicine Special Meeting*, AGARD, NATO.

Ward, W. D. (1976). A comparison of the effects of continuous, intermittent, and impulse noise. In Henderson, D. *et al.* (eds.) *Effects of Noise on Hearing* (New York: Raven Press).

Weaver, E. G., Lawrence, M., Hemphill, R. W. and Straut, C. B. (1949). Effects of oxygen deprivation upon the cochlear potentials. *American Journal of Physiology*, **159**, 199–208.

Webster, J. C. (1969). *Effects of noise on speech intelligibility*. American Speech and Hearing Association Reports, Report 4.

Webster, J. C. (1970). Updating and interpreting the speech interference level (SIL). *Journal of Audio Engineering*, April.

Welch, B. L., and Welch, A. S. (eds.) (1970). *Physiological Effects of Noise* (New York: Plenum Press).

Welford, A. T. (1965). Stress and achievement. *Australian Journal of Psychology*, **17**, 1–11.

Welford, A. T. (1968). *Fundamentals of Skill* (London: Methuen).

Wilkins, P. A., and Martin, A. M. (1981). The effect of hearing protectors on the attenuation demand of warning sounds. *Scandinavian Audiology*, **10**, 37–43.

Williams, H. L. (1973). Effects of noise on sleep: a review. In Ward, W. D. (ed.) *Proceedings of the International Congress on Noise as a Public Health Problem*, U.S. EPA No. 550/9-73-008.

Williams, R. B. Jr. (1975). Physiological mechanisms underlying the association between psychosocial factors and coronary disease. In Gentry, W. D. and Williams, R. B. Jr. (eds.) *Psychological Aspects of Myocardial Infarction and Coronary Care* (St. Louis: Mosby).

Wohlwill, J. R., Nasar, J. L., DeJoy, D. M., and Forunzani, H. H. (1976). Behavioral effects of noisy environment: task involvement vs. passive exposure. *Journal of Applied Psychology*, **61**, 67–74.

Yerges, J. F., and Bollinger, J. (1973). Manual traffic noise sampling — can it be done accurately? *Sound and Vibration*, December, 23–30.

The Physical Environment at Work
Edited by D. J. Oborne and M. M. Gruneberg
©1983 John Wiley & Sons Ltd.

Industrial Music

JOHN G. FOX
*Department of Employment, Social Affairs
and Education, EEC, L-2920, Luxembourg*

SOME EARLY OBSERVATIONS

The twentieth-century introduction of music into the workplace may depend on modern technology but the idea of exploiting man's innate response to music to increase his work efficiency is lost in the mists of time. Army commanders have long used it to get the adrenalin flowing in their warring hosts. The Jesuits in South America in the seventeenth century had a band lead the workers into the fields each morning to overcome the Indians' aversion to manual labour (Lebo, 1955). Sir Francis Drake found room on the crowded *Golden Hind* for musicians.

In the 1930s the early practitioners of industrial psychology began to examine its effects in modern industrial systems; but even before this, empirical observations had gone beyond this intuitive support for the benefits of music and had documented the influence of music on productivity. Glossup (1961) recounts the story of a Royal Navy cordite factory during the 1914–18 war:

The work girls . . . were singing happily at their work, for which they were paid 6d. per hour, with ½d. extra for danger money. A party of brass hats was being conducted round by a select coterie of directors. The girls sang on. The following day a notice was received from the management forbidding singing by the girls in the press rooms. As superintendent on that range, I received the notice, screwed it up and dropped it in the waste paper basket; and my girls sang on. My opposite member on the other shift — being perhaps a more law abiding fellow than myself — obediently imposed the singing ban on his girls. The book, in which was recorded the shift work tally, recorded that, dating from the imposition of the singing ban, the output of the silent canaries fell by something like 10 per cent, while the persistent warblers continued to produce 15 per cent above the planned rate of output of the plant. Two or three weeks later, I received word from the management that 'it was noted that, in spite of orders to the contrary,

211

the workers on cordite range X still continued to sing at their work'. I interviewed the source of the memo—accompanied by the appropriate shift work tally—and pointed out the effect the singing ban had on output. The ban was lifted immediately and output was restored!

A later 'Hawthorne Experiment' might have put less emphasis on the effect of music in such an account. Perhaps there the experimenters might have erred. Perhaps the music effect and the 'Hawthorne effect' are one and the same thing. Certainly had they shown awareness of such data, they (and industrial psychologists for quarter of a century) would have been less overcome by their results.

On another occasion *The Illustrated London News* (Anon., 1916) gave much publicity to a 'Ragtime Laundry'. The 300 women employees of the laundry were subjected to records of 'ragtime' all day long on the principle that 'girls simply can't loaf "in time" with ragtime'.

Of course, it almost goes without saying that this principle, in the light of later research, certainly had some basis: but in any industrial society that demands dignity for the worker it had an unfortunate orientation. The cause and effect of music in relation to productivity was perhaps more acceptably presented by William Green (quoted in Clark, 1929) as President of the American Federation of Labor when he said 'Music is a friend of Labor for it lightens the task by refreshing the nerves and spirit of the worker.'

Systematic studies in the 1930s, however, began to give an objective basis to the claims in favour of the effect of music on factory output. Torrington (1936) reported that the Canley factory of Standard Motors found music influencing productivity beyond their expectations, and Wyatt and Langdon (1937) reported an increase in productivity ranging from 6.2 to 11.3 per cent when music was played in a factory employing women. They considered 'music was an effective antidote to boredom'. It has been suggested that their research was influential in the decision of the British Broadcasting Corporation to introduce the programme 'Music While You Work' for factory workers during World War II.

In the period 1950–70 the transmission of popular music by the many possible means offered by a rapidly developing technology was extensively exploited so that it entered virtually every aspect of working and social life in the U.S.A. and Western Europe. By the end of the 1970–80 decade it probably had become a world-wide feature of life.

The phenomenon has occasioned many studies during this period and many confirm the intuitively expected and previously reported beneficial effects. Others would contradict them. Many extravagant claims have been made for its acceptance and 'equally' vehement protests have been made against it. On review it would seem that it can be concluded that each point of view has some justification.

If any conclusion is to be drawn, it is that experimentation on the use of music as a deliberate social/industrial policy has clearly demonstrated the inadequacies of the general approach, theoretical frameworks, and methodologies of contemporary psychology to permit a definite statement on even one very small aspect of human behaviour. Reviewing the literature at a distance of some years one can feel, almost physically, impelled to the total rejection of methods borrowed from the physical and agricultural sciences which, while relevant and purposeful in the early simplistic experiments of the laboratory, have long outlived their usefulness to experimental industrial psychology. One marvels at the unbounded optimism of legions of experimenters seeking relevance in their results on half-a-dozen subjects using methods which, in an experiment in agricultural science would have involved many thousand seeds, or in an experiment in the physical sciences would have involved untold millions of identical atoms: all without the complexity of the human organism.

The experiments which have made a definitive statement on the value of music for commercial productivity are in the main 'dirty' experiments; those which have, in whole or in part, forsaken the received wisdom on experimental methods. However, that they seem to support inconclusively both favourable and unfavourable attitudes to the music comes less from their lack of experimental rigour than from a lack of understanding of the commercial philosophy behind a 'music service' and, remarkably, its relationship to the psychological theoretical framework in which it operates.

BACKGROUND MUSIC AND INDUSTRIAL MUSIC

Essentially, two services are available: 'background music' and 'industrial music' and the latter can be viewed in two different psychological contexts. Though each may be said to be directed to inducing commercial profitability, they are quite different in their basis and intended operation, and while 'industrial music' might provide a background of music, 'background music' could never effectively replace an industrial programme. Unfortunately in testing the productivity possibilities of music many experimenters have used 'background music' in error for 'industrial music'.

Background music is now almost generally found as 'acoustical wallpaper' in shops, hotels, public transport, waiting rooms, dental surgeries, etc. According to its commercial producers, background music creates a welcoming atmosphere, it relaxes customers, increases turnover, covers disturbing noise, and reduces boredom. Its character is subdued and unobtrusive with a middle register tempo. Usually vocals are not featured. A current extension of this kind of music to aircraft passenger cabins seems to have set aside this latter principle. Surprisingly, since many vocals used could conceivably raise tensions. In all these respects it differs from 'industrial music'. But its greatest difference is that in principle it is a virtually continuous presentation over the working day: in the shop (8 hours) in the hotel (16 hours), or whatever. Continuous exposure may produce a monotonous environment which itself may produce stress. It is used for its effect on the transient customer and not the staff. In this it is everything that industrial music is not.

There have been few, if any, reliable evaluations in this use of music. A number have been examined but none have withstood a critical evaluation. It seems that the most one can say is that a few people are positive towards it, the majority do not notice it, and yet another few are clearly stressed and irritated by it.

BACKGROUND MUSIC AT WORK

Since intuitively, or empirically, 'industrial music' was seen as unsuitable for tasks which demand a high level of mental activity and could be expected to produce negative effects in banks, offices, and the like, the use of background music played at intervals in such establishments has been common. There its aim has been that of 'industrial music': to enhance working performance.

This use has often been investigated and Roberts (1959) reports a number of such studies.

(1) At the Mississippi Power and Light Co., keypunch operators showed an average 37 per cent decrease in the number of errors per 1000 cards punched after the introduction of such music.

(2) Stevenson et al. studied the cheque-typing section of the accounts department of Lever Bros. They found, with other environmental factors considered ideal, the number of cheques ruined by mistakes dropped from 9 per cent to less than 5.5 per cent after music was introduced.

(3) A study by Stevenson et al. at Prentice-Hall Inc. observed workers in the mailing section. On the basis of records kept for 6 months before and 8 months after planned background music was introduced, it was found that productivity had increased by more than 8 per cent over the total period.

Smith (1961) reports similar positive results in a study of IBM keypunch operators. The enhanced performance, however, seems most likely attributable to the increasing skill of the operators. But it might be argued that the music facilitated the learning process. The role of music in the learning process has been suggested in an investigation by Freeburne and Fleischer (1952) on the comprehension of Russian history. Briefly the argument runs: the plateaux common to all 'learning curves' can be attributed, among other things, to boredom in its broadest sense brought on by slow rates of progress. The boredom reduces attention to increase errors and further slows progress. Thus a circle is created which can only be broken by external influences such as remedial exercises — or perhaps music.

In what may be taken as more demanding circumstances Saptala and Kalasnikov (1978) examined the effect of music on engineering design office staff and concluded that it had a positive effect on the staff's work potential and they recommend music as an effective stimulus for mental work.

On the debit side Kirkpatrick (1943) reported that music hindered mental concentration, and McGeehee and Gardner (1949) found no increase in productivity with the introduction of music into a factory where 142 women worked on a complex rug-making operation.

These experiments in measurements of productivity are mirrored in the laboratory studies of the effect of music on an experimental task. For example, Konz (1962) found a background of music improved performance on a matching letters task by 18 per cent; Dannenbaum (1945) concluded that music made people less able to find faults in geometric figures; while Poock and Wiener (1966) found music to be of no benefit in a visual task. In most of these laboratory studies it is rare to find the characteristics of the music well defined and thus it is not clear if it has the qualities of 'background music' which might be predicted to be effective; or if it would be better described as 'industrial music' which one would expect to produce a negative effect. The general conclusion, however, would seem to be in favour of music as a background to cognitive activities. Clearly 'individual differences' will be a significant modifier to this claim; and there must be a cross-over where the music becomes a disruptive factor. Last (1970) claims that if mental effort demanded exceeds 50 per cent any music becomes disruptive. Unfortunately he does not define the scale on which this 50 per cent falls.

INDUSTRIAL MUSIC

An emotional impetus to productivity

A description of industrial music is virtually the antithesis of background music. It is strictly programmed to some favoured timetable; its sound level must significantly exceed the general noise level; it has varying rhythm; vocals make up a large part of the programme; and whereas 'background music' can be almost anonymous, industrial music should contain well-known popular songs or 'hits'.

These characteristics return the music to the type used over the centuries to raise morale, give unity of purpose and an emotional impetus to demanding physical effort or drudgery. The re-discovery of this use for music in modern industry has been occasioned by the social industrial environment that the technical demands of industry have created.

For example, modern technology, by automation and rationalization of work, has compartmentalized work and reduced the volume of team effort to the point where a worker finds himself totally divorced from the total work experience so that the work itself loses its purpose for him. Modern production systems create personal, if not physical, isolation with little opportunity for personal choice or initiative.

In such conditions, morale and the general approach to work is almost robotized. Music in such conditions can compensate in some measure for the inherent failure of the job to satisfy man's self and group identification. If a programme of vocals encourages singing, the singing is significant in raising morale. It generates cheerfulness and group solidarity, and is necessary in an impersonal age.

It is a problem and a solution which it seems transcends political and ideological susceptibilities. Sergeev and Sergeev (1970) report an inquiry in a Soviet telephone factory where a programme of functional music was introduced. Fatigue, power of concentration, nervous tension, and the feeling of well-being at the end of shifts were investigated in the 100 employees. All the parameters showed a positive response to the music. Accident and sickness frequency were reduced and productivity improved. As an indication of cost-effectiveness the authors note that the installation for transmitting the music was amortized within the year.

A Yugoslav report (Anon., 1977) reports similarly on music as an element to improve the conditions and comfort of work.

A study published by 'Muzak' (1966), and carried out by the Institute of Science and Labour at the Mita plant of the Nippon Electric Company, found an increase in the Japanese employees' output after music was installed.

A report in *Fuhrungspraxis* (Anon., 1962) had already claimed increases of 10–25 per cent in productivity in European organizations following the introduction of planned music. The results were not always substantiated statistically but none of the investigators would appear to have cause for bias.

Much earlier Kerr (1945) reported studies carried out in four electronic equipment manufacturers, covering over 1000 employees, which showed increased productivity of 3–4 per cent on the introduction of music along with a reduction in scrappage, the average reduction being 3.35 per cent.

Deeson (1973) quotes a study at the American Machine and Foundry Company's Brooklyn plant in 1962 where a comparison between two departments showed a difference in efficiency of 4.1 per cent in favour of the one which had a music transmission daily as compared with one which had none.

There are many other reports which show an intuitive believe that 'industrial music' achieves an industrial aim. Deeson (1973) notes that since 1954 the

2500 production workers of Gillette Industries Ltd. have had 2 hours of music each day and that, although the company has no evidence that the music directly increases productivity, they are enthusiastic about its role in improving the work environment and believe that it does bring them various benefits.

Often the benefits shown are indirect elements of productivity. United Biscuits installed a transmission system in their London factories. In parallel with the development of their music programmes, labour turnover was reduced from 87.5 to 28 per cent. This almost matches the reduction of 75 per cent in employee turnover after the introduction of music in a U.S. Government Office (McDaniel, 1945).

The argument for the effective use of 'industrial music' — certainly at the commercial level — could rest on the basis of it creating a more socially acceptable environment in the dreary impersonal factories of post-war industry. However, examination of the more controlled investigations of its use must leave the psychologist unhappy to close the file at that point. The clear influence of type of music and the length and timing of transmission periods on the results demands he look in another direction to explain — at least in part — the causal effect.

A neuropsychological stimulus to productivity

A theoretical framework which offers a possible structure to the use of 'industrial music' is the neurophysiological theory of 'arousal' proposed by Hebb (1955). Following Hebb's argument, inputs to the human central nervous system have a dual task: to provide information for subsequent actions, and to provide stimuli to non-specific cortical areas (the reticular activating formation) which in turn determines the level of vigilance, or arousal, to sense, to identify, and to interpret further inputs. The feature of the incoming stimuli which is pertinent to the second role is the variation in successive aspects of the stimuli; so that a series of uniform repetitive inputs, particularly those demanding action, will eventually reduce the human ability to handle such inputs effectively. As this latter condition, leading to a reduced ability, is fulfilled by so many of the tasks of modern industry a steady decline in productivity over the day is inevitable.

To offset this potential decrement some variation in the workers' sources of stimulation must be provided. The arousal model allows various alternatives for providing such variations. Among them is supplementing the monotonous operational input with a more variable input. If this supplementary input is in a different modality from that primarily involved in the task and intrinsically has no information-gathering value, then it can serve the purpose of providing the stimulus for the non-specific reticular system and so a high level of vigilance or attention can be maintained.

Following the arousal model such extraneous stimuli should be relatively rare events in the human input programme or else they become just another series of uniform repetitive inputs which will, in fact, contribute to a reduction in levels of efficiency.

Murrell (1962, 1966, 1970) developed these concepts in his work on the effective use of rest pauses in 'light work' based on monotonous repetitive tasks. In particular he showed the considerable benefit from timing the occurrence of the rest pause (or the extraneous stimuli) with the onset of the drop in arousal—which is predictable following Hebb's hypothesis.

There is no reason to believe that bursts of white noise could not replace the rest pauses. However, a more socially acceptable supplementary variable input would seem to have more chance of success. A possible stimulus with this quality is music.

Various aspects of this theoretical framework for the use of 'industrial music' have been tested, using as the vehicle the simulation of one specific industrial task: fault detection in quality control through visual inspection. The choice of this vehicle was possibly determined by the fact that in psychological terms it mirrors in another form the phenomenon of decrement in vigilance and arousal so well documented, and over-investigated, in military studies of radar target detection and the like. It is, however, one of the jobs of modern industry which demand sustained attention to repetitious, monotonous sensory inputs and which quality assurance plans show to be difficult in terms of productivity (acceptable standards of fault detection).

The studies are difficult to compare since, apart from the few rare cases where it was the focus of the investigation, music has been treated and described as a single, global, independent variable without recognition of its own variable parameters. Thus the music of one investigation is not comparable with that of another.

The general conclusion, however, of studies by Tarrière and Wisner (1962); Ware, Kowal, and Baker (1964); Poock and Wiener (1966); Lucaccini (1968); and Wokoun (1968) was that the playing of music over some period of the time spent on inspection, 'target' detection, or fault finding had influenced performance positively.

Davies, Lang, and Shackleton (1973) similarly demonstrated the value of the extraneous music in a vigilance task. This work has special interest in that the performance measure was detection latencies. In their analysis they show that the music could be considered to have prevented the decrement in detection latencies which occurred in the other conditions of their experiment. From this slightly different standpoint the authors point out that their results are best interpreted in terms of arousal. A reasonable conclusion is that the beneficial effects of the music only appeared with the difficult version of the task which employed a less intense signal.

Hartley and Williams (1977) also showed that music (variable noise) prevented a decline in arousal during a vigilance test. But they also noted that it could be associated with increased deflections of attention away from the detection task due to a second mechanism of filtering (Broadbent, 1958). This experiment would appear to show the music causing the 'selective filter' of the central nervous system to switch to novel sources of information; particularly as the task progresses and becomes more monotonous. In commercial terms the lesson of their study is for the length and the familiarity of tunes in a single music session.

Fontaine and Schwalm (1979) reinforce the 'familiarity' need in the effective use of music. In their experiments it was the familiar music which significantly increased arousal and overall percentage detections, as well as offset the classical vigilance decrement.

Another practical lesson emerges from Corhan and Gounard's (1976) study on types of music and visual vigilance performance. In their work vigilance performance was best when the background stimulation was discontinuous and contained elements of uncertainty such 'as rock music which was more diversified, vigorous and changeable than the easy listening music'.

Finally Davenport (1974) showed the importance of the requirement for an interval schedule for the effective use of music to maintain vigilance.

Industrial studies putting industrial music into an 'arousal' framework seem to have been rare. However, Fox and Embrey (1972) reported a number of experiments on the effect of music on real industrial quality control tasks.

The job used as the vehicle for testing the effectiveness of the background music was the visual inspection of batches of metal fasteners for the purpose of separating out any defective articles which had resulted from the production process. The inspection was carried out under three auditory conditions.

(1) Normal working conditions which had a continuous ambient noise background of 83 dB(A). This was designated the 'noise' condition.
(2) Normal working conditions with industrial music relayed for 10 minutes at 30-minute intervals. The ambient noise and music produced a total background of auditory stimulus of 86 dB(A). This was designated the 'noise plus music' condition.
(3) In a room where the background noise level was 60 dB(A). This was designated the 'silence' condition.

The overall results of the experiment are shown in Figure 1. Although the increase in fault detection is quite large (7.1 per cent) its statistical significance in this study was small ($p > 0.1$). The low significance achieved was of little consequence, however, for the study was one of a series conducted both in the laboratory and in industry and the overall results confidently upheld the prediction from the arousal hypothesis on the effect of music on inspection efficiency. The points of interest are the small difference between the continuous noise and silence conditions and the changes in fault detection

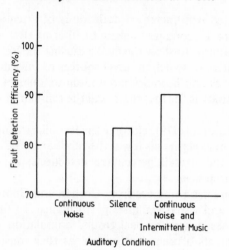

Figure 1. The influence of music on fault detection when inspecting metal fasteners. Reproduced from Fox and Embrey, Applied Ergonomics, 1972, by permission of Butterworth Scientific Ltd

efficiency brought about by superimposing intermittent music on the continuous noise. This is what the arousal concept would predict for a group habituated to noise. Continuous noise adds nothing to the variability or novelty in successive inputs and would not be expected to raise flagging levels of arousal. The music by its intermittency, albeit a cyclic intermittency, has the necessary quality for restimulating the arousal mechanism and so maintains vigilance and fault detection levels when they are likely to drop in the later stages of an inspection period. If the arousal concept has any real relevance then this specific effect of maintaining performance in the later stage of the work period should be demonstrable. The second experiment in the study, in fact, demonstrated this.

The second experiment was carried out in a factory where eight inspectors, whose normal job it was, carried out a quality control inspection of rubber seals of a variety of shapes and sizes. Test sessions lasted 30 minutes at any one time and the job was done either with no music or with a lively programme played during the 15th–20th minutes of the session. It was known that the defect rate was 1 in 100 and that the detection efficiency was normally 47 per cent.

The design of the experiment was essentially a replica of that used in the metal-fastener study without the requirement for special arrangements for a noise versus silence comparison.

A summary of the results is given in Table 1. Again the use of music shows a pronounced effect in improving the detection scores. This time the source of the improvement emerges more clearly. It comes from stemming the fall-off in

Table 1. Mean detection efficiencies and decrements in performance over 30 minutes in an industrial inspection task with and without music (percentages)

	No music (silence)	Lively music programme
Mean detection efficiency	51	69
Decrement in second 15 minutes of task compared with first 15 minutes	27	18

fault detection with time. The difference in detection efficiencies is statistically significant at $p < 0.025$; and the difference between the second half decrements for the two conditions is significant at $p < 0.02$.

The temporal programme

Following through the use of the arousal theory to determine practical schedules of transmission on the shop floor would mean determining the ebb and flow of arousal throughout the day or in Murrell's (1962, 1966, 1970) terms the length of the 'actile period' for a particular task given the specific environment of the shop. The periods of music would then be scheduled to approximate to the end of each successive actile period. Such a welter of investigations is unlikely to precede the installation of a music system despite the fact that most of the authors of industrial evaluations see precise programming as critical to the effectiveness of industrial music. Actually, often a good guess at the length of the actile period can be made from a laboratory study. In industrial inspection it would be about 30 minutes. In the Fox and Embrey (1972) experiments, therefore, 10 minutes of music were transmitted at ½-hour intervals.

In the event many schedules have been prepared empirically on the basis of satisfying the primary purpose of 'industrial music', i.e. creating a suitable social environment. All are reported to be effective. Typically the schedules are based on a 'warm-up and coda' effect. Thus we have music at the beginning of the work day, after all breaks, and just before the end of the day's effort. Given an acceptance of the arousal theory it would seem that after the breaks is superfluous and these sessions would be better placed between the breaks.

Guidance on the total period of music in a day seems equally empirical and variable. Smith (1947) says 12 per cent during the day and 50 per cent on the night shift, Benson (1945) favours 33 per cent and the Muzak Corporation (1960) proposes 42 per cent. Certainly all are agreed that it should be an intermittent feature of the work environment.

The music content

The music content of programmes is obviously important if the desired effect is to be achieved, or indeed if unexpected and unwanted results are to be avoided. Last (1970) makes the latter point with a most unlikely combination of circumstances: 'Hymn tunes played by trombone bands in Advent can induce feelings of isolation and despair in the seriously ill, thus unnecessarily undermining their will to live.' However unlikely such a confluence of events the programme content can clearly interact with personality factors to produce desired and undesirable effects. Skelly and Haslerud (1952) reported that apathetic schizophrenics were more active in response to lively music, while Shatin, Lussier, and Kotter (1958) found that fearful schizophrenics were more easily calmed by stimulating music than by quieter music. Shatin (1970) perhaps gives a line on music content generally. In his experiments the manic patient was given a rousing presentation to start with and this was gradually mellowed: the depressed patient on the other hand was given the reverse selection. The aim was to direct the patient from his extreme emotional condition to a more normally balanced one. Since 'industrial music' is aiming at movement from a low to a higher arousal state, it could be that mellow to stirring is the rule for industrial presentations.

Rhythm

However, it is almost self-evident that slow rhythms will have a soporific effect while faster rhythms will stimulate, perhaps ultimately to irritate, or worse to hyperactivate the reticular activating system to produce a deterioration in psychomotor performance and reduced productivity. But equally a diet of one particular type of music will quickly reduce one's appetite for it. In the experiments reported by Fox and Embrey (1972) the programmes comprised recent popular melodies, well-established dance music, light operas, and marches, in a random order. This mixture seemed effective.

In any event, variability of rhythm is important in two other contexts. Natural rhythms in body functions—such as heartbeat, blood pressure, and breathing—are susceptible to external acoustical influences; altering to enter into phase with the rhythm of a prolonged external source. Work rhythm itself can also be established by virtue of continuous exposure to a constant tempo. For example Anshel and Marisi (1978) give indications that cardio-vascular endurance in a physical task can be enhanced if the work movement is rhythmically co-ordinated with a musical stimulus. If all body functions and work movements had the same periodicity then a single appropriate rhythm for the music could have remarkable results. But in reality this is not so. A prolonged industrial music programme with an unchanging rhythm runs the risk of disturbing the para-sympathetic nervous system or, in a paced task, the operatives' chance of achieving a work rhythm appropriate to that of the mechanical system, be this on the assembly line or typing in the office. A variable rhythm will prevent the build-up of any such unfortunate effects to the point where serious disruption at the human physiological or industrial level takes place.

Loudness

The question of industrial music adding to the total noise exposure of the workforce to put them at risk of hearing damage hardly arises. Certainly the music transmission has to be about 5 dB(A) in excess of the ambient noise level to be effectively heard and appreciated. But if the ambient noise is even approaching levels which are critical thresholds for hearing damage then the introduction of music is a pointless exercise. Hearing damage thresholds are well in excess of the noise-induced fatigue thresholds and if music plus ambient noise exceeds the latter, neither the 'refreshing' nor the 'arousal' effects of music are likely to be apparent. Generally noise plus music should not exceed 80 dB(A) with the contribution of the music to the two components of the total auditory environment adjusted to be 5 dB(A) above the noise.

Paradoxically 'industrial music' has recently offered the possibility of increasing the chances of hearing conversation in the workforce. Ear defenders, although provided by law in most western European countries, often remain unused by personnel. The remote relationship between cause and effect precludes a strong conscious awareness of the hazard while notions of isolation, discomfort, difficulties of communication, etc. create a psychological barrier to wearing them. Thanks to modern technology these real or imagined drawbacks of the ear defender can be overcome as it becomes more than a protection against noise. Fitting a small radio receiver into the defender can allow it to receive transmissions inside a radio loop surrounding the workshop, and on these transmissions communications and 'industrial music' can be received. The total sound energy received at the ear in this way is well below damage levels. In recent years these 'active' hearing defenders have become very sophisticated, capable of attenuating loud ambient noise and at the same time amplifying speech during temporary quiet spells when the defender is still being worn.

There have been many popular reports of this development mainly inspired by manufacturers of ear defenders and industrial music companies. No scientific study has, however, been uncovered. Nevertheless, Fox and Astley in an unpublished series of experiments did find the kind of results which are now claimed in promotional material. A group of approximately 60 girls carrying out a variety of industrial tasks in a single shop were given these 'active' ear defenders. The ambient noise level in the shop was around 93 dBA but there was no history of ear defenders even having been requested or issued.

Overtly—and indeed, principally, since the experiments were financially supported by an 'industrial music' company—the girls were given the defenders to allow them to have 'Music While You Work' in these difficult noise conditions. There was a 98 per cent response to wearing the device. During a 1-month trial period this fell to 95 per cent. Among the users a very complicated picture emerged: about 60 per cent wore them all the time; some 30 per cent wore them only when there was a music transmission; 5 per cent removed them during transmissions; and the remainder had an apparently haphazard pattern of usage. During the same period absenteeism and reported accidents showed a reduction. Unfortunately, the experimental series was not completed. However, the general acceptance of the system was established for at the end of the trial period the work group insisted that the experimental set-up be made permanent. Which it was!

THE NEW INDUSTRIAL SCENE

New technology is fast changing the industrial and commercial scene. Jobs apparently are demanding more cognitive skills which may or may not provide adequate levels of job satisfaction and variable mental activation.

Where adequate levels of job satisfaction exist, music, as in the past, can still play a part as a demonstrable element in the attempt by management to 'humanize work'. Where job satisfaction is at a low ebb music, equally as before, will be an ineffective palliative. Only good management can create job satisfaction.

Industrial music has a surer role in the new scene as a source of variation to a, perforce, unstimulating working environment. Whatever the swing to cognitive activities in industry, jobs are becoming everywhere more formalized and repetitive with little room for variation or discretion. There is much evidence that a little light music will help a willing, if flagging, effort in such circumstances.

While industrial music is making its contribution to future industrial productivity, engineers may give a thought to using the new technology to design systems which will return to management the possibility of designing jobs for people.

REFERENCES

Anon. (1916). A ragtime laundry. *Illustrated London News*, **25**, 599–600.
Anon. (1962). Can productivity be influenced by music? *Fuhrungspraxis*, September, 8–10.
Anon. (1977). Music as an element to improve the conditions and comfort of work. *Ergonomija*, **4**, 49–55.
Anshel, M. H. and Marisi, D. Q. (1978). Effect of music and rhythm on physical performance. *Research Quarterly*, **49**, 109–113.

Benson, B. (1945). *Music and Sound Systems in Industry* (New York: McGraw-Hill).

Broadbent, D. E. (1958). Effect of noise on an 'intellectual' task. *Journal of the Acoustical Society of America*, **30**, 824–827.

Clark, K. S. (1929). *Music in Industry* (New York: National Bureau for the Advance of Music).

Corhan, C. M., and Gounard, B. R. (1976). Types of music, schedules of background stimulation and visual vigilance performance. *Perceptual and Motor Skills*, **42**, 662.

Dannenbaum, A. (1945). The effect of music on visual acuity. *Sarah Lawrence Studies*, **4**, 18–26.

Davenport, W. G. (1974). Arousal theory and vigilance: schedules for background stimulation. *Journal of General Psychology*, **91**, 51–59.

Davies, D. R., Lang, L., and Shackleton, V. J. (1973). The effects of music and task difficulty on performance at a visual vigilance task. *British Journal of Psychology*, **64**, 383–389.

Deeson, A. F. L. (1973). Does music-while-you-work, work? *Works Management*, March, 3–5.

Fontaine, C. W., and Schwalm, N. D. (1979). Effects of familiarity of music on vigilance performance. *Perceptual and Motor Skills*, **49**, 71–74.

Fox, J. G., and Embrey, E. D. (1972). Music an aid to productivity. *Applied Ergonomics*, **3**, 202–205.

Freeburne, C. M., and Fleischer, M. S. (1952). The effect of music distraction on reading rate and comprehension. *Journal of Educational Psychology*, **43**, 101–109.

Glossup, A. A. (1961). Bring on the singing girls. *Engineering* (London), **191**, 408.

Hartley, L. R., and Williams, T. (1977). Steady-state noise, music and vigilance. *Ergonomics*, **20**, 277–285.

Hebb, D. O. (1955). Drives and the C.N.S. (Conceptual Nervous System). *Psychological Review*, **62**, 243–254.

Kerr, W. A. (1945). Experiments on the effect of music on factory production. *Applied Psychology Monograph*, No. 5 (Stanford University Press).

Kirkpatrick, F. H. (1943). Music takes the mind away. *Personnel Journal*, **22**, 225–228.

Konz, S. A. (1962). The effect of background music on productivity in two different monotonous tasks. In *Proceedings of the Human Factors Society Conference* (The Society).

Last, G. (1970). Music at work and the occupational health requirements which it must meet. *Munchener Medizinische Wochenschrift*, **112**, 487–492.

Lebo, D. (1955). An early Jesuit contribution to industrial music. *Music Educators Journal*, **41**, 66.

Lucaccini, L. F. (1968). *Vigilance and Irrelevant Stimulation: A Test of the Arousal Hypotheses* (Ph.D. thesis, University of California, Los Angeles).

McDaniel, R. (1945). How music increases office production. *American Business*, **15**, 22–26.

McGeehee, W., and Gardner, J. (1949). Music in a complex industrial job. *Personnel Psychology*, **2**, 405–417.

Murrell, K. F. H. (1962). Operator variability and its industrial consequences. *International Journal of Production Research*, **1**, 39–55.

Murrell, K. F. H. (1966). Performance decrement — a tentative explanation. In Leopold, F. F. (ed.) *Proceedings of the Second Seminar on Continuous Work* (Eindhoven: Institute of Perception T.N.O.).

Murrell, K. H. F. (1970). Temporal factors in light work. In Singleton, W. T., Fox, J. G., and Whitfield, D. (eds.) *Measurement of Man at Work* (London: Taylor & Francis).

Muzak Corporation (1960). *Music and Muzak* (Muzak Corporation).

Muzak Corporation (1966). *Fatigue and Music* (Tokyo: Institute for Science and Labour).

Poock, G. L., and Wiener, E. L. (1966). Music and other auditory backgrounds during visual monitoring. *The Journal of Industrial Engineering*, 17, 318–323.

Roberts, J. W. (1959). Sound approach to efficiency. *Personnel Journal*, 38, 6–8.

Saptala, A. A., and Kalasnikov, A. A. (1978). Effect of functional music in psychological performance in mental work. *Gigiena Truda i Professional 'nye Zabolevanija*, 6, 11–15.

Sergeev, S., and Sergeev, V. (1970). Music versus noise. *Ohrana Truda i Social 'noe Strahovanie*, 13, 34–35.

Shatin, L. (1970). Alteration of mood via music: a study of the vectoring effect. *The Journal of Psychology*, 75, 81–86.

Shatin, L., Lussier, L. W., and Kotter, W. (1958). Fear in ECT and its alleviation through music. *Psychiatry Quarterly Supplement*, 32, 200–223.

Skelly, C. G., and Haslerud, G. M. (1952). Music and the general activity of apathetic schizophrenics. *Journal of Abnormal Social Psychology*, 47, 188–192.

Smith, H. C. (1947). Music in relation to employee attitude, piecework production and industrial accidents. *Applied Psychology Monograph*, No. 4.

Smith, W. A. S. (1961). Effects of industrial music in a work situation requiring complex mental activity. *Psychological Reports*, 8, 159–162.

Tarrière, E., and Wisner, A. (1962). Effets des bruits significatifs ou non significatifs au cours d'une épreuve de vigilance. *Travail Humain*, 25, 1–28.

Torrington, G. (1936). Working to music. *Spectator*, 156, 785–786.

Ware, J. R., Kowal, B., and Baker, R. A. (1964). The role of experimenter attitude and contingent reinforcement in a vigilance task. *Human Factors*, 6, 111–115.

Wokoun, W. (1968). *Effects of music on work performance*. U.S. Army Technical Memorandum 1-68. (Aberdeen Proving Ground Maryland, U.S.A.: Human Engineering Laboratories).

Wyatt, S., and Langdon, J. N. (1937). *Fatigue and boredom in repetitive work*. M.R.C. Industrial Health Board Research Report No. 77 (HMSO, London.)

Author Index

227

Subject Index